——————— HISTORY, TRAGEDY, THEORY ———————

T0385875

HISTORY, TRAGEDY, THEORY

Dialogues on Athenian Drama

EDITED WITH AN INTRODUCTION BY
BARBARA GOFF

UNIVERSITY OF TEXAS PRESS

AUSTIN

Requests for permission to reproduce material from this work should be sent to
Permissions, University of Texas Press, Box 7819, Austin, TX 78713-7819.

∞ The paper used in this publication meets the minimum requirements of
American National Standard for Information Sciences—Permanence of Paper
for Printed Library Materials, ANSI Z39.48-1984.

LIBRARY OF CONGRESS
CATALOGING-IN-PUBLICATION DATA

History, tragedy, theory : dialogues on Athenian drama / edited and with an
introduction by Barbara Goff. — 1st ed.
    p.   cm.
  Includes index.
  ISBN: 978-0-292-72865-3
    1. Greek drama (Tragedy)—History and criticism—Theory, etc.
  2. Historical drama, Greek—History and criticism.   3. Literature and
history—Greece—Athens.   4. Athens (Greece)—In literature.   5. Athens
(Greece)—Civilizaton.   I. Goff, Barbara E.
  PA3131.H57   1995   95-3809
  882'.010926—dc20

CONTENTS

ACKNOWLEDGMENTS

The conference from which this collection derives could not have taken place without generous support from various sources. It is my pleasure to thank the Department of Classics and the College of Liberal Arts of the University of Texas at Austin for their sponsorship and to acknowledge gratefully the financial support of the Robert M. Armstrong Centennial Fellowship in Classics. I would like to thank Professor Michael Gagarin for his encouragement and for allowing me to exploit his knowledge of organization and fund-raising. The staff of the department, Shelley Brewer, Sarah Duke, and Eileen Steinle, provided invaluable help in arranging the conference. The members of my graduate seminar on "Tragedies and Histories" joined me in thinking through many of the pertinent issues. Thanks also go to the staff of the University of Texas Press, especially Joanna Hitchcock, Kerri Cox, and Carolyn Wylie, for their help and encouragement. Last but never least, I would like to thank my husband, Michael Simpson, to whose knowledge of contemporary theoretical arguments my own discussion is indebted. His critical intelligence made my work possible, and his tireless blue pencil rendered my writing readable.

HISTORY, TRAGEDY, THEORY

ONE

INTRODUCTION
History, Tragedy, Theory

Barbara Goff

The papers in this collection represent the proceedings of a conference, entitled "History, Tragedy, Theory," held in the Department of Classics at the University of Texas at Austin in October 1992. The aims of the conference were: to consider the possibilities raised for accounts of Athenian tragedy by the increasing emphasis, in the broader critical establishment, on socioeconomic context as a determining force within literary texts; and, more generally, to approach the consequent tasks of coordinating descriptions of "history" with the notion of an autonomous "textuality" that has dominated recent critical discourse. The conference was envisaged as part of the general effort, recognizable at present within the classical establishment, to negotiate a productive relationship with recent developments, often contradictory, in literary theory. The reaction of classics to self-consciously theoretical work has often been hostile and defensive, but it has never been exclusively so,[1] and the increasing institutional importance of "theory" has required the discipline to reflect on its assumptions and procedures in a way that should be welcomed by all those who value intellectual commitment.

In my preliminary proposals for the conference I offered the participants three questions as possible points of departure: Has "history" supplanted "theory" as the main term of contemporary literary analysis? Will an emphasis on "history" give classical critics an excuse to retreat into their empirical and untheorized practices? Can we coordinate the gains from poststructuralism and feminism with "history" in our readings of classical texts? It is appropriate first to give a working definition of the terms that informed this conference. "Theory" can usefully be described as the disposition in literary studies to focus on the way that meaning is produced and conveyed rather than on the meaning itself of texts.[2] The term is often invoked to signal particularly those departures in the study of literature that postdate the New Criticism. Crucial to the development of "theory," as its history is now written, are structural linguistics and the reaction to structuralism known as poststructuralism or deconstruction, feminism, and materialism. Why these movements can be characterized as "theories" is that they claim their explanatory power not only accounts for specific texts but also extends beyond the text to account for those forces and structures that enable the text to signify at all. There are crucial differences among these components of the critical context; while structuralism and poststructuralism engage in the main with the language itself of the text, feminist and materialist analyses describe the text primarily by means of its relations to political conditions external to it.

Of these developments, deconstruction seems to have generated the most heat, and among its detractors a corresponding lack of light, in the academy and the media. The critic most closely associated with deconstruction, Jacques Derrida, managed recently to be awarded an honorary degree at Cambridge, but only just, and amid debates as to whether he is responsible for the end of Western civilization as we know it.[3] What deconstruction *is* responsible for is provoking a clash with those theories that focus on the external relations of texts, simultaneously undermining their position and enabling them to redraw it more effectively.

Deconstruction emerged as a technique of reading philosophical texts and went on to generate readings of literary or figurative texts. (I use these terms provisionally; one of the achievements of deconstructive analysis is to render such distinctions unstable.) Deconstruction characteristically involves demonstrating that the dominant figures by which a text organizes itself, if rigorously pursued, unravel the logical fabric of the text. Frequently a text is shown to operate by means of a binary polarity, the terms of which it strives to keep apart in accordance with the law of noncontradiction, but which are ultimately shown by the analysis to inhere in one another and thus again to threaten the text's ostensibly logical organization. The meaning of the text resides in neither pole of the opposition, but is endlessly deferred in the relation between the two poles as they are repeated in the text. Nor may the meaning be referred to referents external to the text, for the analysis also argues that the claimed referentiality of a text is irreducibly metaphorical, based on a distinction between inside and outside that is also shown to be a logical fiction. All texts, both the figurative and the ostensibly descriptive, are reduced to the level of rhetorical acts that strive to deny their rhetorical status in the pursuit of an elusive referentiality or "truth." In the philosophical context, this technique of reading, in its emphasis on the text's irreducible rhetoricity or "textuality," destabilizes the central enabling assumptions of conventional Western metaphysics such as "being," "presence," and "identity." In the specifically literary context deconstruction destabilizes the notion of authorial intention or control, and focuses on the ways that the text can be said to be "about" its own (unsuccessful) strategies of signification rather than "about" any plausible connection between text and the "reality" outside it. Some critics have argued further that deconstructive analysis leads to the recognition that language is fundamentally arbitrary, and that texts are consequently without inherent meaning.[4] This is the position most often seized upon and caricatured by the opponents of deconstruction, especially in the popular media.

An example may flesh out this abstract formulation. An opposition frequently invoked and investigated in Derrida's work is that of "writing" and "speech." In his essay "The Violence of the Letter: From Lévi-Strauss to Rousseau,"[5] Derrida focuses on the work of Lévi-Strauss and deconstructs the opposition between speech and writing underlying Lévi-Strauss' work on the Nambikwara, "The Writing Lesson." Lévi-Strauss' essay centers on the moment when the Nambikwara learn to write by copying the anthropologist himself. The knowledge marks an irreversible fall from innocent nature into corrupt culture. Without writing, Lévi-Strauss claims, the Nambikwara were distinguished by "a great sweetness of nature, a profound nonchalance, an animal satisfaction as ingenuous as it is charming, and . . . the most moving and authentic manifestations of human tenderness" (117). Writing, as opposed to speech, he argues, brings with it deception, hierarchy, exploitation, and violence. But Derrida, in his analysis of "The Writing Lesson," goes on to cite other parts of Lévi-Strauss' work on the Nambikwara in which they appear, *before* the advent of writing, as characterized by "intrigues and conflicts, rises and falls, all . . . at an extremely fast pace" (Derrida 1976:136). Derrida concludes that what lies behind the fantasy of the peaceful preliterate Nambikwara is the equally fantastic "image of a community immediately present to itself, without difference, a community of speech where all the members are within earshot" (136). "Speech" for Lévi-Strauss signifies presence and immediacy, but it is allowed to do so only by the coordination of "writing" with deception and violence. The two polar opposites depend on one another in order to generate any meaning at all. If, however, the opposites depend on one another, logical or temporal primacy cannot be allotted to one at the expense of the other. Derrida shows that Lévi-Strauss cannot maintain the fiction of a primal innocence unmarked by deception and violence; similarly unsustainable is the notion of a community of "speech" unmarked by the difference and deferral that Lévi-Strauss wants to attribute only to "writing." "Speech" cannot, then, be defined as the providential absence of "writing." In the literary context, deconstructive arguments consequently entail that the written text cannot yield transparent access to the "speech" of an author or the "presence" of a referential reality; since such an originary moment cannot have logical or temporal primacy, any attempt to make it do so is similarly consigned to fantasy.

Deconstruction has thoroughly disrupted the traditional humanistic inquiry into literature, and it will be obvious that it poses an especial threat to classics, which as a discipline frequently relies on the notion of reconstructing an authorial voice and tracing influences among a set of canonical writers. Deconstruction has instead made problematic any comfortable or comforting relationship that could be maintained with literary texts, because of its rigorous exposure of the effort required to sustain the humanist categories of analysis, such as truth, intention, and referentiality, against the destabilizing potential of language. It is hardly surprising that the theory's successful hold on critical practice should have given rise to an extreme reaction against it. The philosopher John Searle debated with Derrida about the case of "speech acts" as theorized by J. L. Austin.[6] "Speech acts" constitute a category of performative utterances that are held to take effect in the "real world," such as promises, bets, oaths, and curses. Such acts seem to presuppose consciousness and intention, and thus could be thought of as representing an area of language that deconstruction cannot account for. Derrida countered this argument at length,[7] but whatever the merits on either side, that the argument took place and was necessary enables us to make another point. What deconstruction *has* offered is an irreplaceable propaideutic to the process of thinking through the relations between language and "the world." If we have to account for why language is *not* in a constant state of free play, as deconstruction would claim it is, we have to explain how it does become organized into more or less stable differences and polarities, which are themselves more or less coordinated with lines of political power. Bets are placed and people do lose money; language frequently does produce effects in the "real world," and people frequently comply with its ostensible requirements. If the referentiality of language is in question, the issue of how these effects take place becomes at once more pressing and more complex.

Searle's objection to deconstruction derives from philosophical arguments, but there are also powerful objections to be made on the grounds of history. Some notion of referential language may be presumed indispensable to historical inquiry. Deconstruction, if pursued, therefore renders difficult any relation with history; it jeopardizes the very notion of historical inquiry into "documents" or "evidence" by its insistence both on the metaphoricity of all texts and on the impossibility of there being any "reality" or "referent" that is not also constituted by relations of textuality. It is on this ground that the present critical context most often takes issue with its deconstructive inheritance. On the one hand, some wish to reinstate "history" as a more or less objective context for literary texts so that it may control the otherwise unreliable meaning that deconstructive analysis unleashes. On the other hand, while many found the energies released by the deconstructive project to be wholly radical, there were those who argued that it represented a failure to engage with the way that texts, in empirically verifiable ways, get work done in political and historical scenarios.[8] Within such debates have emerged the various practices that go under the name of "new historicism," a mode of inquiry which at its most productive moments seeks to take account of the history within texts as well as the textuality within history. The "return to history," then, emerges as a reaction to deconstruction, but it is a reaction that takes different forms depending on its precise relationship with deconstruction's destabilizing energies.

"History" in this context is obviously a term that itself needs to be inspected. In recent years it has become a term with considerable political resonance. Francis Fukuyama put the cat among the pigeons with his 1989 article "The End of History?," later expanded into a book, *The End of History and the Last Man*.[9] Fukuyama's thesis is that with the close of the Cold War and the dismantling of the Soviet Union, "history" ends because there is now no viable alternative to democratic capitalism as it is practiced in the United States and Western Europe. Democratic capitalism uniquely satisfies both material needs and psychological desires for recognition, and thus finds no ideological competitors in the present political context. The controversy surrounding Fukuyama's writings indicates at least the need for discussion, whether material or psychological, if not the unqualified success of his thesis. If the end of the Cold War is dated to the fall of the Berlin Wall, then subsequent events in Central and Eastern Europe make it regrettably clear that history, in the sense of alternatives to liberal capitalist democracy, is not yet over, and that the promise of a new world order has not yet been fulfilled. But pointing to counterexamples does not put an end to theoretical debate. The demise of the postwar certainties, both within nations and among them, gives an added urgency to accounts of how cultures produce and reproduce themselves over time.

The example of Fukuyama may serve to show how contested a term "history" can be. A British critic may perhaps be permitted to note that one of the areas in which the present Conservative government of the United Kingdom seeks to intervene is precisely the definition of history as it is taught in schools. As the leader in the *Times* for October 3, 1992, (p. 13) points out, in the debate between "kings, queens, dates and facts" on one side and a "new history" which takes account of "ethnicity, class, and the dispossessed" on the other, Downing Street has seen fit to express a preference for the former, over the heads of its own Education Department.

These examples indicate what can be at stake in the practice of historical inquiry, and the academic discourse of history duly registers these political debates. Such discourse is also conditioned by an increased recognition of the textuality of the documents it studies. The institution of historiography, as well as that of literary study, thus registers changing theoretical imperatives. Again, the renewed convictions of the importance of history to literature, and of literature to history, converge in new historicist practice.

> The one truly distinguishing feature of the new cultural approach to history is the pervasive influence of recent literary criticism, which has taught historians to recognize the active role of language, texts, and narrative structures in the creation and description of historical reality.[10]

Within classics itself, such work as that of Hartog and Ober also complicates the relations predicated by traditional historiography between "historical" and "literary" texts, and applies a specifically literary understanding of texts to the reconstruction of ancient history.[11] Hartog, when confronted with a discrepancy between the Herodotean account and the archaeological remains, suggests:

> Instead of labeling this as a useless remnant of information, why not, rather, suppose that it may acquire a meaning within the text itself, that it is a detail stemming from and explained by the logic of the narrative, that it is the product of a particular representation of the Scythians which the logos is, precisely, in the process of constructing?
> (1988:4)

In *Mass and Elite in Democratic Athens*, a study of ancient political rhetoric in its social context, Ober rejects "a literalist approach [that supposes] that speeches are a more or less accurate mirror of social and political reality" (1989:46) and instead combines "*Annales*-School social history . . . with a major insight of modern literary theory: viewing texts as symbol-systems that must be understood in relation to their receptors" (1989:xiii). Both these works assume that historical texts are determined by considerations other than that of representing a preexistent reality. Texts ostensibly of historical description are shown to answer throughout to their own rhetorical imperatives, and to offer no privileged moments of transparent access to the past.

Recent accounts of history, and of literature, thus give rise to the critical movement known as "new historicism." My account of new historicism, like the conference itself, will concentrate on its significance for literary texts, because it is with respect to these texts that the clash with deconstruction has been most frequently and most compellingly staged. The versions of engagement with literary texts that are grouped under the label of new historicism do not form a monolith, and some versions are at odds with others. In the collection of articles edited by H. Aram Veeser (1989), for instance, many disparate notions of the project are entertained, and internal disagreements are thoroughly aired. Practitioners may, however, be said to be united by frequently distinguishing themselves from practitioners of a positivist historicism which treats the text as a simple mirror of its circumstances, and thereby commits what Edward Said points out is the fallacy of reducing the text to its circumstances (1979:166).[12] Such positivism disregards the more or less independent forces that also constitute specific literary texts, such as those of genre, narrative viewpoint, and poetic language. Stephen Greenblatt's introduction to the issue of *Genre* entitled *The Forms of Power and the Power of Forms in the English Renaissance,* which he also edited, is relevant to this disagreement.[13] A positivist historicism, he claims, seeks "through historical research, a stable core of meaning within the text" (1982a:4). Recovery of such stable meaning is allied to the discovery of a single political vision that

> most often presumed to be internally coherent and consistent . . . has the status
> of a historical fact. . . . Protected then from interpretation and conflict, this vision
> can serve a stable point of reference . . . to which literary interpretation can
> securely refer. Literature is conceived to mirror the period's beliefs, but from a
> safe distance.
> (1982a:5)

Here, the work of interpretation, the work of engagement with textuality, is foreclosed by being made to depend on a prior historical understanding which is itself claimed to be a fact rather than a further matter of interpretation. "History" is invoked to ground and therefore control the possibilities of interpretation. In contrast, Greenblatt goes on to argue for a new historicism that has accepted deconstructive arguments and thus

> erodes the firm ground of both criticism and literature [and] . . . challenges the
> assumptions that guarantee a secure distinction between "literary foreground"
> and "political background," or more generally, between artistic production and
> other kinds of social production.
> (1982a:6)

Deconstruction is understood to erase differences among various kinds of language—here the literary, the critical, and the historical—and reciprocally, literature is found to be produced in ways that do not fundamentally differ from the ways in which other cultural manifestations are produced.

Greenblatt's prescription and practice are paradigmatic for much of new historicism. His work characteristically compares an established "literary" text with a contemporaneous but relatively obscure nonliterary text and finds them

7

to be mutually constitutive. The transcendental authority of the literary is thus dispersed in and by its historical involvement, while the historicity of the non-literary is compromised by its reciprocal relations with the literary. His own contribution to *The Forms of Power and the Power of Forms* is a short piece comparing *King Lear* with a contemporary work on exorcism.[14] A hallmark of new historicist practice is the crossing of "boundaries separating history, anthropology, art, politics, literature, and economics";[15] for instance, one critic finds herself "patiently working through a series of connections between Parliamentary debate, women's manuals, medical writing, novels, and the accession of Queen Victoria."[16] In the introduction cited, Greenblatt claims that the new historicism "has no respect whatsoever for the integrity of the text" (1982a:4). This lack of "respect" may entail finding unmanaged contradiction in the text where New Critics or positivist historicists found unity, but it also entails dethroning the text as the bearer of meaning in favor of "the story's full situation," which includes the text's reciprocal relations with its historical moment. That Greenblatt is writing on a Shakespeare play is germane to our present concern with Athenian tragedy. The "story's full situation . . . that governs its shifting meanings" in Greenblatt's formulation includes, but presumably is not limited to, "the genre it is thought to embody, the circumstances of its performance, the imaginings of its audience" (1982a:3). These latter will, of course, be conditioned by extratextual concerns as well as by the work of the drama itself. The text itself does not determine what it means, but it is irremediably immersed in a particular historical situation whose own internal fissions multiply the possible meaning of the text.

There are problems with Greenblatt's practice, of course. As here articulated, Greenblatt's prescription for critical practice does not clearly engage with the methodological problems for the readers who approach texts generated at a tremendous historical remove, because it seems to intimate the possibility of full historical description. Earlier historicists are condemned for assuming that a text elaborates a single political viewpoint, but new historicism here falls into the complementary error of envisioning the recovery of "the story's *full* situation" (my italics). Both positions thus presuppose a stable point from which to view a complex situation. But Greenblatt does go on to intimate that such historical recovery will always be open to "interpretation and conflict," i.e., that it never will be completely "full." Indeed the material history, the supposed object of the inquiry, will itself have been conditioned by interpretation and conflict that is not necessarily part of its later retelling. To this extent we must recognize the usefulness of the deconstructive claim that the object of historical inquiry is itself textual, and that its meaning has never been self-evident. To suggest otherwise is to perform an escape from interpretation rather than a return to history.

8

In some cases, the new historicism does not look very different from Greenblatt's account of the old, and the intellectual rigor of deconstruction is sacrificed to the goal of limiting and governing the irreducible metaphoricity that it proposes. Thus David Simpson can write: "The exponents of new historical criticism have not escaped the accusation that their popularity may be based precisely on their inclination to avoid or deny theoretical self-consciousness" (1991:13). Much new historicist criticism focuses on the local and contingent dimensions of texts, their irreducible particularity, without necessarily engaging with the task of defining the larger structures or relations that may be said to condition literary production. In fact the refusal of the large historical narrative, with its inbuilt tendency towards teleology, is proclaimed as a strength of new historicism.[17] This pursuit of particularity has been defended as an attempt to model the production of literary texts themselves. Jerome McGann writes:

> Criticism moves in constant pursuit of the text's lost and unrealized points of reference—all the verbal and eventual matters of fact which constitute the work's complex symbolic networks, and without which criticism cannot hope to reconstitute those networks. . . . The project of historicist work, its insistence upon matters of fact and accidentalities, is a critical reflection . . . of poetry's incommensurable procedures.
> (1985:15)

But it can be argued that if new historicism eschews the explanatory power of the large narrative, it implicitly refuses to allow itself a theoretical dimension, and thus endangers its own discursive authority.

It should be noted that all these versions of new historicism, with their emphases on the nonliterary and the historically contingent, have a potential political charge which may be construed as sinister. The politics of new historicism can involve exclusion from the academy. Those junior members of the academy, such as graduate students, who were theoretically equipped in the discourse of deconstruction, could function as authoritatively as their teachers; they possessed an understanding of their own practices and those of the academy. Now a hierarchy is reinstated; substantial research is apparently required before one can make a challenging utterance, and what was common intellectual property in literary texts is again withdrawn. Houston Baker, speaking as a critic of African-American literature, points out that the moment when minorities and women entered the academy in numbers is also the moment when they were told to retreat to the archives.[18]

Much of what new historicism does is conditioned by its intricate and uneasy relations with cultural materialism or Marxist criticism. One might even argue that part of the critical scene is devoted to a struggle between Marxists and non-Marxist historicists to determine how the energies released by new historicism will eventually be identified. An early criticism of new historicism accuses it of complicity with Marxism in that it reduces all texts to demonstrations of existing power relations and does not allow literary texts to occupy positions of dissent or to debate received opinions (Pechter 1987). This position, however, is more readily recognized as deriving from the work of Foucault, and thus is not one with which all materialist critics would easily agree. Foucault's works are part of what made new historicism possible, even if some present practice looks very different. His legacy to new historicism is a radical rethinking of the self and of agency through a new kind of writing of history. The objects of his inquiries—clinical treatment, incarceration, and sexuality—are those institutions which have produced the self as a historically constructed object of knowledge. But his legacy is awkward, for two main reasons. The work abjures notions of diachronic cause and effect in favor of a concentration on breaks and ruptures in the historical process where, it is claimed, there is no connection between the practices of one period and those of the next. This can license the refusal of the grand narrative, which traces continuities and variations, in place of a "thick description" of a particular period. Secondly, Foucault theorizes that the power relations in society are so ubiquitous and diffuse that there is no possibility of autonomous agency, and thus no position from which to resist or dissent. This leads to the position outlined above, wherein texts are complicit with dominant power structures. This kind of conclusion, rather than one which emphasizes literature as the site of autonomous activity carried out by a free self, is said to be characteristic of new historicist practice and of materialist criticism.

While some such analyses may be identified with Marxism or materialist criticism, other versions of cultural materialism take issue with this position. Frank Lentricchia complains that in this model "modes of social opposition . . . in the end merely confirm the original paradigms from which the rebel never departs" and that if "radicalism is a representation of orthodoxy in its most politically cunning form and . . . all struggle against a dominant ideology is in vain . . . Marx, theorist of social change and revolution . . . becomes a servant of the councils of cynicism" (1989:240–241). While there is room for disagreement, new historicist and materialist practices are nonetheless joined by an investment in the notion of history, and cultural materialism shares with other versions of new historicism the founding interest in relations between history and literature. It has an important investment in how we describe the relations of literary production to the events of material history, since it holds that all of a culture's symbolic projections are to some extent determined by its more or less uneven distribution of power and resources. Such relations are usually theorized with the term "ideology." This term has borne different significations historically, and is prevalent in some current discussions of Athenian tragedy. It is also discussed by some contributions to this volume, and it seems appropriate to consider various working definitions in this introduction.

Ideology may be variously described. Ober gives some definitions, in particular the influential one of Finley: "the matrix of attitudes and beliefs out of which people normally respond to the need for action . . . the combination of beliefs and attitudes, often unformulated or subconscious and certainly neither coherent nor necessarily consistent" (1989:8). Ober differentiates this from traditional Marxist notions of ideology, which hold that the ideas of the ruling class are imposed on the lower classes as a means of "false consciousness." Few Marxist critics would nowadays subscribe to this formulation, and most agree with Althusser that the workings of ideology always have a degree of independence from the material base of power and its distribution in the given society. But the definition of ideology offered by Ober lacks the important dimension of conflict, which is crucial to materialist analyses. For such analyses, ideology usually works to justify the inequities of a particular social arrangement and often to mystify its actual processes; ideology strives to render "natural" what is a culturally specific distribution that favors some elements of society over other elements. The notion of ideology entails that texts and other artistic productions do not have a simple relation of either identity with or difference from historical particulars, but are always conditioned by and actively intervene in what is necessarily a struggle over uneven distributions. The notion of ideology is not easily reconcilable with other critical practices. It is not readily incorporated by deconstructive analysis, because deconstruction argues that history and culture are constituted by a series of texts conditioned by the play of language rather than by social relations. The notion of ideology also threatens humanist categories of analysis because it renders untenable the concept of the freely choosing and intending author or reader. The subjectivity of author, reader, or audience is not free, because it is always conditioned by social relations of uneven distribution. Nor is it the case that all new historicists are prepared to work with the notion of ideology; many seek less mediated accounts of relations between texts and their historical situation.

If we accept the importance of ideology to an account of artistic production, such production may be variously understood in its relations to ideology. Some theorists argue that art characteristically constitutes a zone of resistance to ideology; art makes visible the ideological work that is carried on unseen in other areas of culture. Althusser at one point writes:

> I do not rank real art among the ideologies, although art does have a quite particular and specific relationship with ideology. . . . I believe that the peculiarity of

art is to "make us see," "make us perceive," "make us feel" something which
alludes to reality. . . . What art makes us see . . . is the ideology from which it is
born, in which it bathes, from which it detaches itself as art, and to which it
alludes. . . . [19]

In this formulation art always has a relationship with ideology, but also always
maintains a distance from it, and can thus lead us to a greater understanding
of its work. This is the notion of art which seems to inform those readings of
Athenian tragedies which understand them as questioning or subverting the
accepted order of the *polis*. The notion of art as subversion is also relevant
within arguments that draw on deconstruction; if texts inevitably draw attention to their own rhetorical strategies, then they may well also draw attention
to the deceptive rhetoric by which culturally specific norms claim to be natural
and inevitable.

This account of art and ideology, which has just been identified with Althusser, is hard to sustain without modification. It suggests that all relations in
society are conditioned by ideology except that of literary or artistic production. But critiques of this account point out that if ideology is as pervasive as
is claimed, it is reasonable to ask why there are exceptions to its field of operation, and why these exceptions are found in the areas of literary and artistic
production. It is as if readers, writers, and audiences were free of ideological
constraints only as long as they perform these roles. The diagonally opposite
claim, that all artistic production is necessarily complicit with the ruling ideology, can also be plausibly resisted; critics point out that not only is this position counterintuitive, but it can be shown to lead to a point where the criticism has theorized away all possibility of dissent from a ruling ideology. It is
in this position that Greenblatt finds himself at the end of *Renaissance Self-
Fashioning:*

In all my texts and documents, there were . . . no moments of pure, unfettered
subjectivity; indeed, the human subject itself began to seem remarkably unfree,
the ideological product of the relations of power in a particular society.
(1980:256)

While it is unnecessary simply to reinstate the free subject as writer or reader, it
is also unsatisfactory to reduce the specific nature of literary or artistic production to a state where it is indistinguishable from other "ideological state appa-
ratuses," to use Althusser's term, such as educational or religious institutions.

It is possible to point to a way out of this impasse, and those contributions
to this collection which register the critical debates about ideology also reject
any simplified account of its relations to literature. Michelle Gellrich's paper

argues for the importance of not attributing to ideology a monolithic status, in which it is always a self-consistent monologue. Peter Rose's paper points out that the ideological field is one of "struggle and persuasion." It is important to remember that the notion of ideology stems from that of conflict, and in conflict there are necessarily at least two sides. The workings of ideology are rooted in a social contradiction; if specific arrangements *were* natural rather than cultural, clearly the work of ideology in demonstrating their natural rather than cultural status would be redundant. A dominant ideology has constantly to canvass alternatives to itself even if only to attempt to dispel or discredit them.

The issues of the relation of ideology to literature and history become relatively clear, if not simple, if we consider aspects of the work of feminist criticism. Feminist criticism has a serious investment in the notion of ideology, because it operates with an assumption of inequality; despite minor variations in material histories from different times and cultures, feminist critics argue, women have in all periods and places occupied an inferior position in their culture and lacked access to power and resources comparable to that available to men. Our present position in the United States of the late twentieth century gives us a quite unprecedented take on women's historical subjection, due to the real work of political resistance within their own unequal societies that feminists have undertaken in the recent past. Feminist criticism tends to be avowedly non- or antihumanist because it argues that the category "human," allegedly universal, is secretly restricted to that of "male." Most feminists would further complicate the dyad of male and female with other divisions by race and class, and claim that individuals are seen to correspond more nearly to "human" the more they bear signs of the favored ethnic or social categories. If we leave these latter issues aside for the purpose of exposition, we can note that in line with this claim, feminist criticism often finds itself at odds with the humanist notion of literature because it concludes that art and literature are not necessarily "good for" women, do not help them make sense of or enrich their lives, but instead can be complicit in the real political subjection of women. An avowedly "ideological" conception of literature replaces the humanist notion. This can lead to extreme and probably unsustainable positions such as that attributed to Suzanne Kappeler: "Art will have to go." [20]

Relevant to our present forum is the feminist work which has established itself as an authoritative voice on Athenian tragedy. The issue of gender is absent from the conference title but fortunately not from the different contributions; and indeed it could plausibly be argued that descriptions of Athenian tragedy are necessarily inadequate unless they take account of gender. Feminist critics who employ a theory of ideology claim that texts deriving from ancient Athens, nonfigurative as well as figurative, bear the marks of a patriarchal ideology that positions them to promulgate a certain notion of relations between the sexes; this relation is assumed to be unchanging and natural whereas it may be only cultural, sustained for the benefit of men at the expense of women.[21] This is how the argument appears in the work of Nancy Rabinowitz:

> Feminists can then expect to find in literary artifacts reflections of ideology that have fitted men to rule, women to be ruled. But literary texts not only represent ideology; in circular fashion, they support it as well, for they can make what *is* seem like what *has to be*, can make that which is constructed and artificial appear "natural" and necessary.
>
> (1987:127)

That this ideologically charged zone of literature is one of struggle, however, rather than of monolithic certainty, may be indicated by the frequency in Athenian texts of representations of apparently noninferior women within a context of similarly frequent remarks about women's "natural" inferiority. The culture seems to have to rehearse contraventions of the norm in order to produce and reproduce the desired situation, to define and redefine it within different contexts. This argument about the contested nature of the field can be made even if scholarly inquiry never recovers instances of historical Athenian women complaining about their subjection. In fact, a silence from one side of the struggle would be most eloquent testimony to the success of the other. Seen in this light, texts are not reflections of any material reality, because part of their task is actually to constitute a desired reality. Similarly, they cannot be ascribed to the personal concerns of discrete authors, because they are determined by forces larger than that of individual subjectivity. Even when not making explicit statements about specific females, tragedies enter the arena of struggle and persuasion where certain distributions of power are preserved and promoted and others are not. They enter that arena marked with signs of their literary, or rather dramatic, status, so that they cannot be reduced to mirrors of the way things are, nor to authorial reactions to certain events or issues, but rather constitute interventions in a continuing process.

Feminist criticism has had varying relations with "theory" and with "history."[22] Many feminists welcomed the polemical dismantling of binary oppositions that deconstruction performed because so many such oppositions seemed to lead back to the "complementary" but ultimately hierarchical pairing of male and female. Deconstruction thus provided a tool for urgent feminist work; again as Rabinowitz puts it, "feminists . . . can deconstruct the notion of necessity to reveal the tensions contained and even controlled therein" (1987:127). The general theoretical alignment visible in the critical profession was also attractive to feminists because it promised a reexamination of categories previously taken for granted, and such reexamination seemed of necessity politically useful to dissenting parties. Marilyn Skinner writes:

> Theory has become both the discourse and the disciplinary posture of those intellectually and professionally marginalized. Its questioning of self-evident assumptions naturally extends to analysis of the mechanisms for the production and validation of academic knowledge.
> (1992:223)

But at the same time deconstruction, with its dethroning of authorial presence and control, seemed to jeopardize much of the pioneering work in the recovery of texts by women writers who were previously consigned to obscurity. As Joanna Russ intimates in "Denial of Agency" (1983:20–24), if nobody wrote it or it wrote itself, then no woman can have written it, and the status quo, in which women *do not* write, is preserved.

Feminist theory also has a particular and productive relation with "history," whether understood as the practice of inquiry or as the recoverable materiality of the past. Feminism is consistently aware not only of its special provenance in the recent past, but also of its capacity to reconstruct various histories of female agency and subjection that may either validate its present claims or complicate them. This has meant that feminist criticism is almost always engaged in theorizing the position of the reader or critic who approaches texts generated at a distant historical period (at an inordinately great distance, for feminists working within classics) and frequently within a very different set of assumptions. Feminist criticism repeatedly has to face questions such as: To what extent is the criticism reading concerns that constituted the texts in their own historical period, and to what extent is it importing its concerns with too little understanding of the text's irreducible historical difference? The issue of historical distance between text and reader is of course a problem not only for feminist criticism but for all historicizing projects. Such criticism needs to negotiate a way between the fallacy of a full recovery of the past that would be untainted by the critic's own investments, and the solipsistic assumption that since only the act of reading animates the text, the text is constrained to give us back ourselves.

Feminist criticism has secured itself a relatively respectable position within classics, as it has within the study of other languages and literatures, partly because of changes in the demographic profile of college faculty[23] and partly because many of feminism's goals can be presented as congenial to a liberal humanist philosophy. But classics as a whole has historically been resistant to any self-consciously theoretical enterprise, even in its time to the New Criticism. The discipline emerged in the Renaissance as a humanist undertaking that endeavored to reconstruct "the ancients" fully in order to enter into a dialogue with them. Its guiding assumptions are overwhelmingly positivist and empiricist. Hugh Kenner, in the *Times Literary Supplement* for April 30, 1993, describes the characteristic activity of classicists as "pattern-matching" and even invents a professional journal titled *Classical Patterns Quarterly*. Here is his account of our research:

> Pattern-matching means finding a sequence of letters, or a close variant of such a sequence, wherever it may turn up in the multi-million-character corpus we call Greek and Latin Literature. The finds end up as lists. So lexicographers collect every context in which a "word" (which is nothing but a pattern) appears. Better texts are sorted from worse ones by spotting patterns of degeneracy. Recurrent mannerisms help scholars ascribe authorship.

Kenner is not alone; Professor Thomas Rosenmeyer similarly describes "classicists, in their capacity as classicists, . . . as trackers and transmitters" (1988: 44). Evidently a discipline so constituted will not place a very high premium on self-conscious examination of its assumptions. That there are competing notions of the discipline, such as Amy Richlin's claim that classics is "an area study and includes the work of linguists, literary critics, philosophers, historians, epigraphers, papyrologists, art historians, and archaeologists, among others" (1992:xii), does not by itself alter this picture. The resistance to theory can be variously explained. Karl Galinsky, in his introduction to a recent collection of essays on Roman poetry, gives four possible reasons: antimethodism, the antihumanism of modern theory, classicists' respect for text and author, and the theoretical establishment's devaluing of aesthetic pleasure (1992:21–26). These explanations all depend on a broadly humanistic notion of the inquiry into literature. To them we can add a demanding training in language that may present texts as more urgently requiring translation and paraphrase than intricate unraveling. The student is encouraged to establish a single meaning rather than to entertain a multiplicity of meanings. Finally perhaps we can add to Galinsky's list the corporate culture of a discipline under economic threat that, reasonably enough, does not want to be seen to undermine its own premises.

The discipline's resistance, however, is constantly overcome in many different ways and places—particularly, I shall suggest, in the study of Athenian tragedy—and there are many signs that classicists are reaching an informed accommodation with the more taxing practices of recent literary criticism. In this context the publication in 1988 of Rosenmeyer's *Deina Ta Polla: A Classicist's Checklist of Twenty Literary Critical Positions*, is an eloquent sign.

While it was heartening to see a discourse on theory aimed precisely at classicists, it was disheartening that they should be encouraged to use a "checklist"—unwittingly validating Kenner's description!—rather than to engage seriously with the issues. The kind of intellectual commitment envisaged is described thus:

> It is best to be familiar with the variety of choices, to make the history of critical stances one's own, and then, against the background of informed sophistication, to wade into the interpretive fray in a spirit of spontaneous generosity, without aligning one's steps narrowly with this or that model.
> (1988:5)

Engagement with theory is presented as selection from a smorgasbord, a benign eclecticism that apparently cannot be considered to have wider consequences in, or be conditioned by, the rest of the critic's existence. Such a formulation is obviously inadequate in the case of, e.g., feminist theory and, many would argue, in other cases, too.

In this atmosphere the "return to history" in related disciplines can generate a certain amount of complacency among classicists, because it is easy for them to claim that, owing to the synthesizing nature of their discipline, they have always been doing literature-with-history and history-with-literature. They are thus the keepers of the flame, and practitioners in other literatures have merely been temporarily seduced away from the stable bedrock of documents and evidence. Even in this more congenial climate, however, the profession may still be heard to sound a note of caution about its ability to engage with the new historicism. As I have pointed out, new historicist practice often depends on the juxtaposition of established literary texts with those that are obscure and nonliterary. The Presidential Address to the meeting of the American Philological Association in December 1989 expressed doubt as to whether we have access to enough nonliterary texts from the ancient world to mount intelligent comparisons. Another version of this argument is to claim that we do not have access to sufficient numbers of *any* kinds of texts and that our knowledge of ancient history is too lacunose to make it part of our analytic equipment. There are some ready, if not clinching, responses to these arguments. One is to wonder what we as classicists have collectively been doing since the Renaissance. A more cogent response is to point out that the accumulation of documents and evidence does not constitute knowledge or understanding without a theorized frame of reference within which to perceive it. Some theoretical parameters must be in place for the document or piece of evidence even to be recognized as such. Furthermore, one can argue that some of the materiality of history itself goes unperceived because of contemporary bias. The field of women's history suggests that this may be the case. I quote Lefkowitz and Fant's introduction to the second edition of *Women's Life in Greece and Rome*:

> When we began collecting ancient sources on women's lives, in the late 1970s, we, and our publishers, expected to cover the field in a single medium-sized volume. We now know that an enormous quantity of ancient material on women's lives exists; but long and patient labour is required to discover and make sense of it. (1992:xxiv)

In the late 1970s, then, the traditional parameters of inquiry made it impossible to *see* the contributions of women to history. A shift in theoretical notions of what constitutes history actually makes more information available.

The third term in the title of the conference is tragedy. What are the relations implied by the title among these terms? I shall begin by explaining the privileged position that the conference awards to tragedy rather than to other genres. I would make the perhaps unwise claim that within the discipline of classics, Athenian tragedy occupies a special position both in terms of the discipline's relation to other areas of the humanities and in terms of the work that is currently being achieved in the criticism of tragedy.[24] The specialists who write on Athenian tragedy are dealing with what is readily acknowledged as a common possession of the West. It is chiefly tragedy, from among classical genres, that enters the arena of current debates on the goals and methods of higher education. Here at the University of Texas, during deliberations about a proposal to require courses in multiculturalism, Professor Steven Weinberg said in opposition to the proposal, "I doubt that a college [that] graduates people with an A.B. who have never read Dostoevsky or Tolstoy or a Greek tragedy is really living up to its obligation."[25] Few other genres from the ancient world would find it easy to replace tragedy in this triumvirate. Tragedy has been understood to have intimate relations with both poetic theory and historical critique. Numerous theoretical discourses, from Plato to Brecht, make their claims with large reference to tragedy. In *Death of Tragedy* (1961), George Steiner uses Athenian drama as a touchstone by which to write a history of Europe. Critics have persistently cited tragedy as a sign of the peak of human social achievement. Shelley's *A Defence of Poetry* claims:

> The connexion of scenic exhibitions with the improvement or corruption of the manners of men, has been universally recognized. . . . The drama at Athens, or wheresoever else it may have approached to its perfection, coexisted with the moral and intellectual greatness of the age.[26]

Shelley's writing, of course, addressed an audience which acquired a classical education as a "natural" adjunct to its social preeminence and was thus disposed to grant classical civilization exceptional status. Contemporary classicists, however, find it less easy to make such hegemonic claims, although that such claims can be registered even outside the specialized discipline is indicated by Weinberg's speech. But tragedy also seems to hold a singular place within the discipline, in terms of the theoretically aware work done on it. This situation may arise partly *because* tragedy provides a point of intersection between the specialized discipline and a wider culture. At least since the Cambridge ritualists of the early twentieth century, tragedy has been exceptionally fertile ground for those critics who draw on anthropological discourses of myth and ritual. Structuralist analysis, because it is interested in myth, has frequently been drawn to produce new readings of tragedy. Radical deconstructive analysis has assailed the heights of the *Oresteia*,[27] and it is hardly necessary to point out that tragedy is one genre that has insistently demanded the attention of feminist critics.[28] Tragedy has also offered itself to psychoanalytic critics, and has provided the very terminology for some of psychology's central constructs. There is a certain circularity to my argument, of course; classicists who are theoretically aware have found it congenial to work on tragedy and correspondingly tragedy has proved constantly productive of new theoretically informed readings. This circularity can escape the gaze of the practitioners: comments such as "Lévi-Strauss's view of myth as exploring and validating the opposition between nature and culture . . . is substantiated by a great deal of Greek tragedy" sidestep the problem of the investment of the observers in what they claim to observe dispassionately.[29] But that the study of tragedy is carried on by people especially disposed to reflect on their interpretive practices does seem to be a feature of the current critical scene.

How does the theoretical dimension of writing on tragedy engage with more historical accounts of it? Since production of drama entails public events in front of a specific audience, one might expect all varieties of drama to insist on their relations to their historical circumstances. Similarly, it can be argued that dramas have a distinct temporal dimension which is that of performance, so that the notion of a "present time" is indispensable to the functioning of a drama.[30] There is no narrative framework which could suspend the play in a completed past and thus insulate it from its contemporary circumstances. This immediate relation to history might also be described in terms of action; dramas actually take place and have themselves the status of a historical event. They are even on occasion said to cause other events, such as the miscarriages which allegedly attended the first scenic revelation of the Eumenides. Of course, this notion of a necessary relation to history as an adjunct of performance is thoroughly flawed; not all dramas are staged (although this seems an unlikely condition of dramas in ancient Athens) and dramas are not always staged but may constantly be read, recited, or subjected to other kinds of textual elaboration such as editing. All of these possibilities were instantiated for tragedy in ancient Athens. Moreover, any attempt to discuss Athenian tragedy in terms of a historicity of performance comes up against the reality of its temporal survival, which is both attested and assisted by the hegemonic claims for its cultural relevance that I quoted above. The problem of interpretation at a historical remove is thus compounded by the extreme mediation by which we approach the plays; tragedy cannot appear to us free of the transhistorical meanings which successive groups of readers have assigned to it. The historicizing critique of Marx famously came up against this problem. It is not impossible for Marx to explain why tragedy emerges as a uniquely developed form of art from an undeveloped social and material base. Rather, "the difficulty lies not in understanding that the Greek arts and epic are bound up with certain forms of social development. The difficulty is that they still afford us artistic pleasure and that in a certain respect they count as a norm and as an unattainable model."[31] If certain artistic forms are at such a historical remove from us that in fact they can no longer be produced within contemporary culture, why do they still excite a response in contemporary audiences? Marx's solution to this conundrum has not been found very satisfactory,[32] but many other attempts to comprehend this relation seek to eradicate any sense of historical difference by taking refuge instead in changeless human nature as an explanation of tragedy's survival. Such accounts of tragedy, which refer it to the categories of free will and fate, for instance, or individual and society, suppress the work that is involved in reading (or watching) these plays—the obstacles that they put up to comprehension—in favor of an effortless transparency between present concerns and those of the past.

Alongside such generalizing, universalizing accounts of tragedy there have always been those that do seek to position tragedies in a more precise relation to their historical provenance. To many of these, however, can be attributed the fallacy described by Said whereby the text is reduced to its circumstances; the text is said to mirror its world accurately, without regard for the specific conditions that make it a text. This makes the interpretation of plays an exercise in discerning which contemporary Athenian lurks underneath the guise of the tragic personage. Delebecque, in *Euripide et la guerre du Péloponnèse* (1951), mounts a reductio ad absurdum of historical particularity in which tragic characters are discovered with alarming regularity to conceal Alcibiades, and numerous dramatic utterances are "Euripide" darkly commenting on the progress of the war. Such historicizing interpretation evidently endangers any claim we might wish to make for tragedy's cultural hegemony, because it offers to reduce *all* tragic discourse to matters of fact and accidentalities. My own work makes me particularly aware of this tradition in the case of Euripidean drama, which frequently seems to register more strongly than Aeschylean or Sophoclean the pressure of contemporary events. Perhaps it is only an accident of transmission, however, that is responsible for this impression; for instance, without one fortuitously preserved manuscript, **L**, the explicitly Athenian plays like *Hiketides, Herakleidai,* and *Ion* would be lost. The alleged permeability of the Euripidean dramas to their social environment, however, is frequently read only in the supposed dramatic irrelevance of characters' utterances. A cavalier attitude to the interior necessities of the dramatic fabric is then imputed to the author, as a sign either of his incompetence or of his developed moral sensitivity. The pursuit of historical particularity, moreover, is often accompanied by an unquestioning identification of the Athenian past with the present of the commentator. The sensibility of Euripidean drama to disruptive social currents is often associated in the criticism—at least that of the twentieth century—with a claim that "we" are uniquely placed to understand "Euripides" because of our particular historical experiences. This is as true for Murray before the First World War (1913:16), as for Grube in the middle of the Second (1941:12). Again Delebecque offers a startlingly precise formulation of the relationship:

> Il suffisait d'ouvrir les yeux, sans passion, sur le choc des peuples et les batailles de l'heure . . . pour mieux saisir, sous leur véritable aspect, les Athéniens plongés dans une guerre qui dura vingt-sept ans, et pour rajeunir Euripide en lui donnant peut-être une physionomie morale plus éloignée de la légende.
> (1951:7)
>
> It was necessary only to open one's eyes, dispassionately, to the clash of peoples and the battles of the period . . . in order to understand the Athenians better, as they really were, plunged into a war which lasted twenty-seven years, and to bring Euripides up to date by allowing him, perhaps, a moral physiognomy somewhat removed from his legend. (my translation)

The reconstruction of a specific historical dimension to Euripidean drama, then, often depends on a misguided notion of identity between past and present, and has tended to be reductive in its accounts of individual plays.

Sophoclean drama, in an inevitable converse, seems studiously to have ignored the social currents of the fifth century. It has often been held up as a sign not only that "the poet" can be "above the fray," but also that Sophocles, biographically, was so.[33] That the biographical tradition, for what it is worth, offers numerous counterexamples of historical and political engagement on the part of a historical Sophocles has not been allowed to interfere with later investment in the Olympian detachment that qualified the dramatist to speak in terms of moral universals. There are of course exceptions to this rule, such as the work of Knox.[34] The work of Vidal-Naquet on *Philoctetes* and *Oedipus at Colonus* has further opened up Sophoclean drama to a generalized socioeconomic pressure.[35] In the case of Aeschylean tragedy, the generalizing impulse of traditional humanist criticism has been briefly halted by the historical particularity of the *Persae* and the *Eumenides*. But treatment of the latter play has often placed "Aeschylus" in various partisan positions over the reform of Ephialtes, thus falling into the positivist trap of the single political viewpoint censured by Greenblatt above. The main thrust of much criticism has still been to treat Aeschylean drama as chiefly concerned with human relations to the divine rather than with relations within specific social formations.[36] Winnington-Ingram opens his study of Aeschylus with the words "Aeschylus was a dramatist of ideas—religious ideas" (1983:1).

The present critical scene offers a number of possibilities for describing tragedy's relation to its historical provenance. In several of these, as I indicated above, the notion of ideology is prominent. The tradition deriving from the work of Vernant and Vidal-Naquet has had a tendency to posit ideology as a relatively monolithic structure operating in "society" but not, crucially, in tragedy, which is privileged instead to question social arrangements. Vernant writes of tragedy: "It does not reflect that reality but calls it into question" (1990:33). A modification of this position is legible in Goldhill 1990, where the notion of ideology is elaborated by that of a specifically "civic" ideology. This civic ideology is upheld in the ceremonies which open the festival of Dionysus and precede the plays. The dramas that follow constitute not only a questioning of the dominant norms but also "a questioning of the very basis of those norms, the key structures of opposition on which 'norm' and 'transgression' rest" (1990:127). The plays do not simply invert the teachings of the preplay ceremonials but interrogate and complicate them. There are problems with this formulation; the first is that there can still be perceived a dichotomy between the preplay ceremonials and the plays themselves, which are somehow less ideologically determined than the preceding displays. A second, more cogent objection is that the Athenian civic ideology, as described by Goldhill, lacks the crucial component of inequality; it operates at no one's expense because it has to distort no social relations.[37] If the civic ideology's ideal of unity is in fact to be achieved at the expense of one group's aspirations, the plays, on this model, would presumably make some of this particular tension legible. Another kind of inequality that might be thought to operate within the civic ideology is that between Athenians and their empire. It could be argued correspondingly that the civic ideology binding the citizens was bought at the price of the subjection of other Greeks. But again in Goldhill's account the tragedies are not interested in this relation and do not render it visible.

I have no wish in this introduction to preempt Professor Gellrich's discussion of the work associated with the Paris-based school of classicists, but it seemed appropriate to cite the foregoing accounts of the relation between tragedy and history as foils to other significant views which also condition the current scene. In my discussion of these I shall again largely confine myself to work on Euripidean drama. This work is most familiar to me and, moreover, because of the characteristics of Euripidean drama outlined above, provides a plausible index to what is available in terms of working notions about tragedy's historical dimensions. One strand of this work, which is most clearly articulated in the writing of David Kovacs, insists on reclaiming tragedy, especially Euripidean tragedy, for "the norm," in response to the perceived inadequacies of accounts of its subversive potential. Thus the tragedies can and should be read "in this straightforward and unsuspicious way against the background of fifth-century norms, the critic invoking no standards or ideas that would not have occurred naturally to an ordinary Athenian in the audience" (1987:x). The tragedies thus work to reinforce what all Athenians accept, and this social coherence is guaranteed in part at least by the figure of the author, who always intends the audience to have one, and only one, attitude towards his characters (1987:7). This account presents at least two difficulties. The first is the notion that there was on any topic one thing that the Athenians thought. Here the criticism falls into the trap of the "old" historicism as defined and censured by Greenblatt. Secondly, Kovacs places an unwarranted faith in the figure of the author. Controlling all the text's meanings (and thereby ensuring that it has very few), the author brings the text to coherence and completeness, but he is simultaneously controlled by audience expectations and by the norms of his culture. The paradox disappears if the author is conceived of as knowing the norms and identifying wholly with them, and furthermore if he resides within a society that can always reconcile one norm with another. If we accept instead the notion of a culture always in some form of conflict with itself, the norm-producing author becomes less probable.

A more interesting attempt to explore the ways in which tragedy may be said to uphold and preserve a dominant consensus is mounted by Synnøve des Bouvrie (1990) on the particular ground of the representation of women. She draws heavily on anthropological models and explicitly eschews the notion of ideology which, she claims, connotes "deception" and "illusion":

> The notion of "ideology" should be avoided since it conveys overtones of optional, conscious exertion of power, whereas the phenomena I will discuss . . . belong to the inevitable patterning of social life.
> (1990:51)

In fact many would argue, as I have suggested, that the workings of ideology also belong to the "inevitable patterning of social life." Des Bouvrie also explicitly rejects the notion that plays constitute any kind of intellectual or reflective activity (e.g., 1990:115); instead of entering into an arena of debate, plays reinforce their culture's values and goals, with all the resources of ritual display and emotional identification at their disposal. She refutes the notion of the author's prized individuality as the guiding force behind the tragedy, but substitutes an anthropological account of culture which eventually erases the constitutive differences of tragic theater so that drama is largely indistinguishable from ritual. Again des Bouvrie rejects the notion of conflict within the culture, so that her refusal of Romantic conceptions of the artistic process, which involved the poet teaching the culture as an "unacknowledged legislator," is ultimately replaced by an equally Romantic conception of a culture untroubled by disagreement over its social relations, its values, and its goals, which are taken to be ultimately conformable with one another.

Justina Gregory's *Euripides and the Instruction of the Athenians* (1991) attempts a slightly different tack. Gregory accepts the Athenian notion of the dramatist as *didaskalos* (teacher), especially of people in the city. This is to say, tragedy necessarily has an avowed political dimension (1991:6–9). The political dimension of Euripidean drama is found to reside especially in its reworking of aristocratic values for consumption and use by a democratic audience that has need of tragedy in order to maintain political stability (1991:9–12). Tragedy, or at least the Euripidean version, thus enters a realm of potential conflict between aristocrats and democrats, in order to exert a stabilizing influence by its mediation. This approach has many positive possibilities, but the "wholesome aim" (1991:8) of the tragedies is attributed entirely to "Euripides," who is thus represented as standing outside the fray. Moreover, the issues on which Euripidean tragedy allegedly chooses to exert itself turn out to be curiously familiar; the encounter with necessity (1991:12) is the starting point for tragedy, and then resolves itself into "the relationship between life and death; the nature of moderation; the claims of justice; the definition of nobility; the uses of language and intellect" (1991:11). In this respect, then, a renewed emphasis on "history" has not yet led to the renewed readings that one might have expected.

The essays in this collection are sited within this problematic. They vary considerably in terms of their explicit allegiances to notions of "theory" and "history," and it is difficult to construct among them any significant consensus. During the conference, in fact, fundamental differences were productively aired. It may appear anomalous that no historians as such were invited to speak at the conference; the reason for this is not a lack of interest in their separate but related inquiries but because the questions in front of the conference, and the possibility of posing them, derive from theoretical rather than historical reflection, and center exclusively on tragedy. I should like to elucidate the more or less explicit agreements and disagreements among the papers before sketching what I consider as the future possibilities and tasks for a historicizing criticism of tragedy. The order of the papers in this volume largely reproduces that of the conference; the passage from one paper to another is determined not by chronology or authorial identity but rather by the types of argumentation deployed and the notions of history and of theory which are brought to bear on the chosen texts.

Michelle Gellrich's paper examines part of the context for the conference's agenda with an account of how classics has relied on structuralism and anthropology, mediated through the work of French critics such as Vernant, Vidal-Naquet, and Detienne, to avoid both an engagement with deconstruction and a critical understanding of the discipline's own relation to historical inquiry. She suggests that the Paris-based school of critics has elaborated notions of history and ideology that, while highly influential within classics, foreclose many productive possibilities and are particularly vulnerable to a deconstructive critique. The new sociocriticism, she argues, replaces the unitary figure of the "author" with an equally monolithic "culture" or "ideology" that predates the text and thus delimits its meanings. Recovery of the parameters of the extraliterary context is held to permit a full identification between the text and the contemporary reader. This context resolves into the binary oppositions and polarities characteristic of structuralism, so that even if the dramatic text or performance inverts or questions the norms of its culture, it is said to do so within a binary logic and thus to be forced ultimately to confirm the preexisting structures and loci of power.

Gellrich opposes this position by mobilizing deconstructive arguments to suggest that the posited context is not a normative given but a text that itself requires interpretation, and she points to the ways in which tragedy is constitutive of its context rather than logically and temporally subsequent to it. She suggests too that the fantasy of identification between text and reader, said to be made possible by recovery of the context, fails to take account of the resistance of the past to interpretation. Not only does the past resist, but when it does speak, it refuses to speak in categories that we recognize. Gellrich argues instead for a more acute awareness of "other voices" in tragedy, and at the close of her paper offers a deconstructive reading of the *Bacchae* that unpicks the notion of binary opposition, said to inform many recent analyses, and replaces it with an exploration of the centrifugal tendencies in the text's competing voices.

Marxist analysis has historically found itself in frequent opposition to "theory" generally, and particularly to deconstruction. Peter Rose's paper opens with an investigation of the ways in which "the messiness of history and politics" is effectively bracketed by much of the present critical emphasis on ambiguity and ambivalence. In the case of his chosen text, the *Ajax*, he shows how criticism of various brands has engaged with the drama's politics only as a preface to demonstrating how some other issue is in fact paramount in the play. This is a measure, Rose suggests, of the text's success; it has managed to reinscribe the conflicts from which it emerged as human universals.

To restore a specific historical dimension to the text, Rose argues, is to solve the problem of making the past speak without forcing it to say only what we want to hear. The relation between history and text is mediated by ideology, and the discussion of ideology in this paper is complementary to that of Gellrich, in that ideology is held to be not a monolithic worldview but a site of "persuasion and struggle." Since ideological production is seen as determined particularly by class conflict, the focus of discussion shifts to conflicts within Athens, where the political struggle between elite and mass for cultural hegemony constitutes the external problematic to which the *Ajax* is said to respond. The unfinished nature of the struggle produces the "internal contradictions" and "structured silences" of the play. If there are plural "meanings" to be deciphered in the drama, they are not in open-ended play but in a struggle for supremacy.

Rose concentrates on Sophoclean modifications of the myth and on disjunction between the mythical and rhetorical structures of the play. Sophocles endeavors to transform the archaic, heroic, but troubling, figure of Ajax into the representative of a particular social and economic class, a *strategos* writ large. This figure transcends the aristocratic code but simultaneously denigrates the democratic alternative, and thus promotes a "justly hierarchical" paternalism. The mass of Athenians are brought to identify with this figure, despite his removal from them in class terms, by the hostile representation of his Spartan opponents. The play thus validates tendencies in Athenian society that are "aristocratic, militaristic, paternalistic," and in so doing it responds to a need for Athens to envision herself as repository of humane culture at the same time as she acts ruthlessly toward her subject allies. This kind of identification can heal internal political breaches, but Rose suggests it is bought at the price of contradictions in the drama that conversely make legible the effort to overcome them.

Rose's analysis of the *Ajax* relies on the organizing intentions of a particular author and thus is open to deconstructive objections, which would locate the contradictions of the text in the nature of representation as well as in political process. The work of David Rosenbloom also assumes authorial intention, although for him the author Aeschylus stands at odds with Athenian culture and his dramas constitute a meditation on the threat to Athenian freedom posed by the acquisition of a maritime empire. For Rosenbloom, as opposed to Rose, the impetus to tragedy stems from conflict between Athens and her allies rather than from internal struggle. In further contradistinction to Rose, and moreover to Gellrich, Rosenbloom does not mobilize a notion of ideology but models a particular history as directly producing the general contours and the specific details of Aeschylean dramaturgy.

Rosenbloom sees the genre of tragedy as implicated at all points with the Athenian empire. The experience of the Persian Wars provided a paradigm of action for Aeschylus' plots, which characteristically dramatize liberation on the personal and civic scales. But for Athens, freedom at home was accompanied by domination abroad, and Rosenbloom argues that Aeschylus constantly investigates this contradiction and its consequences. In the heart of the powerful city he repeatedly stages the downfall of the powerful. In particular, Rosenbloom marshals a wealth of historical and textual detail to suggest that Aeschylean tragedy is informed by the figure of naval power. Naval power is marked with a sinister ambiguity, developed as it was in response to the barbarian, the Persian. Naval power is also compromised as a route to empire because it belies Athens' traditional virtues with the aggressive exploitation of allies by siege and blockade. Rosenbloom mounts a specific analysis of the *Oresteia* that shows how Agamemnon is represented predominantly in naval metaphors, which are abandoned when the *Eumenides* celebrates the traditional agricultural fertility of the Attic countryside. The historical situation of imperial Athens, modeling itself after the enemy, is seen as the generative paradox that makes possible tragedy's ceaseless investigation of the categories of self and other.

Helene Foley opens her paper with a useful restatement of the issues before the conference, framed with reference to the Paris-based school of classicists. While their work has provided to classicists more sophisticated equipment with which to approach the historical situation of the tragedies, she suggests that the very possibility of historical inquiry has simultaneously been jeopardized by contemporary developments in theory. Such developments have instead directed increased attention to the ways in which texts refuse stable readings and insist on a ceaselessly deferred indeterminacy. Foley considers that a productive way of reading is offered by relating tragedy to the notion of "democratic ideology" rather than to specific historical detail. But this approach, too, will prove unsatisfactory if democratic ideology is taken to be univocal and monologic. She suggests that any attempt to posit the historical dimension of tragedy as source and guarantee of a coherent identity or agenda is undermined by the generic and institutional qualities of the drama. Her arguments thus lead her to a position similar to that of Gellrich, but her engagement with the notion of "democratic ideology" does not allow room for an argument about tragedy's response to the materiality of political conflict, as does the work of Rose and Rosenbloom.

Foley's chosen text is the *Antigone,* and she takes issue with two recent readings of this play that both claim to read it in relation to democratic ideology but that nonetheless reach diametrically opposed conclusions about the play itself. Foley examines in particular the work of Sourvinou-Inwood, who argues that a twentieth-century audience must shed its own preconceived assumptions when it approaches an ancient text. Similarly, the work of Bennett and Tyrrell postulates an "imagined audience" for whom the dramatist originally wrote and whom therefore the twentieth-century audience must strive to become. Despite the apparent similarities in their projects, these two historicizing readings fail to generate a consistent account; Sourvinou-Inwood concludes that Antigone is the typical "bad woman" whom the polity must contain, whereas for Bennett and Tyrrell she is the simply laudable defender of democratic values. Foley criticizes both bodies of work for their unquestioning assumptions both that an untroubled identification with audience (or author) is possible and that the ancient audience is undifferentiated in its reactions. Against both the readings she argues that the very form of a tragedy, its dialogue and debate, militates against the attribution to it of a "clearly defined, logically consistent, and easily assimilable viewpoint." Moreover, tragedy takes place in the context of a democratic arena "that prided itself on being open to public exchange of ideas and differences of opinion." *All* the characters in the *Antigone* speak "democratic ideology," and *all* the cases both for and against its protagonist have already been made on stage. Foley questions why historicizing readings consistently present themselves as unilateral and antidialogic, and suggests instead that tragedy encourages its multiple and varied audiences not to reach a single preordained judgment, nor to confess an inability to judge, but to engage in a demanding *process* of judging, as democratic practice regularly requires.

With the paper of Bernd Seidensticker we move from consideration of one female character, Antigone, to consideration of women generally as they are represented on the tragic stage. The representation of women in Athenian drama has always provoked extended discussion of how a given history relates to given texts, or, to cast the question in more familiar terms, why tragic women are so unlike what we conclude real Athenian women to have been. Seidensticker challenges the common assumption that there is in fact a difference, in this case, between literature and life.

The main thrust of his argument foregrounds lived history as a determinant of the text, for he holds that the women of tragedy by and large conform to the norms set out for them by the regular practices of their culture. Not only are

these norms frequently articulated in tragedy, but they are articulated by female characters, and the majority of women represented on the stage present
no critique of such prescriptions. Moreover, the female characters who overtly
refuse to conform still abide by the traditional parameters of female identity.
Women who act on their own initiative in tragedy often do so as a result of
masculine disruption of the female sphere, the domestic environment, and
they regularly confine their actions to that sphere. They even perform their
most threatening acts, the murders of their men, with the traditionally feminine weapons of fabric and poison; at the close of the dramas, whether in
triumph or defeat, they return to the domestic interior.

Seidensticker agrees that this account of tragic women, which he illustrates
with Clytemnestra, Deianira, and Medea, cannot entirely empty such figures
of their transgressive force, but he maintains that these women do not constitute the extreme exception to the rule of female identity that is often claimed.
Instead, he suggests that such female figures are the response of the tragic genre
to the fifth century's unprecedentedly rapid political and social change. The
new politicization of fifth-century life entailed a corresponding diminution in
the significance of the domestic sphere, traditionally identified with the female,
which in turn led to the unusually marginal status of women within Athenian
culture. Seidensticker argues that tragedy provides the forum for discussion
and management of the new stresses consequent to this imbalance between the
genders. In particular, he argues that the tragedians do not merely dramatize
problems and develop ambiguities, as is claimed most prominently, he suggests, by the Paris-based school. In their capacity as teachers of the *polis,* they
also attempt to offer solutions. Seidensticker argues that the tragedians consistently show the necessity of balance in relations between the sexes, as well as
the elusive and fragile nature of that balance. Finally he suggests that the tragedians manage, through their equivocal representation of the female, to challenge the masculinist bias of their audiences while not fundamentally upsetting
traditional assumptions about female identity and role.

This model of tragedy's interventions in its culture, whereby it issues challenges but confines its critique within traditional limits, is most obviously at
variance with Gellrich's emphasis on tragedy's centrifugal tendencies. Similarly,
the model implicitly rejects a notion of political conflict such as informs the
work of Rose and Rosenbloom. Tragedy *cannot* be implicated in a political
conflict between the genders, because it is offering a space for its symbolic
resolution. This focus on the integrative energies of the tragic genre anticipates
the work in this collection of Richard Seaford.

It is perhaps not surprising that the Paris-based school of classicists, prominently including Vernant and Vidal-Naquet, should appear within this collection as proponent both of "theory" and of "history." Froma Zeitlin, often as-

sociated with this school, continues the problematic identification by setting her analysis in an entirely different terrain from much of her work. Her contribution to this collection suggests a further historical contextualization for tragedy in its relation to other aesthetic products of its culture. The later plays of Euripides in particular, she suggests, show a heightened awareness of the visual dimension of the *polis* and indicate that theatrical practice may have contributed to the development of graphic and plastic arts. Theater shares with art an interest in educating the spectator to "recognize, evaluate, and interpret" the visual field.

Zeitlin suggests that Euripidean drama, in its relation to the visual arts and especially in its emphasis on ecphrasis, indicates a growing historical consciousness that is especially aware of multiple and conflicting traditions. The past is displayed to the citizens of the *polis* not only in the theater but also in a rich visual environment that repeatedly informs them of their civic and national identity by means of mythic iconography. But this past is always a contested field. Zeitlin examines the ecphrastic moments of *Ion, Phoenissae,* and *Iphigenia at Aulis,* and suggests that each indicates a relation not only with visual arts but also with a narrative history shaping the "tragic interference" between myth and contemporary political concerns. In particular, the ecphrastic episode of the *Iphigenia at Aulis*—the chorus's viewing of the ships—seems to adumbrate the development of memory systems. The scene thus seems to invoke the epic ideal of *kleos* and commemoration, but suggests that in a more complex age transmission of cultural memory is more difficult and demands its own techniques. The resistance and final compliance of Iphigenia, which plays in characteristically Euripidean fashion with the possibility that "the Trojan War will not take place," is also staged in terms of sight and of memory, but the final acquiescence is cast in terms of the late-fifth-century ideal of Panhellenism. The rescue of Iphigenia and the substitution of the deer, as described by the Messenger speech, is a notorious coup in the visual plane but leaves open, at least as far as Clytemnestra is concerned, the question of what really happened.

For reasons of copyright Richard Seaford was unable to contribute to this volume the paper that he delivered at the conference. He produced a new paper especially for this collection, a paper that engages on different ground with the same issues as his original presentation. His paper forms a fitting conclusion to the collection, as it mounts a deliberate confrontation between history and theory and issues direct or indirect challenges to the work of many of his fellow contributors.

Seaford identifies as "mainstream" the notion that tragedy is a genre marked by ambiguity and ambivalence, resistant to closure and subversive of the order of the polis. He argues instead for a historically informed understanding of the functioning of ambivalence which would, for instance, account for differences between Aeschylean and Euripidean treatments of certain forms of ambiguity in terms of historical change in the workings of law courts and in the notion of rhetoric. He suggests a dual strategy of reconstructing the place of ambivalence in Greek culture while simultaneously investigating the development of our own critical preconceptions, and to the latter end he analyzes Nietzsche's notion of the Dionysiac and demonstrates its inadequacies. But the main focus of his paper is on the vote of Athena at the end of the *Eumenides,* which he takes as a paradigmatic case for investigating whether tragedy succeeds in establishing order and closure at the end of its turbulent, destructive action. Seaford relates the narrative structure of the drama to the workings of etiological myth and ritual, which subsume ambivalence into a collective cohesion necessary for the survival of the *polis.* He thus seeks to show that the ambivalences in the ending scenes of the *Eumenides* are practical rather than insoluble, and that elements such as the gender confusion in the figure of Athena function as part of the solution to the crisis rather than as its deferral.

Seaford states the issues clearly: a historical understanding may make legible the ways in which a text subordinates its transgressive forces to a final ordering, even though the questions thus answered, or even *that* the questions get answered, might offend current critical sensibilities. Seaford thus stakes out a position which clearly challenges the analyses of Gellrich and Foley, while his notion of the cohesive *polis* might itself be interrogated by the work of Rose or Rosenbloom.

In the light of this productive variety and disagreement it would be foolish to propose a five-year plan for successful writing on tragedy. It is clear, however, that the "return to history" in related disciplines presents certain challenges to classicists working in this field, among them the challenge of not assuming that their traditional positivist practices have finally been validated. It is incumbent on classicists to theorize their practices as fully as possible, not least if they want to continue to make sense to students who are increasingly habituated to quite demanding relationships with texts. The significant work that has been done on the gender tensions that inform tragedy could well be extended to take account of the constitutive tensions among classes and between Athenians on the one hand and subject Greeks on the other.[38] Such conflict would need to be sited within a specifically fifth-century context, one that is understood to be at least partly conditioned by the work of the tragic representations themselves. Tragedies may leave signs both of how they try to disguise or resolve such conflicts and of how they fail to do so. To read tragedies in this way, with an advantage of historical perspective that was not available to contemporary audiences, is again to come up against a necessity to theorize our positions as readers who are produced both by a history that includes ancient Greece and also by a very different present. Here the demands on theoretical awareness are considerable. While a full objective recovery of the past remains unlikely, it seems important to reconstruct the past in a way that foregrounds its obstinate differences, rather than its similarities, in relation to our own assumptions. The dialogue that we mount with "the ancients" will then always be critical, in both directions, rather than a narcissistic monologue. Here the work of reception-theorists can be extremely useful in assisting us to think through the historical differences, and continuities, that produce the necessity to engage with these texts.

In this connection I should like finally to draw attention to recent developments in the performance of Greek tragedy that focus very sharply the issues of tragedy and history. While the conference was proceeding, *Les Atrides* was playing in New York to considerable critical acclaim and controversy. In this production, the French director Ariane Mnouchkine prefaces the *Oresteia* with a performance of the *Iphigenia at Aulis* to produce a ten-hour cycle of four plays held in a huge open-air arena. The ancient Athenian form of the tetralogy is thus preserved, but the satyr-play with the happy ending—well, maybe a happy ending—precedes the tragic action. A review in *Newsweek* (October 5, 1992) comments thus: "It is, simply and overwhelmingly, our story, the story of the human race in its attempt to shake off the endless cycle of violence and replace it with the rule of law." *Newsweek* makes the appropriate genuflection to the immense capacity for survival that tragedy seemingly displays, and to its ceaselessly rediscovered relevance. But perhaps the relevance is determined not so much by the timeless quality of tragedy as by the very specific demands of our own late-twentieth-century politics. The timeless human story of *Les Atrides* was enacted in New York within some very particular parameters. The Furies, who must be appeased before the resolution of the action can be achieved, were in this production costumed as bag ladies. The emergent democracy at the end of the *Oresteia*, then, apparently proclaimed its foundation on the conciliation and under the authority of those who are, outside the theater and on the streets of New York, among the more excluded elements of American society. The production seemed to claim a double achievement of justice, both in the narrative resolution of the trilogy and in the social conditions of its theatrical materialization. Yet that pointed turning to a contemporary context might easily cast the production's achievements into doubt. Again, according to *Newsweek*, the theater company was made up of actors from more than twenty countries and the performance style drew on Oriental models. "In a time of burgeoning ethnic enmity," says the magazine, "the stage becomes a synthesis of East and West." American society is still divided by enforced inequalities along ethnic lines, but the production in New York ensured that the *Oresteia* proclaimed, again, that justice had in fact already been done; the very cast that acted the plays could apparently unite different nations and overcome any violent history that might otherwise divide them.

Newsweek reports that the director Mnouchkine considers the *Oresteia* timely because "what's happening in Eastern Europe is terrible." What's happening in Europe may well be considered to have become yet more terrible since this review, but events during the collapse of Communist regimes have been characterized not only by political and cultural disintegration. The British newspaper *The Guardian*, in its article on *Les Atrides* (August 29, 1992), pointed out that one of the marks of the post-Communist era in previously Communist societies has also been the staging of Athenian tragedies. In Poland, for instance, as Solidarity grew in importance, an *Antigone* was staged that cast Creon as a Communist official and the chorus as workers in the Gdansk shipyards. In 1990, six months after the execution of Ceaușescu, Andrei Serban produced *An Ancient Trilogy*, comprising *Medea*, *Trojan Women*, and *Electra*, in Bucharest. This production was in ancient Greek. The miners who arrived in the capital in truckloads interrupted rehearsals in search of subversive material, but were placated by being told that this was only ancient Greek, a harmless diversion of pedagogues.

These newspaper accounts show Greek tragedy in interesting and compelling guises. Its power seems to reside in its helplessness—it can always take refuge in its status as a timeless classic that thereby claims a lofty irrelevance to any real struggle. Then it may reappear as one of the many codes in which the disenfranchised and threatened can communicate with one another. But it is not, perhaps, a coincidence that the Western media choose to report precisely *these* movements of post-Communist culture. Are these reviews a simple celebration of what in Greek tragedy really is human and timeless and can therefore unite disparate cultures? Or is the East's production of Greek tragedy useful to the West as most compelling proof that the "others" wish to Westernize? These reviews tell us that the post-Communist countries can help us to discover once more the marvels of our Greek heritage. So in this narrative what post-Communist societies teach the West is the superiority of Western products. The Romanian audiences are reported as responding enthusiastically to the ancient theatrical debates over violence and social justice. The reviews allow us to see them watching. But is our spectating of their spectatorship anything other than a confirmation of what we already think we know—that for us the problem of justice is solved, whereas for them it is only just beginning? In these latest media descriptions of tragedy's survival, *our* productions of Greek drama are effectively said to fantasize the problems of violence and justice from which we are essentially free; but *their* stagings are said to fantasize only the solutions. The East Europeans were represented in Fukuyama's argument as having enacted for us the end of history; now that the end of history hasn't come about, they are seen to be stuck in tragedy, unable to achieve anything but theatrical resolutions. We would do well to reinstate the principle of lectio difficilior, and choose instead that reading, of Greek tragedy or any other cultural artifact, which gives us the most trouble.

NOTES

1. See, e.g., the review articles by W. R. Connor and David Konstan in Culham and Edmunds 1989.
2. See Hillis Miller 1987:283.
3. See for instance the leader in the *Times Higher Education Supplement* for May 8, 1992, p. 12, and the letters in the issue of May 15, 1992, pp. 2 and 13.
4. See especially de Man 1977.
5. Derrida 1976:101–140.
6. See Derrida 1977*a* and Searle 1977.
7. See Derrida 1977*b*.
8. The position of deconstruction in the academic establishment was severely compromised by the discovery of anti-Semitic newspaper articles written in his youth by the prominent deconstructive critic Paul de Man. For some this proved that deconstruction was the corrupt enterprise they had always claimed. For others, the articles revivified the question of the political and historical efficacy of language. Derrida's own writings are occasionally marked by political engagement. Two recent newspaper articles by him have been collected into *The Other Heading: Reflections on Today's Europe* (1992). "Language" and "identity" are still at issue, but in a specific—and urgent—European context.
9. Fukuyama 1989 and 1992. See *New Left Review* 193 (May/June 1992): 89–113 for a spectrum of responses to the book. I cannot tell why the question mark has disappeared between article and book.
10. Lloyd S. Kramer, "Literature, Criticism, and Historical Imagination: The Literary Challenge of Hayden White and Dominick La Capra," in *The New Cultural History*, Lynn Hunt, ed. (Berkeley 1989). Quoted in Simpson 1991:2. This recognition has, of course, been the main drive in the work of Hayden White for many years.
11. See Hartog 1988 and Ober 1989.
12. Said quotes Michael Riffaterre on this fallacy.
13. See Greenblatt 1982*a*.
14. See Greenblatt 1982*b*.
15. Veeser 1989:ix.
16. Newton 1989:152
17. See, e.g., Veeser 1989:xii, xiii.
18. In an unpublished lecture given at Colgate University in fall 1990.
19. L. Althusser, *Lenin and Philosophy* (London 1971) 203–204, quoted in Eagleton 1978:83.

20. Quoted in Richlin 1992:xvii.

21. There are various accounts of why this patriarchal ideology is necessary or valuable in the specific historical conditions of ancient Athens. See for instance Meiksins Wood 1988:118.

22. Newton (1989:154–155) argues that feminist history generated the focuses and practices that later came to be associated with Foucault and with new historicism. She also claims that this pedigree is ignored by these later developments.

23. Such changes, of course, are generally brought about chiefly by feminist political initiatives rather than by any progressive evolution.

24. There are no prizes awarded for pointing out that conference participants also have professional interest in a hegemonic tragedy!

25. Quoted in *On Campus* (University of Texas at Austin, October 28, 1991), p. 3.

26. See the edition of Reiman and Powers (1977:490).

27. See Goldhill 1984.

28. Feminist work on classical tragedy is not confined to classicists, of course; see for instance the seminal work on the *Oresteia* in Millett 1970.

29. Segal 1981 (1986): 32.

30. See, e.g., Elam 1980:117–119.

31. Quoted in Eagleton 1976:11.

32. But see the argument following in Eagleton 1976:12–13.

33. See for instance the complaints about this tradition in Whitman 1951:3–4.

34. Bernard Knox (1957 and 1982) details Sophoclean reservations about the workings of the Athenian *polis*.

35. See Vidal-Naquet 1990a and 1990b. It is striking that even this type of work can ignore historical particularity. The placing of a drama at Colonus, site in 411 B.C. of a particularly abrupt decision on citizenship, is sidelined in favor of much more generalized speculation on categories of citizen. See 1990b, n. 33.

36. Christian Meier's useful work examines the *Eumenides* as a sign of the emerging political dimension of Athenian life rather than of any particular partisan position. His analysis is flawed by the divorce of the political sphere from that of the social or economic, and more particularly by his extraordinary denial that the drama involves issues of gender (see 1990:82–139).

37. It is perhaps relevant that the article confines itself to comment on *Ajax* and *Philoctetes*, and thus largely avoids the need to address civic ideology's relation to Athenian women.

38. Hall (1989) considers tragedy as *the* main cultural site in which Greeks formulated their superiority over non-Greeks.

REFERENCES

Culham, Phyllis, and Lowell Edmunds. 1989. *Classics: A Discipline and Profession in Crisis?* Lanham, New York, and London.

Delebecque, Edouard. 1951. *Euripide et la guerre du Péloponnèse*. Paris.

de Man, Paul. 1977. "The Purloined Ribbon," *Glyph* 1:28–49.

Derrida, Jacques. 1976. *Of Grammatology*. Trans. Gayatri Chakravorty Spivak. Baltimore and London.

————. 1977a. "Signature Event Context," *Glyph* 1:172–197.

————. 1977b. "Limited Inc: abc," *Glyph* 2:162–254.

————. 1992. *The Other Heading: Reflections on Today's Europe*. Trans. Pascale-Anne Brault and Michael B. Naas. Bloomington and Indianapolis.

des Bouvrie, Synnøve. 1990. *Women in Greek Tragedy: An Anthropological Approach*. Oslo.

Eagleton, Terry. 1976. *Marxism and Literary Criticism*. London.

————. 1978. *Criticism and Ideology*. London.

Elam, Keir. 1980. *The Semiotics of Theatre and Drama*. London and New York.

Fukuyama, Francis. 1989. "The End of History?" *The National Interest* 16:3–18.

————. 1992. *The End of History and the Last Man*. London.

Galinsky, Karl. 1992. "The Interpretation of Roman Poetry and the Contemporary Critical Scene." In *The Interpretation of Roman Poetry: Empiricism or Hermeneutics?* Karl Galinsky, ed., 1–40. Frankfurt.

Goldhill, Simon. 1984. *Language Narrative Sexuality: The 'Oresteia'*. Cambridge.

————. 1990. "The Great Dionysia and Civic Ideology." In *Nothing to Do With Dionysos? Athenian Drama in Its Social Context*, John J. Winkler and Froma I. Zeitlin, eds., 97–129. Princeton.

Greenblatt, Stephen. 1980. *Renaissance Self-Fashioning*. Chicago.

————. 1982a. "Introduction." In *The Forms of Power and the Power of Forms in the English Renaissance*. Stephen Greenblatt, ed., 3–7. (*Genre* 15)

————. 1982b. "*King Lear* and Harsnett's Devil Fiction." In *The Forms of Power and the Power of Forms in the English Renaissance*. Stephen Greenblatt, ed., 239–242. (*Genre* 15)

Gregory, Justina. 1991. *Euripides and the Instruction of the Athenians*. Ann Arbor.

Grube, G. M. A. 1941. *The Drama of Euripides*. London.

Hall, Edith. 1989. *Inventing the Barbarian: Greek Self-Definition through Tragedy*. Oxford.

Hartog, François. 1988. *The Mirror of Herodotus: The Representation of the Other in the Writing of History*. Trans. Janet Lloyd. Berkeley and Los Angeles.

Hillis Miller, J. 1987. "Presidential Address 1986: The Triumph of Theory," *PMLA* 102: 281–291.

Knox, B. M. W. 1957. *Oedipus at Thebes*. London and New Haven.

————. 1982. "Sophocles and the Polis." In *Sophocle: Entretiens sur l'antiquité classique* 29. Jacqueline de Romilly, ed., 1–27. Geneva.

Kovacs, David. 1987. *The Heroic Muse*. Baltimore and London.

Lefkowitz, Mary R., and Maureen B. Fant. 1992. *Women's Life in Greece and Rome*. London.

Lentricchia, Frank. 1989. "Foucault's Legacy: A New Historicism?" In *The New Historicism*, H. Aram Vesser, ed., 231–242. New York and London.

Lévi-Strauss, Claude. 1955. "The Writing Lesson." In his *Tristes Tropiques*, 312–325. Paris.

McGann, Jerome. 1985. "Introduction: A Point of Reference." In *Historical Studies and Literary Criticism*, Jerome McGann, ed., 3–21. Madison.

Meier, Christian. 1990. *The Greek Discovery of Politics*. Trans. David McLintock. Cambridge, Mass.

Meiksins Wood, Ellen. 1988. *Peasant Citizen and Slave: The Foundations of Athenian Democracy.* London and New York.

Millett, Kate. 1970. *Sexual Politics.* Garden City, N.Y.

Murray, Gilbert. 1913. *Euripides and His Age.* New York and London.

Newton, Judith Lowder. 1989. "History as Usual? Feminism and the 'New Historicism.'" In *The New Historicism,* H. Aram Veeser, ed., 152–167. New York and London.

Ober, Josiah. 1989. *Mass and Elite in Democratic Athens: Rhetoric, Ideology, and the Power of the People.* Princeton.

Pechter, Edward. 1987. "The New Historicism and Its Discontents: Politicizing Renaissance Drama," *PMLA* 102:292–307.

Poole, Adrian. 1987. *Tragedy: Shakespeare and the Greek Example.* Oxford.

Rabinowitz, Nancy. 1987. "Female Speech and Female Sexuality: Euripides' *Hippolytos* as Model." In *Rescuing Creusa: New Methodological Approaches to Women in Antiquity,* Marilyn Skinner, ed., 127–140. Lubbock, Texas (= *Helios* 13.2)

Reiman, Donald H., and Sharon B. Powers. 1977. *Shelley's Poetry and Prose.* New York and London.

Richlin, Amy. 1992. "Introduction" in *Pornography and Representation in Greece and Rome,* Amy Richlin, ed., xi–xxiii. New York and Oxford.

Rosenmeyer, Thomas G. 1988. *Deina Ta Polla: A Classicist's Checklist of Twenty Literary-Critical Positions.* (Arethusa Monographs.) Buffalo, N.Y.

Russ, Joanna. 1983. *How to Suppress Women's Writing.* Austin.

Said, Edward. 1979. "The Text, the World, and the Critic." In *Textual Strategies: Perspectives in Poststructuralist Criticism,* Josué Harari, ed., 161–188. London.

Searle, John. 1977. "Reiterating the Differences: A Reply to Derrida," *Glyph* 1:198–208.

Segal, Charles. 1986. "Greek Tragedy and Society: A Structuralist Perspective." *Propyläen Geschichte der Literatur* I.98–217 and 546–547. Berlin. (Reprinted in *Interpreting Greek Tragedy: Myth, Poetry, Text.* [Ithaca and London, 1986].)

Simpson, David. 1991. "The Moment of Materialism." In *Subject to History: Ideology, Class, Gender,* David Simpson, ed., 1–33. Ithaca and London.

Skinner, Marilyn. 1992. "Literary Theorists at Second-Rate Universities." In *The Interpretation of Roman Poetry: Empiricism or Hermeneutics?* Karl Galinsky, ed., 215–226. Frankfurt.

Steiner, George. 1980 (1961). *Death of Tragedy.* New York.

Veeser, H. Aram. 1989. "Introduction." In *The New Historicism,* H. Aram Veeser, ed., ix–xvi. New York and London.

Vernant, Jean-Pierre. 1990. "Tensions and Ambiguities in Greek Tragedy." In Vernant and Vidal-Naquet 1990:29–48.

Vernant, Jean-Pierre, and Pierre Vidal-Naquet. 1990. *Myth and Tragedy in Ancient Greece.* New York.

Vidal-Naquet, Pierre. 1990a. "Sophocles' *Philoctetes* and the Ephebeia." In Vernant and Vidal-Naquet 1990:161–179.

———. 1990b. "Oedipus between Two Cities: An Essay on *Oedipus at Colonus.*" In Vernant and Vidal-Naquet 1990:329–379.

Whitman, Cedric H. 1951. *Sophocles: A Study of Heroic Humanism.* Cambridge, Mass.

Winnington-Ingram, R. P. 1983. *Studies in Aeschylus.* Cambridge.

TWO

INTERPRETING GREEK TRAGEDY

History, Theory, and the New Philology

Michelle Gellrich

In recent study of Greek tragedy, classicists have been scrutinizing questions of theory and method in an effort to redefine the priorities of research. The result has been the emergence of what some have called a "new philology," an interdisciplinary approach whose assorted tools have been put together from borrowings in several areas, chiefly literary, historical, and anthropological study.[1] To characterize generally the new philology, it seems to be fed by two methods: structuralism and a kind of sociocriticism drawing heavily on Jean-Pierre Vernant and members of the École des hautes études en sciences sociales. The latter trend has aligned classics with the most current manifestation of poststructuralism in a related discipline—namely, the new historicism in Renaissance studies, whose proponents reject what they take to be the narrow textualism of deconstruction in favor of a broader concern with social forces of production.[2] Although history has never gone out of favor among classicists, recent critics of Greek tragedy have nonetheless sought to present themselves as departing from a prevailing text-centered criticism. We should note, however, that the textualism from which they seek to depart is not deconstruction but formalism, especially in the guise of the so-called New Criticism.

Because the status quo to which classical sociocritics are responding is different from what it is in other areas, we should be cautious about assuming deep affinities between historical approaches now winning the day in various fields of literary study. More importantly, we need to probe the question of how new the historicism being practiced on Greek tragedy is. To what extent does it preserve or disrupt the values of traditional philology, as they are epitomized, for example, in August Boeckh's pioneering work on what was then the new philology, *Encyclopaedie und Methodologie der philologischen Wissenschaften*? In particular, how successfully does the current liberal strand of classical scholarship, with its commitment to pluralizing historical discourse by including marginal groups, move away from formalism, authorial intent, and a narrow contextual determinism, which are commonly targeted as the positions from which older studies launched their claims?

I will argue that recent studies in Greek tragedy, by merging the earlier practice of structuralism with an apparently poststructuralist sociocriticism, have bridged a gap filled in other fields by a prolonged encounter with deconstruction. In the process, they seem to have confirmed that there is no need to deal with the brand of theory represented by thinkers such as Jacques Derrida and Paul de Man. But the result of this trend has not been altogether satisfying, for few classicists have availed themselves of the tools provided by deconstruction for a critique of the concepts of structure and history, which are at the heart of contemporary interpretations.[3] This is not a belated attempt to vindicate deconstruction, whose limits have become increasingly apparent. But so have its achievements, and in the aftermath of its heyday we are in a position to judge its bearing on matters vital to our field, especially historical inquiry. I emphasize this point, for despite the frequent contention that deconstruction has eclipsed history, it is clear from a variety of developments that it has instead generated a productive debate about history.[4] If classicists have not been major participants in this debate, it is partly because our field is not well poised to enter the fray with those sorting out the details of the deconstructive critique. One of my efforts in the present paper is to encourage this encounter, since it would assist in breaking through problems that continue to limit criticism on Greek tragedy, despite its avowed intentions to break with certain practices of the past.

Let me begin by setting out characteristic assumptions in recent studies of Greek tragedy, drawing on essays anthologized in *Nothing to Do with Dionysos?* as well as on the work of Jean-Pierre Vernant and his associates.[5] A point of departure is offered by the preliminary remarks of Froma Zeitlin and John Winkler in the anthology just mentioned:

> We, the editors and our contributors, are particularly interested in the extra-textual aspects of tragedy (along with its satyr-plays, of course) and of comedy, thus violating one of the familiar premises of formalist criticism, that "the text is the thing and the only thing!" Instead, we will look behind the masks and under the costumes and peer out into the audience, and investigate the various elements that went into a finished performance.... We will consider how individual plays or groups of dramas directly or indirectly pertained to the concerns of the body politic, which were reflected or deflected in the complex conventions of the stage. (1990:4)

The interest in the extratextual and specifically in the body politic is here directly opposed to the premise of textual autonomy that generated many works of criticism on Greek drama in the past few decades. Stemming from this redefinition of commitment are three central principles of interpretation, which are not necessarily featured with equal prominence in the work of all the sociocritics, but which nonetheless circulate freely.

First is the principle that texts have historical contexts, which usually refers to mental contexts made up of categories of thought, types of reasoning, beliefs and values, and forms of sensibility about the modalities of agents and actions. These elements may be reified for purposes of study as the "mind of the people," a *mentalité*, but are in reality inseparable from a dense network of social practices. The historical context is usually taken to be prior to and determining of texts—it delimits the conditions in which texts appear and the possibilities for thought and action in them. Sometimes, however, as in the work of Vernant, the term "context" is modulated against others, such as "undertext," *sous-texte*, and is treated as genre-specific; types of institutions or categories of work elaborate segments of the broader social context in their own peculiar way, and thus are conceived as bearing the marks of a distinctive consciousness—for example, the tragic consciousness.[6]

Second, the notion of context as a structure of ideas, beliefs, and values is frequently equated with the term "ideology." Though vaguely indebted to Marx, who is often refracted through the lens of either Dumézil or Foucault, ideology is typically not construed in the strict Marxist sense of "an inverted genealogy of culture, that makes for 'illusion' and 'mystification' by treating ideas as primary where they should have been treated as derivative."[7] More common is the looser sense of ideology as a system of ideas or mental habits that both determine and coexist with social practices, including, for example, the performance of drama. However the term is used, it is almost invariably understood hierarchically as the underlying framework of a superstructure that includes literary texts.

Third, the single most notable characteristic of this mental and social context is that it is organized as a system of binary oppositions. Although Geoffrey Lloyd's *Polarity and Analogy* (1966) showed how fundamental polarity is in archaic Greek thought, his thesis took on tremendous momentum in classical studies from the work of Lévi-Strauss and de Saussure. In its structuralist form, binary opposition was first and most explicitly elaborated in the analysis of Greek myth as a logical system of classification.[8] Subsequently, however, the pattern has been construed as ubiquitous, permeating modes of thought and social practices in ancient Greece, including tragedy. Thus the structure of myth has often been taken as prior and exemplary, if not determining, of other structures coordinate with it or built upon it.

This ensemble of assumptions leads to characteristic forms of critical practice. Interpretation is a matter of reconstructing the context in an effort to understand the life of the text, the vital forms of thought and action that give rise to it. In an early and influential essay, "Tensions and Ambiguities in Greek Tragedy," Vernant asserts: "It was the context that made it possible for the author to communicate with his fifth-century public, and that same context makes it possible for the work to rediscover its full authenticity and to convey its full significance to the reader of today."[9] The hermeneutic ideal at work here recalls the familiar activities of recognition *(Wiedererkenntnis)* and reenactment *(Nacherleben)*, central to traditional philology and elevated to the status of definition by Boeckh. But this is not to say that the new sociocriticism recapitulates Romantic hermeneutics. It certainly rejects the subject-centered thinking associated with the work of Boeckh, Schleiermacher, and Dilthey, who tend to look for meaning in the psychological identity of reader and author. But empathy remains a pivotal activity in both modes of interpretation, for it is the vehicle that closes the temporal gap between interpreter and subject by enabling one to enter into the mind of the other. The salient difference between Romantic historicism and the current historicism is that the latter conceives of this closure as an identity between reader and the collective (rather than authorial) mind that can be hypostasized from the web of social practices.[10] To enter into this mind is to lay claim to the key for decoding the work of art. Moreover, a mimetic conception of literature is at the core of this model, for the text reflects its background, even, paradoxically, when it seems to deflect it. Literary distortion, as we will see, is often treated as a "version" of a previously given context. This is partly because ideology, if not "reality," is understood as swallowing up even what appears initially as deformity or dissent.[11]

Before I turn to a critical assessment of these principles, let me illustrate how they have been implemented in readings of Greek tragedy. Oddone Longo, in the leading essay of *Nothing to Do with Dionysos?*, entitled "The Theater of the *Polis*," claims that the patron or sponsor of the Dionysian contests—the institution that organizes the dramatic performances—orients and controls the representations to which the dramatic text is preliminarily submitted. "The patron (let us call it more generally the *polis*, understood as a social institution) operates toward the public with an end in view that might be roughly formulated as 'consolidating the social identity, maintaining the cohesion of the community'" (1990:14). Plays are therefore not just expressions of communitarian values, but they are circumscribed by institutional constraints to create an area of consensus in a highly differentiated society. "The reinforcement of community cohesion, in a context of social rituals and spectacles that clinch the axioms of the community's own ideology, is not just the 'goal' pursued by the patron; it is also the 'request,' the 'expectation' of the public itself" (14). This is an example of the way in which ideology may be construed in the work of the new social historians, and the result is a view of Greek tragedy as culture affirming and bound in by the hegemonic forces of political order. The point is worth underscoring, for such a view runs counter to a tendency discernible in other critical traditions, notably those affiliated with Nietzsche, to treat tragedy as subverting cultural norms or setting dilemmas that challenge the premise of coherence and consensus in the *polis*.

A similar result is even more apparent in another essay anthologized in *Nothing to Do with Dionysos?*, Winkler's "The Ephebes' Song: *Tragoidia* and *Polis*." Arguing a novel thesis about the tragic chorus on the basis of combined evidence from such specimens in the graphic arts as the Pronomos Vase and controversial records about the *ephebeia*, Winkler concludes with a thoroughgoingly didactic conception of tragedy. He interprets plays at the Dionysian festivals as elaborations on the theme of proper and improper civic behavior, chiefly of proper male citizenship in its military aspect. Moreover, Winkler's chorus of ephebes becomes the focus for tragedy conceived as an object lesson for citizens, especially the young, who distill a moral from the calm choral center in which "the tragic turbulence is surveyed and evaluated" (43). There are many interesting and detailed arguments in this reading, but in the end tragedy has been effectively reduced to a discourse that confirms a highly restrictive hypothesis about how the *polis* drills its citizens. Winkler's argument has much in common with Longo's, and both are affiliated, if only indirectly, with Hegel's rationalizing account of Greek tragedy, which also treats the chorus as the authoritative moral center mediating the tragic conflict. But now the moral center is accented in specifically military tones, as the hoplite-oriented ideology is taken as a determining context for the meaning of plays. Understanding this ideology is the critical imperative for entering into the sensibility that produces tragedy.

Simon Goldhill's essay, "The Great Dionysia and Civic Ideology," qualifies this tendency. He examines four usually neglected preplay ceremonies, which propagate the dominant military ideology of the *polis*: (1) the libations poured by the ten generals; (2) the display of tribute by cities in the Athenian empire; (3) the reading of the names and honors accorded those who had greatly benefited Athens in some way; and (4) the parading of male war orphans who were raised at the city's expense. The tragic plays, however, do not affirm the values implicit in these ceremonies, but strain them to the breaking point: "Rather than simply reflecting the cultural values of a fifth-century audience . . . rather than offering simple didactic messages from the city's poets to the citizens, tragedy seems deliberately to make difficult the assumption of the values of the civic discourse" (1990:124). Thus Goldhill would want to recognize a "more complex dialectic between the proclamation of social norms and their possibility of transgression" (1990:127) in tragic drama, and in so doing he implicitly questions the kinds of tendencies apparent in the theses of Longo and Winkler. Civic ideology, however, is still construed as ultimately structuring, since it shapes the forms of subversion in drama. For instance, in Sophocles' *Ajax* it is the background that generates a tension between fifth-century hoplite values and Ajax's epic heroic code, which he passes on to his son, Eurysakes, in a gesture that is meant to recall and also to question the preplay ceremony of the orphans in military uniforms. For Goldhill and others, tragedy is an epiphenomenon, a superstructure that exhibits or reinforces the values in the base.

As assumptions about context and ideology generate a host of common critical practices among the new social historians, so do assumptions about the pervasiveness of binary opposition in Greek thought. The most significant works on classical tragedy to appear over the past five to ten years have taken a structure assumed to inhere in the texts analyzed and turned it into a methodological tool. Interpretation follows the habits of thought in the object studied. Zeitlin sees this as a distinguishing mark of the scholarship of Vernant, and suggests in her introduction to *Mortals and Immortals: Collected Essays of Jean-Pierre Vernant* that there is some vital bond between French attitudes and the heritage of classical culture, "which seems to have penetrated deeply and silently into the mental practices of French society and is, in part, replicated there in its modes of discourse" (1991:9). The mirroring effects between observer and observed are taken as the strength of the French sociocritics, whose "discovery" among the Greeks of a mental activity organized around binary opposition is matched by a shared conviction that society is indeed an intelligible system governed by a logic. Embedded in this mirror play, once again, is the hermeneutic injunction to seek merger with the culture under scrutiny. Now this merger admittedly proceeds in the face of Vernant's explicit assertion that "the writings which have come down to us from ancient Greek civilization embody ideas sufficiently different from those expressed in the framework of our own intellectual universe to make us feel not only a historical distance, but also an awareness of a fundamental change in man." [12] The warning that Greek culture is "quite separate from ours" and that "the psychological categories of today cannot be applied with any precision" is one that guides Vernant's research and that reveals the influence of the historical psychologists Ignacy Meyerson and Zevedei Barbu. [13]

This orientation toward the Otherness of the Greeks, however, is qualified by a penchant in the work of those associated with the École des hautes études en sciences sociales to see an extraordinarily high degree of cognitive coherence and rule-governed thought in Greek society. Rejecting, as Vernant does, the idea of "a scattered and heterogeneous pantheon, a mythology of bits and pieces," [14] need not commit one to the antithetical view of a world ordered in every nook and cranny by a logic that conforms with the structuralist expectation of binary system-building. Yet the embrace of dualistic thinking in this form of criticism can force such interpretive choices, which repeat at the level of method the pattern assumed to inhere in the object studied. Once again, as in the case of Longo's and Winkler's theses, we are presented with a hyper-rational image of a society, an image shaped by the assumption that everything worth studying among the Greeks is organized as an oppositional structure. A lingering Hegelianism continues to haunt this criticism, which appears to bear out the maxim that "whoever looks at the world rationally finds the world in turn takes on a rational appearance." [15] Among the difficulties with this view is its marginalizing of evidence that does not confirm the expectation of binary order. Overall such a perspective underestimates elements in the so-called social order that thrive on the edges of dominant cultural antitheses and inflates its own predilection for systematicity. We will return to this point shortly.

An early attempt in the study of Greek tragedy to evaluate the structuralist bent for seeing binary opposition is Helene Foley's "The Conception of Women in Athenian Drama." [16] Focusing especially on the overarching structuralist oppositions of nature/culture and domestic/public, Foley investigates the uses and limitations of the terms in comprehending gender differences in Greek dramatic texts, and doubts their flexibility as tools for probing the meaning of tragedies. Plays do not merely reflect dichotomies in the relations of the sexes, preserving a strict identification of women with nature and the domestic and of men with culture and the public. Instead, they use these dichotomies as cultural clichés to explore larger cultural questions or to turn such clichés on their head. Not only must interpreters be wary of approaching binary oppositions as keys that unlock a dramatic code, according to Foley, but they must approach these oppositions as historically relative and not merely fixed a priori in their content and alignment. This is an important argument for a flexible, undogmatic appreciation of binarism. Polarities are not so much specious or unviable as misleading, unless they are used with interpretive caution and refinement. Above all, the critic must remain alert to patterns of inversion, whereby oppositional terms shift their position in a hierarchy.

Charles Segal's studies of Sophocles and Euripides are well known for implementing structuralist methods in the interpretation of Greek tragedy and also for demonstrating how tragic drama complicates "the precoded patterns of the social norms," rearranging, transforming, distorting, or interweaving the codes in new and unpredictable ways. [17] Broadly integrating a variety of influences associated with the new sociocriticism, Zeitlin's essays, "The Dynamics of Misogyny: Myth and Mythmaking in the *Oresteia*" (1984) and "Playing the Other: Theater, Theatricality, and the Feminine in Greek Drama"

(1990), also exemplify techniques of structuralist analysis.[18] To take one illustration, Zeitlin argues that the *Oresteia* is concerned with world building and that "the cornerstone of [its] architecture" is the hierarchization of binary values to create order out of conflict (1984:160). Aeschylus' solution to the war of opposing forces "places Olympian over chthonic on the divine level, Greek over barbarian on the cultural level, and male above female on the social level" (1984:159). The male-female conflict, however, actually subsumes the other two and sexualizes them, so that social evolution becomes identical with a divine evolution from female to male dominance. In this study, the centrality of binary opposition as an organizing principle is explicitly linked with hierarchy, with the privileging of a term and a host of others continuous with it in a scheme of power relations. This interpretive move reveals Zeitlin's tendency to treat the logic of myth and the logic of tragedy as homologous, that is, as exhibiting similar structures and functions—notably, the mediation of contradiction.

I now return to my leading questions. To what extent do the readings I have noted take us beyond the limitations of formalism, authorial intent, and a narrow historical determinism that disregards competing voices in the life of the *polis*? And do they break with traditional philological principles that foster such limitations? Let's begin with an examination of the text-context model.[19] Contextualization of one sort or another is ineluctable in criticism. It is not the act but the form or style of contextualization that should be scrutinized in recent readings of tragedy. The historical background assumed to be composed primarily of mental habits embedded in social practices is typically posited as a stable point of reference in interpretation, an objective structure that frames the questions we put to the text. It assumes much the same status as "historical facts" in the old philology, which are construed as empirically verifiable data beyond the vagaries of individual bias, emotive distortion, or political interests. This is the case even in such controversial historical reconstructions as Winkler's in "The Ephebes' Song." That he is elaborating upon a certain view of the *ephebeia* still shrouded in debate does not change the fact that his reading aspires to establish empirical evidence about the institution as the ambient condition for the performance of tragedy. But Winkler's reading also illustrates, without ever explicitly pursuing, a point that has emerged forcefully in poststructuralist and deconstructive critiques of history—that the historical context is itself a text. It is constituted by reference to texts that must be interpreted and is thus itself an interpretive construct, not a simple documentary account that presents the past in its own right. The binarism of the text-context model obscures this point, by creating the illusion of an interpretive activity that is controlled by reference to a noninterpretive, objective set of facts.

The view of historical context as necessarily mediated by language and thus dense with motives—our own as well as those of the writers on whom we draw—may in principle be admitted by the critics I am examining. But the consequences of this acceptance have not really been examined. The textualizing of history, a move that has migrated from semiotics and deconstruction, is a problem at the core of debates being conducted by an increasing number of historians and philologists. Its controversial status is obvious, for it undermines a revered philological goal—namely, to read words in such a way as to arrive at a literal meaning that stands, as Boeckh would say, "in real connection with historically given circumstances."[20]

The result of entertaining a concept of history as textual, however, is not opening the floodgates to an abysmal subjectivism and relativism—though, once again, the habit of binary thinking would dictate that these are the only alternatives to objectivity. Rather, in disavowing scientific neutrality, this orientation insists upon the irreducibly human construction of history as a story of interests and actions that will inevitably be judged in multiple and competing ways by individuals with their own interests and actions. Such an insistence encourages the development of models of historical inquiry that, on the one hand, do not succumb to the illusions of unmediated reality fostered by the documentary ideal and that, on the other hand, do not abandon respect for the rigors of empirical analysis. An alternative to the documentary model that has assumed some prominence is the dialogical model, imagined by the historian Dominick LaCapra as a conversation with the past in which we both speak with it via its textual remainders and learn to listen to the ways in which it can talk back—that is, not only respond but show recalcitrance to our assumptions and ignore our ways of imposing order.[21] I do not mean to suggest that "dialogy," which embodies LaCapra's deconstructive reworking of a notion elaborated by Bakhtin, is the answer to problems posed by traditional philological approaches to history. Its ultimate usefulness may be chiefly heuristic, for it offers a perspective on the past that assumes neither the spectator's masterly objectivity nor the complete openness or manipulability of what we call facts.

By contrast with the documentary model, the dialogical makes a concerted effort to open channels for reading the resistance of the past to our questions, as well as to tune in competing voices that challenge the notion of a unified, coherent historical field lending itself to comprehensive formulation. It stresses the varieties of possible backgrounds that might be supplied and the complexity of reading that emerges when one strives to incorporate such heterogeneity. Indeed close reading of the sort encouraged by formalism retains a central role in this approach, for resistance to the urge for total interpretive coherence can be read only by submitting to the centripetal forces at work in language. The retention of a formalist strength seems to me salutary at a time when social critics have been following a reactionary swing of the pendulum away from the text.

A chaos of interpretations is not the necessary result of history pursued as a dialogical activity with the past. But such an approach does encourage the forthright acknowledgment that context, no matter how "thick" the description of it, is never a monolithic frame that provides *the* adequate point of reference for literary analysis. The new sociocritics would, presumably, applaud the revision for which I am speaking, since restoring the socially marginal is central to their concerns. Yet their formulation of the text-context problem often unwittingly ends up undermining the goal for which they strive. For they define determining background in fairly restrictive ways, even while trying to respect difference.

Though in principle dedicated to uncovering the heterogeneous character of the *polis*, the readings I have mentioned usually hypostatize power in dominant institutions or groups, characterized via the sociopolitical structure based on ephebic initiation and hoplite status. Political power appears embodied in one rigorously defined male segment of the population, and this power ultimately controls the production of tragedy, including the representation of women. This view is especially prominent in the essays by Longo, Winkler, and Goldhill anthologized in *Nothing to Do with Dionysos?*. But it is also apparent to a lesser degree in Zeitlin's significant concession in her essay, "Playing the Other" (1990). Exploring the implications of theater and theatricality in Greek drama, she focuses on four principal elements that she believes were commonly associated in the society with the feminine domain: (1) the representation of the body; (2) the arrangement of stage space as a commerce with the inside and the private; (3) the plot itself as a product of contrivance and cunning; and (4) the condition of performative mimesis, "playing the Other." To submit men and masculine values to the experience of these conventionally feminine elements identified with Dionysus, the god of theater, amounts to a profound testing of the dominant ideology; actor and spectator alike are initiated into "new and unsettling modes of feeling, seeing, and knowing" (87) that force them to imagine a "fuller model for the masculine self" (85). Yet in the end, Zeitlin concedes, "tragedy arrives at closures that generally reassert male, often paternal, structures of authority . . ." (86–87). Subversion is ultimately absorbed, as men return to the lucid rationality of the hoplite citizen.

Zeitlin's thesis about the predominance of the feminine in Greek tragedy and Winkler's thesis about tragedy as a hypermasculine initiation rite present us with ultimately disjunctive views of how context shapes dramatic performance. These views could admittedly be assimilated via Vidal-Naquet's frequently employed insight in "The Black Hunter and the Origin of the Athenian *Ephebeia*"[22]—that adolescent male rites of passage typically involve role inversion or improper conduct as a component part of making the final transition into manhood. Yet to adopt this position is to subordinate and parenthesize the feminine (something Zeitlin is reluctant to do), again under the assumption that ideology and the conventional hegemony have the final say. But must we make this choice?

If we retain the implications of gender in these two theses without feeling compelled to discount one in favor of the other, then it becomes feasible to entertain a line of argument different from what each taken by itself entails. Namely, we may be led to consider whether tragedy presents a view of masculine identity that eludes ideological formulation because it reveals the presence of the feminine in the masculine. We may not go far enough when we say that tragedy temporarily inverts gender roles or that it presents male and female as complementary and mutually defining. Masculinity, in its dramatic self-presentation in the theater, is not a consistent state arrived at via a temporary flirting with the feminine, as a category distinct from it. Because it is constituted by and represented in forms that are culturally stereotyped as feminine, it already contains within the sediments of its social formation the very properties that characterize its supposed opposite. Theater thus lays open as a social fiction the internal coherence of gender in Greek society. To the extent that playing the other is an activity that structures ritual as well—a point borne out particularly by Euripides' *Bacchae*—one would want to explore more deeply how masculine identity is simultaneously constituted and undone in a variety of social practices other than overtly theatrical ones. In any case, the vitality of tragedy as I am describing it would have to be linked with a place neither totally within nor totally without the *polis*; it would be neither simply ideological or purely nonideological, but a performance opening up some space in between. This space that escapes the logic of purely oppositional thought may very well be "the Dionysiac," but to do it justice we would have to overhaul our vocabulary and our habitual tendency to think along with the axiom of noncontradiction—a point to which I will return. By acquiescing to the view that the hierarchy of gender is preserved in the dramatic conflation of the masculine and the feminine, we arguably fail to read the resistance of tragic voices to the systems that the dominant culture would want to put upon them. We revert to the cultural fiction of male hegemony, without looking at the fissures, which make openings not for simple subversions of social order, but for dismantlings of its very structure. If such dismantlings seem alien to what we think we know about the binary construction of Greek society, that may be because we have grown complacent with structuralist insights into the logic of social organization and with the reduction of literature to a code within that organization. In the process, we have suppressed the capacity of literature to operate in ways that cast doubt on the self-consistency of ordinary assumptions about personal roles and identities.

As my comments suggest, the control of textual meaning in recent interpretations is still too often situated in a single center, precisely as it was in older forms of reading, which focused on the author rather than on a predominant social group as a fulcrum. The diversity of culture, which social critics strain to emphasize, and the competition between rival interests finally capitulate to a ruling elite. This notion of a monopoly on power, with consequences that permeate literary representation, has perhaps been encouraged by Foucault, who is a major influence on the social historians. But much in the later Foucault tells against it, specifically the capillary understanding of power as diffuse, nonlocalized, noncentralized, and always circulating. The importance of Foucault's move toward what he called "genealogy" and away from an archaeologically centralized episteme such as he articulated in *The Order of Things* is not only that it shows increased responsiveness to heterogeneity, but that it discourages the tendency to treat ideology as monolithic and ironclad. To approach ideology as if it *were* monolithic is to accept the illusion propounded by those in power—that they exercise total control. Ideology never exerts a stranglehold on culture, extending its fingers octopuslike into all the narrow recesses of life.[23] Its great enabling lie is precisely that it does. One of the ironies of recent interpretations is that they reveal the continuing force of the myth of ideology, at the same time as they would take up arms against the oppression it exerted in its time.

As I have remarked, efforts to arrive at an objective account of the past have traditionally been bound up with the correlative impulse to close the gap between observer and observed through recognition (reknowing what was known) and empathy. Once again, a dialogical, nondocumentary approach to the past that remains sensitive to heterogeneous voices and to the interests of theory could assist in revising the philological goal of interpretation as merging with the object of study. This goal reflects what has been called, borrowing from Freud, the anxiety of transference—a repetition-displacement of the past onto the present, which can cause either fear of losing oneself to the past or a desire to converge with it in total unity.[24] Like psychoanalytic transference, the variety found in textual interpretation may produce either a lively denial of similarity with the past, an assertion of its absolute difference, or a sense of identification with it, an insistence on its reenactment in our own lives. The latter alternative is characteristic of sociocritical efforts to reconstruct the *mentalité* out of which tragic drama springs. But to see in the work of French thinkers a reflection of the mental habits contained in ancient Greek society is, perhaps, to witness a narcissistic response to the anxiety of transference. For what guides scholarly activity in this case is a fantasy of full merger.

Such a fantasy is not, in fact, borne out in the best criticism produced by this tradition. Vernant's work, as I have noted, strives for a balance between the tendencies to make strange and to make familiar a wide host of Greek concepts, including, most recently, that of the image, the *eikon* or *eidōlon,* which, significantly, does not begin its famous career in Western culture by meaning "an imitative artifice reproducing in the form of a counterfeit the external appearance of real things." [25] The characteristic suppleness of Vernant's readings escapes the kind of reductiveness to which I'm referring. But derivative work sometimes falls victim to projection and posits its own historically circumscribed preoccupations as intrinsic to the material studied. The challenge is not to avoid transference in interpretation, but to find ways of opening a conversation with texts, both historical and literary, that can respect their difference from our own interests while also seeking grounds of agreement. This is especially imperative in the case of tragedy, which tests the sociopolitical norms of its own day as well as the rage for order founded on patterns of exclusion and scapegoating. The problem with readings of tragedy that seek to demonstrate its ideological character is that they are impervious to ways in which performances elude ideological constraints. In other words, such readings overestimate the role of social substructure in producing the meaning of texts. In so doing they ironically repeat the scapegoating the plays often critique, for they adopt too singular a view of context and power, and thus enact strategies of exclusion that ultimately guarantee the coherence of their own perspective.

This brings me to another point—the ongoing tendency in recent criticism, once again common to traditional philology, to treat cultural context as operating in a one-way relation of influence on literary texts. That lines of force are drawn almost always from the direction of determining background, whether it be conceived as "reality" or "ideology," betokens a persistent assumption that literature plays a secondary and receiving role with respect to history. In the field of tragedy, this tacit subordination of literature runs counter to the enormous cultural significance that critics typically accord the genre, such as Vernant does when he construes tragedy as a signal turning point in the life of the Greeks between mythical and heroic modes of thought on the one hand, and legal and political ones on the other. The conflict contained in this moment of transition may be appreciated most starkly, he maintains, in such episodes as the dispute over *nomos* in Sophocles' *Antigone,* where the term exhibits opposing meanings that block communication between the protagonists, though they do not themselves perceive this "zone of opacity." [26]

Vernant acknowledges that tragedy may actually initiate historical change, and not simply respond to it; indeed he frequently draws evidence of a break with heroic ideals from the plays themselves. Yet his method leads him for the most part to espouse a mimetic vocabulary for literature even when his claims run counter to mimetic assumptions. That Vernant's insights resist his critical bias suggests again that traditional formulations of the text-context problem may not be adequate in accounting for the cultural importance of tragedy. Rather than regarding tragedy as a mimetic enactment of an evolving social clash between religious and political ways of configuring the world, we need to imagine how tragedy may itself be this event and how the history it supposedly reflects has been largely derived from tragic texts themselves. We will then be in a position to judge whether much of the history thematized in the new social criticism has been retrogressively projected as context and, in the process, ironically elevated as a prior engendering force of a secondary literary manifestation.

I have tried to show that our habits of critical thinking about tragedy operate in accordance with a binary logic that falsifies the complexities of interpretive choice. The critique of binary structure, of course, has been probably the single most potent tool activated by deconstructive reading, and in closing I would like to turn to it once again. In his paper "Structure, Sign, and Play in the Discourse of the Human Sciences," delivered at the Johns Hopkins Humanities Colloquium in 1966, Derrida posed the intractabilities of a method based on binarism.[27] For classicists, it is significant that this paper was delivered alongside Vernant's "Greek Tragedy: Problems of Interpretation," which was based upon commitments to structuralism. Though he did not target Vernant directly, Derrida did target Lévi-Strauss and the role of binary opposition in his ethnographic analyses, which rely on the central antithesis of nature and culture. Here as in later works, Derrida's reading uncovers moments of "methodological scandal," when a phenomenon is encountered that cannot be explained in terms of a dominant opposition, the function of which is to organize the system. In the case of Lévi-Strauss, Derrida locates such a moment in the anthropologist's encounter with the incest prohibition, which does not tolerate the nature/culture opposition and "which seems to require at one and the same time the predicates of nature and those of culture" (1972:253). For the incest prohibition is simultaneously both universal and spontaneous, not dependent upon any determinate norm (this makes it natural), *and* dependent on a system of norms regulating a particular society, thus capable of varying from one social structure to another (this makes it cultural). It thus eludes the logic of identity that a binary system assumes and questions the integrity as well as the organizing capacity of Lévi-Strauss's principal opposition, nature and culture, which in turn subordinates a whole host of others.

The chief strategies enacted in Derrida's essay are worth recollecting, since they bear on recent readings of Greek tragedy. First, Derrida understands texts, in this case Lévi-Strauss's, as aiming at meanings built around a crucial opposition of terms: nature/culture, male/female, *polis/oikos*, and domestic/public. Inevitably, where there is dichotomy, there is hierarchical order, with one term conceived as secondary to, derivative from, and inferior to the other. This hierarchy marks the form of the text's ideology. Second, this hierarchical relation is complicated to the point of being undone in a text, for the prior, original, superior term always turns out to be inhabited by the secondary one. This is not a matter of demonstrating an inversion or reversal of power, but an unraveling of the logic of oppositional thinking; the center of the system cannot hold because neither term obeys the principles of identity, exclusion, and complementarity that the order of binary thought assumes. Third, the destabilized opposition used to begin the deconstructive reading is shown to be linked with a web of other terms that it organizes and of which it is a part.[28]

I can argue most economically for the pertinence of this deconstructive critique to recent scholarship on Greek tragedy by examining some common strategies used in the interpretation of Euripides' *Bacchae*. The play is especially suited to the discussion at hand, for it has received much attention as an exploration of the binary opposition between nature and culture, female and male. My remarks are necessarily sketchy; they hardly amount to a careful reexamination of the text, and they do not attempt to historicize the critique of binary structure, though I believe another essay could very well develop such an approach.

Efforts to read characters and actions in the tragedy in terms of the antitheses nature/culture and male/female have always encountered problems: Dionysus seems to defy these categorizations. Critics such as Segal in *Dionysiac Poetics and Euripides' Bacchae*, and Foley in *Ritual Irony: Poetry and Sacrifice in Euripides*, speak of inversion, reversal, and ambiguity to describe how such defiance is represented.[29] But their insights and the questions they feel the play leaves unanswered strain such categories and reveal the limitations of critical language in wrestling with Dionysus and, by extension, the theatrical performances over which he presides. To approach the god as though he is a *coincidentia oppositorum* who confuses existing polarities, and by extension to treat the character of Pentheus and the female maenads in the language of inversion, is to show the decisive claim that the logic of noncontradiction exerts on our ways of understanding—the logic that one and the same thing cannot at the same time and in the same respect oppose itself. Contradictions can only unfold temporally, marked by the passage of time. This ontological and epistemological stricture fundamental to Aristotelian logic is preserved in the concepts of inversion, reversal, and ambiguity. For they assume intact oppositions, or structural polarities, the elements of which sequentially change place in the usual hierarchy—men play women, women play men, the state of nature re-places the state of culture. This is why the notion of festival implemented by Foley, with all its associations of a world topsy-turvy, seems an apt description of the dramatic action. As a category festival does not imply "anomie," as Douglas Turner has observed, but "simply a new perspective from which to observe structure" and ultimately to return to it.[30]

It has become a usual gesture in discussions of Dionysus to note how he exceeds or defies basic polarities, yet these concessions, though a step in the direction of acknowledging the challenges he poses for interpretation, stop short of the mark. Dionysus appears to signify not a discrete being with a definable identity but a condition prior to or other than "identity." He does not so much destroy or confuse distinctions as configure the nondifferentia-tion out of which such distinctions eventually arise—notably, the foundational ones of female/male and nature/culture. Rather than being structured by op-positions that he simply overturns, he has no center and thus escapes the ulti-mately rational play of oppositional structure named by the terms "ambiguity" and "reversal." That is why there is difficulty, for example, in treating his mask as a disguise, for disguise implies a discoverable personality beneath. Yet Dionysus lacks an essence, an inherent, unchanging nature, and Foley's re-marks on his mask suggest this, for they point to its palimpsestic character, that is, its capability of being read in at least two ways at once—as divine and human, as tragic and comic.

> The tragic irony for which the play is justly famous has a visual level. That is, the audience sees by this mask that the stranger is a god, but Pentheus has no such theatrical cues by which to recognize him. The audience is being asked to be conscious of a costume and a theatrical convention. Thus, for the audience Dio-nysus' mask represents smiling divinity in human disguise; for the characters, a man.[31]

Though Dionysus speaks often in the language of manifestation and epiphany, his appearance disrupts notions of revealed truth, for truth itself implies a cor-respondence with an essence. He defies the conceptual schemas implicit in the language of our criticism, for such language is itself typically proscribed by Aristotelian expectations.

The exigencies of trying to deal in a critically compelling way with Dionysus do not end with him. Once we find a strategy for questioning the habits of binary thought that laden our interpretive tools, we can see that the play does not offer evidence of a once-secure order thrown into confusion by the pres-ence of Dionysus. The condition of life as a system of fine-tuned, if repressive, distinctions is cast back in the play to some vague past for which we haven't any dramatic proof besides the suspect assertions of Pentheus. From start to finish we behold characters acting, speaking, and thinking in ways that throw doubt on there ever having been a pristine moment of stable structure that has since been unhinged. The Theban women are already maenads, Pentheus is already excessive and ready to break under strain, Cadmus and Tiresias have already donned Dionysiac garb. Dramatically, it is significant that normality is marginalized in the tragedy to the point of being a doubtful hypothesis, rather than a secure given. Moreover, as the dramatic action unfolds, we find increasing reason to believe that being female, though ideologically defined in terms of the interior, the *oikos*, the domestic, is not exclusively attached to these terms and already contains the terms that define the masculine other—the exterior and the public. For as others have pointed out, maenadic conduct, with its urge toward exposure and display, is as female as the activity of cooking and weaving.[32] Similarly, Dionysus' transformation of Pentheus is staged not as a coercive magical spell that turns a virile, law-abiding military man into a soft, delicate, passive woman, but as a process whereby elements that were already part of Pentheus are brought forth for the seeing.

Dionysus, then, is not an exception to the rule of polarities, a god who throws a world of orderly distinctions into disarray, but a figure who enables insight into the tenuous character of the binarisms on which civilized life is based. Such an insight may be construed as inviting the audience to accept a greater measure of integration or complementarity into its categories of exclusion, but it cuts more deeply than this by exposing the illusion of pure identities on which such ideas of integration and complementarity are predicated. The power of the *Bacchae* is here—in the erosion of strategies for building a centered structure, without which culture would not be possible but with which it has repressed a lie that is exposed in the dramatic action.

There is little clarification to be had from the conclusion of the play. Textually damaged though it is, it does not appear to rest with the premise that Dionysiac ritual is a healthy inversion of the restraints of civilized life—a momentary, reconstructive break that ultimately vitalizes the social order. The character of the god continues until the end to baffle efforts at defining the precise relationship between ritual and culture—and by extension, between tragedy and culture. Is the *Bacchae* ideological or anti-ideological? Does it affirm or cast doubt on the socially consolidating role of Dionysiac ritual? The options we pose with such questions restrict us to modes of reasoning indicted by the play itself.

Culture is not so much "the Other" or "the outside" of nature as a condition that actually contains within the structure of its normalcy the terms it excludes, notably violence. And because the play, via the ritually proscribed murder of Pentheus, makes us doubt that ritual violence is safe and culture affirming, it leaves us contemplating the fiction of social order as the taming of primal darkness. The myth of Dionysus on which Euripides was drawing may well posit such a culture-affirming function for ritual, but we should be cautious about assuming that the tragedy, just because it uses myth, is homologous with it and satisfies the same collective needs.

If the critical vocabulary we use in the interpretation of the *Bacchae* reveals the limits of binary analysis, deconstruction may act as an instrument for getting us past some recurring impasses, since it provides a critique of the Aristotelian biases that continue to drive our ways of making sense. It may also encourage a salutary defamiliarization of the literature that we seek to assimilate via conventional notions of artistic order and centered structure. Of course, it goes without saying that deconstruction may become an inflexible template for reading. This is precisely what has happened in disciplines that have gone through full-fledged deconstructive phases—which isn't an argument to forgo what might have been gained before orthodoxy smothered insight. The new sociocriticism has gone some distance in testing orthodoxies of a different kind in the field of Greek tragedy. But if it does not go far enough, that is because it remains wed to assumptions basic to the traditional philological enterprise—assumptions with which it may after all be quite comfortable.

NOTES

1. See, for example, Harrison 1986. For the new philology in the related discipline of medieval studies, see *Speculum* 1990 *(The New Philology)*.

2. For an assessment of the new historicism in Renaissance studies, see Pechter 1987. For an assessment of the new sociocriticism in classical studies, see Rosenmeyer 1988:47−51.

3. See Peradotto 1983. A notable exception is Pucci (1977 and 1980).

4. See especially LaCapra 1983 and 1985 and White 1987.

5. Winkler and Zeitlin 1990; Vernant 1991; Bergren and Zeitlin 1982; Vernant 1972*b* [1981].

6. See Vernant 1972*b* [1981:7].

7. Burke 1950:104.

8. See especially Vernant 1974 [1980:186−242] and Burkert 1979.

9. Vernant 1972*b* [1981:6].

10. On hermeneutics and classical philology, see the essays in Kresic 1981.

11. On ideology in the new sociocriticism, see Rosenmeyer 1988:49−50.

12. Vernant 1965 [1983:x].

13. Vernant 1965 [1983:x]. For a survey of the major influences on Vernant's work, see Zeitlin 1991:3−24.

14. Vernant 1991:271−272.

15. Hegel 1970:23.

16. Foley 1981.
17. See Segal 1981 and 1982 (esp. p. 25).
18. Zeitlin 1984 and 1990.
19. For discussions of this model, see White 1987:185–213 and LaCapra 1983:13–83.
20. Boeckh 1886 [1968:77].
21. See especially LaCapra 1983:25 ff.
22. Vidal-Naquet 1981:147–162.
23. See LaCapra 1985:71–94 and Appiah 1991; also Rosenmeyer 1988:49–50.
24. See LaCapra 1985:71–94.
25. Vernant 1991:152.
26. See Vernant 1972b [1981:17–18].
27. For Derrida's and Vernant's essays, see Macksey and Donato 1970.
28. For elaborations of this summary, see Norris and Benjamin 1988 and the essays in Arac et al. 1983.
29. Segal 1982 and Foley 1985:205–258. Segal makes reference in the introduction (p. 4) to his use of Derrida, but he does not sort out the sharp differences between structuralism and deconstruction, both of which he claims to use in his readings.
30. Quoted in Foley 1985:237.
31. Foley 1985:248.
32. Foley 1981 and McNally 1984.

REFERENCES

Appiah, Anthony. 1991. "Tolerable Falsehoods: Agency and the Interests of Theory." In *Consequences of Theory*, Jonathan Arac and Barbara Johnson, eds. (Selected Papers from the English Institute 1987–1988, n.s. 14.) Baltimore.

Arac, Jonathan, et al., eds. 1983. *The Yale Critics: Deconstruction in America*. Minneapolis.

Bergren, Ann, and Zeitlin, Froma, eds. 1982. *Texts and Contexts: American Classical Studies in Honor of J.-P. Vernant.* (= *Arethusa* 15).

Boeckh, August. 1886. 2nd ed. *Encyclopaedie und Methodologie der philologischen Wissenschaften.* Berlin. [Tr. and ed. John Paul Pritchard. 1968. *On Interpretation and Criticism.* Norman.]

Burke, Kenneth. 1950. *A Rhetoric of Motives.* Berkeley.

Burkert, Walter. 1979. *Structure and History in Greek Mythology and Ritual.* Berkeley.

Derrida, Jacques. 1972. "Structure, Sign, and Play in the Discourse of the Human Sciences." In Macksey and Donato 1970.

Foley, Helene. 1981. "The Conception of Women in Athenian Drama." In *Reflections of Women in Antiquity.* H. Foley, ed. New York.

———. 1985. *Ritual Irony: Poetry and Sacrifice in Euripides.* Ithaca, N.Y.

Foucault, Michel. 1970. *The Order of Things: An Archaeology of the Human Sciences.* New York.

———. 1985–1986. *The History of Sexuality.* Vols. 1–2. Tr. R. Hurley. New York.

Goldhill, Simon. 1990. "The Greater Dionysia and Civic Ideology." In Winkler and Zeitlin 1990:97–129.

Harrison, Robert Pogue. 1986. "The Ambiguities of Philology," *Diacritics* 16:14–20.

Hegel, G. W. F. 1970. *Vorlesungen über die Philosophie der Geschichte.* Vol. 12 of *G. W. F. Hegel: Werke in zwanzig Bänden.* Ed. Markus Michel. Frankfurt.

Kresic, Stephanus, ed. 1981. *Contemporary Hermeneutics and Interpretation of Classical Texts.* Ottawa.

LaCapra, Dominick. 1983. *Rethinking Intellectual History: Texts, Contexts, and Language.* Ithaca.

———. 1985. *History and Criticism.* Ithaca, N.Y.

Lloyd, G. E. R. 1966. *Polarity and Analogy.* Cambridge.

Longo, Oddone. 1990. "The Theater of the *Polis*" In Winkler and Zeitlin 1990.

Macksey, Richard, and Donato, Eugenio, eds. 1970. *The Structuralist Controversy: The Languages of Criticism and the Sciences of Man.* Baltimore.

McNally, Sheila. 1984. "The Maenad in Early Greek Art." In Peradotto and Sullivan 1984.

Norris, Christopher. 1983. *The Deconstructive Turn: Essays in the Rhetoric of Philosophy.* London.

Norris, Christopher, and Benjamin, Andrew. 1988. *What Is Deconstruction?* London.

Pechter, Edward. 1987. "The New Historicism and Its Discontents: Politicizing Renaissance Drama," *PMLA* 102:292–307. New York.

Peradotto, John. 1983. "Texts and Unrefracted Facts: Philology, Hermeneutics, and Semiotics," *Arethusa* 16:15–33.

Peradotto, John, and Sullivan, J. P., eds. 1984. *Women in the Ancient World: The Arethusa Papers.* Albany.

Pucci, Pietro. 1977. *Hesiod and the Language of Poetry.* Baltimore.

———. 1980. *The Violence of Pity in Euripides' Medea.* (Cornell Studies in Classical Philology 41.) Ithaca, N.Y.

Rosenmeyer, Thomas. 1988. *Deina Ta Polla: A Classicist's Checklist of Twenty Literary-Critical Positions.* (Arethusa Monographs.) Buffalo, N.Y.

Segal, Charles. 1981. *Tragedy and Civilization: An Interpretation of Sophocles.* Cambridge, Mass.

———. 1982. *Dionysiac Poetics and Euripides' Bacchae.* Princeton.

Singleton, Charles, ed. 1969. *Interpretation: Theory and Practice.* Baltimore.

Speculum: A Journal of Medieval Studies. 1990. (Vol. 65: *The New Philology.*) Cambridge, Mass.

Vernant, Jean-Pierre. 1972a. "Greek Tragedy: Problems of Interpretation." In Macksey and Donato 1970.

———. 1972b. *Mythe et tragédie en Grèce ancienne.* Paris. (Trans. Janet Lloyd. 1981. *Tragedy and Myth in Ancient Greece.* London.)

———. 1974. *Mythe et société en Grèce ancienne.* Paris. (Trans. Janet Lloyd. 1980. *Myth and Society in Ancient Greece.* New Jersey.)

———. 1991. *Mortals and Immortals: Collected Essays of Jean-Pierre Vernant.* Ed. Froma Zeitlin. Princeton.

Vernant, Jean-Pierre, and Vidal-Naquet Pierre. 1965. *Mythe et pensée chez les Grecs.* Paris. (Trans. Janet Lloyd. 1983. *Myth and Thought among the Greeks.* New Jersey.)

Vidal-Naquet, Pierre. 1981. "The Black Hunter and the Origin of the Athenian Ephebeia." In *Myth, Religion, and Society,* ed. and trans. R. L. Gordon. Cambridge.

White, Hayden. 1987. *The Content of the Form: Narrative Discourse and Historical Representation*. Baltimore.

Winkler, John J. 1990. "The Ephebes' Song: *Tragoidia* and *Polis*." In Winkler and Zeitlin 1990.

Winkler, John J., and Zeitlin, Froma I., eds. 1990. *Nothing to Do with Dionysos? Athenian Drama in Its Social Context*. Princeton.

Zeitlin, Froma I. 1984. "The Dynamics of Misogyny: Myth and Mythmaking in the *Oresteia*." In Peradotto and Sullivan 1984.

———. 1990. "Playing the Other: Theater, Theatricality, and the Feminine in Greek Drama." In Winkler and Zeitlin 1990.

Zeitlin, Froma I., ed. 1991. *Mortals and Immortals: Collected Essays of Jean-Pierre Vernant*. Princeton.

HISTORICIZING SOPHOCLES' *AJAX*

Peter W. Rose

For Michael Scufalos

In 1981 Fredric Jameson began his book *The Political Unconscious* with the exhortation "Always historicize!" (Jameson 1981:9). In 1991 he begins his book on postmodernism with the cautious observation: "It is safest to grasp the concept of the postmodern as an attempt to think the present historically in an age that has forgotten to think historically in the first place" (Jameson 1991:ix). Thus, when the enabling institutional power behind this symposium, i.e., Barbara Goff, invites participants to consider the question "Has 'history' supplanted 'theory' as the main term of contemporary literary analysis?" I am confronted once again with the eerie feeling that the field of classics operates in its own special time zone. For the rest of the "first" world, history has ended;[1] there is as little danger of history supplanting theory as there is of real alternatives to capitalism resulting from U.S. presidential elections. But the specific sense in which Professor Goff means "history" in connection with the field of classics is made clear by a subsequent question of hers: "Will an emphasis on 'history' give classical critics an excuse to retreat into their empirical and untheorized practices?" What is here called "history" is recognized by others as pure antiquarianism, history as "just one damned thing after another"—the random accumulation of the flotsam and jetsam of the past for the sole reason that it is there (Jameson 1988:152–157). Within classics, empirical and untheorized research is ultimately enlisted in the service of celebrating an ahistorically conceived fixed human nature. As Michel de Certeau has put it, "In history as in other fields, one day or another a practice without theory will necessarily drift into the dogmatism of 'eternal values' or into an apology for a 'timelessness'" (de Certeau 1988:57).

Jameson's declaration that we live in "an age that has forgotten to think historically" implies a view of thinking historically in which, at the very least, the past is envisioned as potentially both intelligible and relevant to the present. Both concepts—the past's intelligibility and its potential relevance—are great theoretical stumbling blocks for many classicists. Here the currency of a certain version of poststructuralism, alluded to by Professor Goff as a "gain," is ironically part of the problem—precisely to the extent that it seems to offer a highly sophisticated theorization of the historical as an illusion, a mere "effet du réel."[2] Derrida's critique of concepts of origins and of temporal linearity as the "repression of pluri-dimensional symbolic thought" (Derrida 1974:85–86) and his insistence that there is no access to a "real" outside the process and play of signification (1978:278–293) have led many of his followers to dismiss the very idea of history as being meaningful at any level.[3] Foucault's vision of history as an accidental sequence of discursive systems governed by rules which are "empty in themselves" (Foucault 1977:151; cf. Shumway 1989:112) constitutes a parallel assault on both the intelligibility and the relevance of history, at least as traditionally understood.[4] For many classicists who are by and large still most comfortable with the old New Criticism as an extension of the old philology, deconstruction now offers a way to be very subtle and analytical about language—indeed, to see ambiguity and ambivalence as once again the whole point of literary texts, while bracketing indefinitely the messiness of history and politics.[5] In this sense poststructuralism is quite at odds with another gain cited by Professor Goff, namely feminism. The extensive and impressive feminist work on antiquity generally assumes access to some "real" of history—"women's lived reality," as Phyllis Culham stubbornly puts it (Culham 1990:161).[6] This work also assumes that the more scrupulous that access is, the greater its relevance to contemporary struggles for the full emancipation of women.[7]

What I do think is a tremendous gain from poststructuralist meditations on history—I am thinking especially of Foucault and de Certeau—is that they have forced us to meditate on precisely what Professor Goff has asked—namely, what are the enabling questions by which we choose our data and construct our discourse of the past? What is at stake in the theoretical models we adopt and the phenomena we constitute as relevant evidence? We need somehow to consider what institutional and disciplinary interests and constraints set the parameters of our inquiries and whether there are more vital interests that transgress the disciplinary ones.

The questions lurking around the topic of this symposium—such as "Should we 'historicize' Greek tragedy? and if so, in what sense? on what level? and to what ends?"—do not lend themselves to straightforward or uniform answers. There are obviously many different modes in which and levels on which sensitive readers have approached the interface between the texts of Greek tragedy and the range of other texts, in the broadest sense of the term, surviving from fifth-century Greece. For not only are "events" texts, but, as Foucault reminds us, "to say something is itself an event" (Foucault 1991:126) and "the cultural product is also part of the historical fabric" (1991:129).

Certainly my title, "Historicizing Sophocles' *Ajax*," was not intended to suggest that this play has not been previously "historicized," as the term is widely understood. On the contrary, at least since Welcker in 1829, interpreters have seen varying versions of fifth-century political struggles reflected in the text.[8] The majority of interpretations of the *Ajax* over the last forty years do not ignore political and social issues in the play, but they cover these briefly and often tentatively. The truly interesting interpretative problems are seen as located at some other level, for instance: in the religious-ethical sphere (Kitto 1960 and 1986; Winnington-Ingram 1980); in the development of the dramatist's artistry or tragic poetics (Reinhardt 1979; Seale 1982; Heath 1987); in the eternal mystery of the hero's transcendence of mortality (Whitman 1951); in the opposition between civilization and raw nature (Segal 1981); in the internal contradictions of an archaic ethical code (Knox 1964); in the relation between mind and action (Goldhill 1986); in the quest for a purely personal sphere vis-à-vis the limitations of "the political" (Davis 1986; Meier 1988:207; Di Benedetto 1983) or, within the political framework, "the transvaluation of values" (Bradshaw 1991). What N. O. Brown, in offering his own version of an historicized reading of the play, dismissed scornfully as "bloodless abstraction[s]" (Brown 1951:18) are perhaps the clearest indications of the text's ideological success. The immediacies of intractable, historically constituted conflicts are transformed into universal claims; a specific political-historical type becomes an emblem of mortality in general; fifth-century Athens becomes society or civilization *tout court*. Moreover, any critical exercise aimed at reversing this allegorization of immediacy seems inevitably doomed to appear an exercise in banal empiricism. The reason is perhaps that what is truly past is truly irrelevant: in reading a work of antiquity it is perhaps only such allegorical projections of our own concerns that Tiresias-like give blood to these flitting ghosts of struggles past and allow them to speak to us.

As Jameson has stated the seemingly impossible bind: "The dilemma of any 'historicism' can . . . be dramatized by the peculiar, unavoidable, yet seemingly unresolvable alternation between Identity and Difference" (Jameson 1988:150). Either we are guilty, it seems, of projecting our own concerns onto the past or, again to quote Jameson, if "we . . . affirm . . . the radical Difference of the alien object from ourselves, then at once the doors of comprehension begin to swing closed and we find ourselves separated by the whole density of our own culture from objects or cultures thus initially defined as Other from ourselves and thus as irremediably inaccessible" (Jameson 1988:151).[9]

The problem then is not to dismiss the richest and subtlest readings of the play available to us, but to attempt to redeploy them in a framework that offers some meaningful supersession of this dilemma of Identity and Difference. My own approach, which I cannot fully elaborate here, entails a Marxist reading of the texts as ideology, produced by a society that, for all its radical differences, was eminently a class society.[10] By ideology in the Marxist sense I do not refer to what is an increasingly common use of the term by classicists, i.e., a statically conceived worldview or so homogenized an entity as "civic ideology." I refer rather to an eminently combative arena of persuasion and struggle.[11] It is because our own lives are so saturated with the ruses of ideology in a society riven by class conflicts that we have some stake in grasping the workings of ideology in a very different society. Ideology itself—like the workings of the unconscious—has, as Althusser argued, no history (Althusser 1971:159–162), yet its content at any particular historical juncture is per force historically specific. Here I think Althusser's notion of the problematic to which any particular ideology is a response can be helpful. He argues that the unity of an ideology derives not simply from its own internal structure but from a combination of that structure with the set of questions posed for ideology by a particular configuration of social and political realities. The terms in which the text generates its own representations of reality are explored for the internal contradictions and structured silences that point to a problematic outside the text, a problematic to which it attempts to respond (Althusser 1969:62–86; cf. Macherey 1978).

Let me sketch broadly the shape of my approach. I trace a number of overlapping movements that structure meaning in the text. Specifically I look at the shape of the myth, the rhetorical structure that constitutes the *apologia* for Ajax, and the dialectical structure that attempts to square the logic of the myth with the logic of that *apologia*. Finally, I explore how the contradictions of the play entail responses to the contradictions of Athens herself. In my analysis I speak often of plural meanings not because I accept or espouse for this drama the sort of open play of multiple meanings so dear to poststructuralists. To be sure, the attempt to "overcome contradictions," in Lévi-Strauss's well-worn phrase,[12] entails not infrequently the exploitation of ambiguities. But to conceive of fifth-century rhetorical practice solely in terms of the sophists' theorizations about the constitutive power of language or the slipperiness of meanings is to ignore the very high stakes for which their pupils "played" with the language of the assemblies and the courts. There is a world of difference between Gorgias' self-described *paignion* (plaything) and the debate reported by Thucydides over the Athenian response to the Mytilenean rebellion. All sorts of tricks and ambiguities may be exploited in both sorts of texts, but while Gorgias may delight us with the play of signifiers and confront us with the elusiveness of fixed meanings,[13] Cleon and Diodotus bend all their intellectual energies precisely toward fixing meanings of key value terms in ways that imply absolute, life-and-death consequences. To this extent I subscribe to Ober and Strauss's insistence on the close links between Greek tragedy and practical rhetoric (Ober and Strauss 1990:237–270) as opposed to Goldhill's attempts to insist in Kantian terms on the sharp disjunction between rhetoric and tragedy (Goldhill 1990:128).[14] The ends of tragedy may be less direct than speeches in the courts and in the assembly, but they are not just exercises to show the slipperiness of signification.

THE MYTHIC STRUCTURE

The dramatist's choice of a particular *mythos* is perhaps the most obvious structure of meaning in the tragedy. The very choice of the myth entails a prima facie presumption that the myth and version chosen reflect some specific problematic as a focus of interest. Let me sum up briefly the details of Sophocles' handling of this myth and suggest some of the implications of his inclusions, omissions, additions, and modifications. The award of the arms of Achilles was presumably the central narrative focus of the lesser epic treatments and, as far as we can tell, of the first play of Aeschylus' lost trilogy. Sophocles begins his play after the contest has been decided and after Ajax's mad attack on the cattle. Thus there is no opportunity for direct debate or a full dramatic juxtaposition between opposing political, physical, military, or psychological types.[15] Sophocles chooses the version of the award decision that attributes it to a vote of the Greek army.[16] This makes the decision a direct judgment by the community about its own leadership. By the same token such a decision is open to charges of corruption, envy, or stupidity. In Sophocles' version the charge of bias is made and denied, but the question is left open. The text states no explicit criteria for the contest unambiguously agreed upon by all concerned, but a wide variety of potential criteria are suggested. Athena's sermon in the prologue seems to invite the audience to view the two heroes' relative piety—their capacity for *sōphrosynē*—as the ultimate criterion; certainly many modern readers have accepted that view. Menelaus could be understood to imply that the criterion of obedience to the city's laws, which in some unexplained way is figured as the opposite of having a large body (1071–1078), is the decisive basis.[17] Agamemnon makes an even sharper opposition—explicitly tied to the contest—between men who are "broad, wide in the shoulders" and those who always succeed (*kratousi*) because they have the right mental posture (*hoi phronountes eu*, 1246–1252).[18] Ajax clearly sees the sole criterion as proofs of strength—"works of the hand" (*sthenei . . . erga . . . cheiros*, 438–439), i.e., achievements on the battlefield in a contest precisely about supreme martial prowess (*kratos aristeias,* 443)—as does the chorus of his followers, who speak of a "contest over supreme prowess of hand" (*aristocheir . . . agōn,* 935–936). Odysseus, in defending Ajax's right to battle, describes him categorically as "the one best man I've seen of [all] the Argives who arrived at Troy except Achilles" (*hen andra idein ariston Argeiōn,* 1340–1341), where the word "one" and the genitive of comparison insist upon the full superlative force of the word "best" (*ariston*).

While it was open to Sophocles to allude to a wide range of actions by both heroes, he suppresses most of the very rich tradition about Odysseus, while he includes a particularly full and complex array of material about Ajax, even adding a few points of his own. In addition to oft-noted allusions to the Homeric picture of Ajax,[19] Sophocles includes and dramatically intensifies the madness of Ajax. He is perhaps the first to insist on Ajax's return to sanity and the full consciousness of his choice of suicide. Sophocles perhaps has added the conscious intent to kill the generals and invents a full and curious history of a feud between Ajax and Athena extending back to the day Ajax departed from his homeland. Di Benedetto (1983:72) has emphasized the fact that this story is clearly based on the moralizing reminder Odysseus gives Achilles in the embassy (*Iliad* 9.252–259). Tecmessa—unknown earlier—may also be a Sophoclean addition, one always seen exclusively—and always to Ajax's detriment—in terms of the strong echoes of the famous scene in *Iliad* 6 between Hector and Andromache (e.g., W. E. Brown 1965–1966:118–121; Kirkwood 1965:51–70). But already in the *Iliad* the eminently decent but essentially unheroic Hector is sharply contrasted with the potentially savage, true hero Achilles (Whitman 1958:208–212). The figure of Tecmessa, the spear-bride whose homeland has been destroyed by the very man to whom she is now devoted, strongly echoes not only Andromache but also Achilles' spear-bride Briseis, whose poignant lament over the corpse of Patroclus (*Iliad* 19.287–300) evokes a tragic predicament far nearer that of Tecmessa than of the legal wife of the losing city's self-deluded hero. Thus beyond the direct Homeric associations of Ajax fully deployed throughout the text, Sophocles has chosen to enrich the Homeric texture of his protagonist by endowing him with strong echoes of both the human rootedness of Hector and the absolutist isolation of Achilles. The net effect is a further concentration of interest on Ajax at the expense of the relatively colorless Odysseus.

Apart from Odysseus' close ties to Athena and Agamemnon, slurs on his parentage and veracity are the main points from the tradition incorporated by Sophocles—though he seems to have aimed as well at incorporating some sense of the decency and good sense suggested by Odysseus' tactful speech in the *Odyssey* to Ajax's ghost (11.558–562) and his warning to Eurycleia not to boast over the fallen suitors (22.407–418).[20] But Sophocles excludes any specific allusion to an *action* of any kind, military or political, by Odysseus. This, I believe, is the primary reason behind his exclusion of any reference to the battle over Achilles' corpse, the decisive criterion in the *Little Iliad* (cf. Jebb 1962:xvi) and, it seems, Pindar (*Nemean* 8.28–32). Any enhancement of Ajax's martial stature could only be bought at the risk of reminding the audience of a concrete occasion where the tradition also assigned Odysseus a distinguished martial role.

Sophocles' version is thus concentrated not, as the earlier myth would suggest, on the juxtaposition of two broadly representative types of military leader, but on the response of all parties concerned to the fact that one of them has lost in some fundamental communal assessment of his worth, has reacted with extreme hostility, and has been thoroughly humiliated by the intervention of a force beyond his control. The audience first learns of the response of Ajax's rival, Odysseus, and that of the goddess who is his enemy, Athena. These responses are followed and balanced by those of Ajax's friends, the chorus and Tecmessa, his spear-won bride. The central third, roughly, of the play is concentrated on Ajax's personal response to his situation and culminates in his suicide. The final section of the play, a little more than a third, explores first the response to Ajax's death by his dependents, especially his weaker half-brother Teucer, then the response of the generals Menelaus and Agamemnon; and finally, a brief reappearance of Odysseus to offer his response to the now-completed career of his former rival. In such a structure the reduction of Odysseus' role is quite striking.

Despite these and other subtleties in the deployment of the mythic raw material, Sophocles does adhere to the central facts of the myth: Ajax loses the contest of the arms and dies. Whatever face is put upon the contest and whatever view we are induced to take of the hero, his defeat and disappearance from the world are immutable givens, the logic of the myth.

THE RHETORICAL STRUCTURE

The play's rhetorical structure is the movement that tends toward the validation of Ajax as the best available political leader. In this movement, the poet, not unlike a brilliant trial lawyer in an apparently open-and-shut murder case, employs all the resources of his art in the early portion of the play to give the impression that the whole case against Ajax has been laid out in all its starkness. But even in the predominantly negative portion of the play, a few mitigating elements are unobtrusively slipped in. As the play progresses, these are built upon with a variety of factors that culminate in a crescendo of defense. Not only does the broad dramatic situation of the myth—i.e., the conflict between rival leaders—suggest the contemporary world of political trials and ostracisms,[21] but the specific details of both the indictment and the defense are best understood not simply in psychological or religious terms, but politically.

The Indictment

Let me sum up the case against Ajax. First of all he is mad. His madness consists fundamentally in the faulty perception imposed on him by Athena (51–65), which leads him to mistake the cattle and herdsmen of the army for the chiefs and rivals whom he wishes to punish for his defeat in the contest of the arms. This faulty perception is dramatized on the stage by Ajax's inability to see Odysseus, his confidence that he can see the goddess,[22] and his declaration that he is about to torture Odysseus inside the tent where, as Athena and Tecmessa inform us, there is really only a pathetic ram tied to a pillar. More central to the indictment of Ajax than his madness are his "sane" intentions to kill the generals and the pitiless ferocity of his imagined revenge.

The indictment of Ajax for a criminally antisocial pursuit of the revenge code is paralleled by an indictment of his failure to adhere to the other half of that code—the injunction to help one's friends—for Ajax's pursuit of revenge and his later suicide clearly involve grave difficulties for his dependents.[23] The chorus of Ajax's Salaminian followers, Tecmessa, and Teucer all complain in various ways that Ajax has brought suffering on his friends; and the mute figure of Ajax's defenseless son Eurysakes may initially be counted in the same indictment. Many modern readers have seen Ajax's suicide, which deprives these friends of their greatest protector, as only confirming the dangers brought about by his initial madness and, therefore, as a repetition of that madness.

What, one may wonder, is particularly political about all this? The madness that perhaps most interested fifth-century Greek thinkers was the criminal madness of those who had too much power—like the Spartan king Cleomenes or the Persian kings Cambyses and Xerxes.[24] The moral view of this madness presented it as a vehicle by which a just divinity induced the excessively powerful to commit crimes so serious as to entail grave consequences for their communities, for their immediate dependents, and for themselves. Punishing the excesses of these overly powerful madmen helped to make the world safe for democracy. For we cannot ignore the fact that the clearest evidence for this moral view of madness is in the fifth-century Athenian democrat Aeschylus and the pro-Athenian historian Herodotus.

The sermon that Athena preaches to Odysseus and the audience at the end of the prologue seems to place us very fully within an Aeschylean moral and political set of ideas—an indictment of the criminality of ruling-class figures presented as a type:

τοιαῦτα τοίνυν εἰσορῶν ὑπέρκοπον
μηδέν ποτ' εἴπῃς αὐτὸς εἰς θεοὺς ἔπος,
μηδ' ὄγκον ἄρῃ μηδέν', εἴ τινος πλέον
ἢ χειρὶ βρίθεις ἢ μακροῦ πλούτου βάθει.
ὡς ἡμέρα κλίνει τε κἀνάγει πάλιν
ἅπαντα τἀνθρώπεια· τοὺς δὲ σώφρονας
θεοὶ φιλοῦσι καὶ στυγοῦσι τοὺς κακούς.

So now, as you look upon these events, see that
You yourself speak nothing arrogant to the gods
Nor take up haughty airs if, more than someone else,
You are heavy with might or the depth of great wealth:
Know that a single day can bend down or raise again
All that is human. Those who are sensible
The gods do love; they hate those who are bad.
(127–133)

Ajax here seems to be linked with those figures of great power and wealth whose very advantages, social and political, are viewed by Aeschylus as a major factor in their vulnerability to madness, to being carried away by excessive confidence into violations of *sōphrosynē*—a term whose components ("save" and "think") together designate that defensive, deferential mental posture essential to survival. In political contexts this sort of "safe-think" amounts to recognizing the actual hierarchy of power and adjusting one's behavior accordingly. In the aristocratic states it was the virtue of "knowing your place." The Athenian empire recommended it to its subject states.[25]

The political dimension of Athena's categorical indictment of Ajax as an exemplar of the rich and powerful seems to be reinforced by the chorus insofar as they defend Ajax in Pindaric terms as a typical victim of the envy that attaches to "the haves" (*Ajax* 154–157; cf. Pind. *Nemean* 8.22). It is confirmed in Ajax's relentless insistence on defining his own worth in rigorously aristocratic terms of his ancestry, the continuity of his line, the nature *(physis)* he has as a consequence of his ancestry, the obligations he recognizes as a *eugenēs*. Thus the final judgment of the audience on Ajax can be based not on a vaguely defined illustration of the human condition, but on a precisely conceived representative of a particular social and political class.

The Case for the Defense

What is the case for the defense? Sophocles does not exactly answer or refute any of the charges. His argument is essentially narrative: in the course of the play he gradually silences and mystifies the most serious charges, while dramatically highlighting Ajax's positive aspects through a sustained contrast to the hero's inferiors.

In the early part of the play the audience is hit by a veritable barrage of verbal and visual images of blood, of cutting throats, of hacking and hewing flesh, flaying alive, and other assorted mutilation.[26] Ambiguity between horror and sympathy enters with the extraordinary tableau (Taplin 1978:108) in which Sophocles displays the hero, now sane and grieving, surrounded by his animal victims—"a wreck amid the wreck of corpses" (*Ajax* 308–309), as Tecmessa describes him. Ajax, proclaiming a uniqueness that no reader of the *Iliad* could deny him,[27] invites us to be moved by the sight of his degradation:

> No longer may you see
> *This* man, I'll speak out
> A great declaration, a man of the army such as never
> Troy saw come from the land
> Of Greece: but now dishonored,
> I lie here, laid low in the way you see.
> (421–427)

That grim spectacle is before our eyes until Ajax is closed inside his tent at line 595. During the whole scene, allusions to the slaughter are increasingly rare. When Ajax reemerges from the tent, the animal corpses are presumably no longer visible, and he merely alludes to the blood stains which he will wash off (*Ajax* 655). Arguably this statement could be both literal and symbolic. Thus when Ajax is seen for the last time on the shore preparing his suicide, his costume and person may be free of visual reminders of the degrading slaughter of the animals. The only other allusion to it in the play is a brief, relatively colorless one by Menelaus (*Aj.* 1060).

On the other hand, there is a crescendo of pathetic allusions to Ajax's own self-slaughter and blood[28] and an increasingly heavy emphasis on his supreme, protective martial prowess.[29] It is possible to argue, as many have, that the play simply gives a balanced picture of both sides of the same coin: the same mentality and values that make psychopathic murderers also produce very valuable soldiers in wartime. The view is seductively modern and has been best argued by the greatest of the pietists, Winnington-Ingram (1980:11–56). It ignores, however, the rhetorical movement of the play. In drama, timing is everything.

Other important motifs undergo this same sort of rhetorical transformation. The goddess Athena in the prologue can pass—despite dramatic hints of gratuitous cruelty—as a valid representation of divine justice punishing the excessive pride of a violent aristocrat. Yet through comments of the chorus, Tecmessa, and the messenger, not to mention Ajax himself, the motif of divine intervention is fundamentally transformed on the one hand into an image of purely arbitrary impositions external to the will or responsibility of individuals, and, on the other, into a celebration, in a post-Solonian, post-Simonidean world, of a purely human excellence, freed of the Homeric image of heroes as merely the passive vehicles of divine qualities.[30] The circular cliché that the gods are responsible for everything is both valorized as an excuse and challenged to Ajax's advantage.[31]

The image of Ajax's *philoi*, helpless infant and wife, as well as his vulnerable half-brother, which contributes initially to the negative view of Ajax, is transformed into an overwhelmingly sympathetic spectacle as the wife and child huddle pathetically to protect the corpse from the brutal Spartan threat (1171–1181; cf. 1409–1411),[32] while the lesser half-brother rises to heroic stature by accepting the prospect of death in defense of the corpse. This movement of Teucer from utter despair to heroic resolve echoes closely—albeit in a lower register—Ajax's own resolve to choose death rather than dishonor.[33] Even the initial image of the hero's insane isolation (*monon*, 29–30) is finally transformed into a stirring evocation of his unique lonely stance as defender (*mounos*, 1276; *monos monou*, 1283).[34]

Ajax *Strategos*

But if we are really to understand some of the subtler and more comprehensively political aspects of the rehabilitation of Ajax in the latter portions of the play, we must consider the images of social and political relations therein, and explore how these relate to fifth-century Athenian realities. Here I would say that Sophocles uses all the means at his disposal to present in Ajax an abstracted image on a grand scale of an Athenian *strategos*.[35] The usual translation of *strategos* as "general" blurs the crucial point that Athenian *strategoi*—whatever their prowess on land—tended to distinguish themselves most by their military activities at sea.[36] Concomitant with Sophocles' presentation of Ajax as a *strategos* is his characterization of Ajax's followers as Athenian sailors—that is, just like the majority of his audience. The potential class tensions within Athenian society between the aristocrats from whom the *strategoi* were chosen and the *dēmos* who rowed the ships seem to be evoked in the more Aeschylean tone of the prologue, with its indictment of wealth and power.[37] But these elements are progressively blurred through the rest of the play, first by a validation of a fundamentally hierarchical view of society—i.e., a view in which it is affirmed that there are "big" people and "little" people and the little must depend on the great (*Ajax* 154–163)[38]—and secondly, by dramatic exploitation of the "Spartan menace," embodied in Menelaus and Agamemnon—compared to these tyrannical thugs Ajax is bound to look good.

Quite apart from Athenian associations of Ajax external to the play,[39] I am struck by the cumulative impact of its language, which repeatedly associates Ajax and his followers with sailing, with Athens, and with Salamis, in terms that clearly imply the glorious Athenian victory there in 480 B.C. In line 3 of the play the tent of Ajax is described with the untranslatable adjective *nautikē*, "of or pertaining to ships or sailing." The chorus enters apostrophizing Ajax, who "holds the solid base of sea-surrounded, wave-tossed Salamis." The chorus itself is first addressed by Tecmessa as "sailors of Ajax, of the race that springs from the Erectheidai, sons of the soil" (201–202). Tecmessa's words imply with striking directness that Ajax's followers are to be viewed quite literally as Athenian sailors. Ajax's penultimate words before his suicide are an apostrophe to the "sacred soil of my own Salamis, firm seat of my paternal hearth" and "glorious Athens and the race kindred to mine" (*kleinai t'Athēnai, kai to suntrophon genos*, 861). The final lyric utterance of the chorus is a passionate wish that they might "be where the wooded fortress stands, wave-beaten upon the sea, pass beneath Sounion's level summit and offer a greeting to holy Athens" (*tas hieras . . . Athānas*, 1219–1221). Even their image of Sounion as a "fortress" (*problēma*, 1219) fuses the very headland of Attica with Ajax, whom they have just called their "bulwark" (*probola*, 1212). At their most sympathetic moments, Ajax and the chorus are most intimately and directly fused with the land and city of Sophocles' own audience.

If one is willing to grant that this sort of language is intended to evoke for the Athenian audience a very strong identification with Ajax and his followers, to interpellate them, in Althusser's term, as ideological partisans of Ajax,[40] then I believe it is legitimate to ask what image of the Athenian political situation is offered in the play. It is one which fits Thucydides' famous description of Athens as "in name a democracy, but in reality rule by the first [i.e., the best] man" (2.65.9–10). Thucydides was specifically describing the regime of Pericles, but his description fits the virtual monopoly of executive power held by members of the Athenian aristocracy from the inception of democracy at least until the rise of Cleon in the 420's (Ostwald 1986:78, 82; Davies 1971:xvii–xviii).[41] The centrality of the navy-oriented military commander in Athenian life clarifies, I think, the function of Sophocles' consistent association of Ajax—who was for Homer and Pindar the land-hero par excellence—with the sea, sailing, and even imagery of sea storms and ports.

More problematic is the fundamentally degraded image Sophocles offers of the Athenian *dēmos*. Sophocles chooses to convey a particularly unheroic image of the ordinary sailors, while pulling out all the stops in evoking a Homeric image of their military and political dependence on the prowess of the single, superior warrior.[42] Expressing their utter dependence on Ajax, they compare themselves to the most timorous of birds, the dove (134–140; see Jebb 1962 and Stanford 1963*b* ad loc.). They are ready to run away as soon as they learn the extent of Ajax's crimes (245–253), and after observing his state of mind subsequent to his rampage, conclude that he is still mad and better off dead (635–640). Their repeated laments about the hardships and dangers of foreign wars and their expressed longing for a specifically Athenian home (Burton 1980:37) surely seem calculated to interpellate (again in Althusser's sense) the majority of the Athenian audience—to invite them to see themselves represented on stage—but at what price? By contrast the old men who make up the chorus of the *Agamemnon*, who were too old for war ten years before the action of the play but tell Agamemnon bluntly to his face that they thought he was wrong to go to war (799–804) and respond with scornful defiance to Aegisthus' threats of imprisonment and torture (1619–1671), offer the audience an infinitely more heroic image of the ordinary Athenian citizen than these time-trimming cowards in the prime of life. To remind the audience that, given the option, they, like the chorus, would prefer drinking parties and sex to the hardships of war (*Ajax* 1185–1210) does not at all render superfluous their putative dependence on great *strategoi*. On the contrary, the chorus goes on to recall that Ajax had been their only protection in the past (1211–1215) and their only hope of joy in the future (1215–1216).

The pervasive emphasis on the military prowess of Ajax is thus by no means evidence that his contribution to society is dated, an historical irrelevance—as Knox and others have tried to suggest (Knox 1961:24–25). On the contrary, it draws upon very legitimate military fears of ordinary Athenians. Their democracy was subjected to military attack by oligarchic Greeks under Spartan leadership immediately after its inception (Hdt. 5.74–78); it was soon threatened with obliteration by the vast empire of Persia, and—however one reads finally the balance sheet of empire[43]—Athens' prosperity was recognized by its citizens as a direct consequence of the capacity of its navy to guarantee grain routes and extort revenues from its so-called allies. It is then certainly possible for these Athenians to view their successes and survival as not so much their own achievement, but rather as the consequence of efforts by such uniquely talented *strategoi* as Miltiades, Themistocles, Cimon, or Pericles. I believe Sophocles, while not offering a precise dramatic portrait of any particular *strategos*, did expect his audience to have the greatest ones in mind as they judged the fate of Ajax.[44]

Beyond those elements in the play that reinforce and validate a hierarchical, patriarchal, and paternalistic image of Athenian society, Sophocles clinches his rehabilitation of Ajax by his exploitation of the Spartan menace—by the introduction of thoroughly mean-spirited, snobbish, and tyrannical types who evoke in broad and blatant terms the audience's fears of and resentments toward Sparta, as both a rival power and a political system. The most explicitly political allusion in the whole play—one which not even the most fervent exponent of an apolitical Sophocles can deny[45]—is Teucer's militant rejection of Menelaus' claim to sovereignty over Ajax and his followers:

πoῦ σὺ στρατηγεῖς τοῦδε; ποῦ δέ σοι λεῶν
ἔξεστ' ἀνάσσειν ὧν ὅδ' ἤγαγ' οἴκοθεν;
Σπάρτης ἀνάσσων ἦλθες, οὐχ ἡμῶν κρατῶν·

How are *you* general over *him*? Where do you claim
Sovereignty over the troops *he* led from home?
As Sparta's sovereign you came, not as ruler over us!

(1100–1102)

It is of course easier to imagine such lines having more of an impact the nearer we set the date of the play to the bitter disputes between Sparta and Athens over hegemony before, during, and after the war with Persia. But the fact that Sparta consistently viewed the existence of the Athenian empire as a threat to Sparta's own "natural" hegemony over Greece and that the audience lived in a world where the conflict of Greek *polis* against Greek *polis* was an unchallenged fact of life meant that such a line was bound to raise a cheer among Athenians at virtually any point during the fifth century. In the context of Athens' own usurpation of tyrannical powers over her allies, especially after 450 (Meiggs 1973:152–174), this fervent anti-Spartanism might to some extent represent a disingenuous displacement of potential anti-Athenian sentiment to a more acceptable object. But such displacements are the very stuff of imperialist ideology.[46]

It is by tapping this enormous reservoir of anti-Spartan hostility in his audience that Sophocles consolidates his defense of Ajax as outlined above. Indeed, failure to recognize this very source of dramatic energy may account for so many critics' perception that this portion of the play lacks dramatic interest (e.g., Gellie 1972:26). Spartan complaints about Ajax's *hubris* are here undermined by their own *hubris* in denying burial to his corpse and in threatening his helpless dependents.[47] Ajax's impiety toward Athena, already rendered ambiguous by the messenger's speech, emerges in the debate with the Spartans as a positive virtue—a model for Teucer's "thinking big" in the face of Spartan attacks on free speech and independent action (Linforth 1954:26); so too with

Ajax's pride in his noble lineage. Contrasted with the hollow snobbery of the Atreidai in their own thoroughly corrupt family line, Ajax's sense of his own worth is fully validated by the bowman[48] Teucer's pseudodemocratic defense of his own lineage and his stirring account of Ajax's glorious achievements on the field. So too the issues of violating the vote, transgressing the law of the community, and attacking the community's leaders are dramatically mystified by the injection of the Spartan-Athenian conflict. What is clearly a crime when the whole Greek army at Troy is presented as an image of a single Greek *polis*[49] becomes hopelessly murky when that army is transformed into an image of many competing, would-be independent Greek *poleis* in a conflict-laden military alliance—an image far nearer the reality of Sophocles' Greece. In this context all the platitudes of the Atreidai about law and order emerge as an irrelevant mask for their fundamentally tyrannical view of the political hierarchy.

The theme of Ajax's madness itself—which seemed so central to his indictment as a figure deluded by excessive power and which has so impressed contemporary pietists (e.g., Winnington-Ingram 1980; Goldhill 1986:180–198)— gradually shifts until it resonates with a very different pattern, one that, as far as our remains of tragedy allow us to see, was first elaborated in conjunction with an impassioned appeal to Athenians' hatred of tyranny. Bernard Knox, in delineating his tremendously influential portrait of the Sophoclean hero as a type, noted that the earliest appearance chronologically of the pattern is in the *Prometheus Bound,* where we also find the earliest full literary delineation of the tyrant (Knox 1964:45–50; Podlecki 1966:103–122). Particularly suggestive are the denunciation of Prometheus by the tyrant's toady Hermes as "mad with no small sickness" (*memēnot' ou smikran noson,* 977) and the reply, "I may be sick, if it be sickness to hate one's enemies" (978). Hermes also exhorts Prometheus to "be sensible" (*orthōs phronein,* 1000), to which Prometheus replies that never through fear will he become "woman-minded" (*thēlonous,* 1003). Also relevant is the reaction of the chorus of seemingly timid Oceanids. Initially they side with Hermes in urging wise counsel (*euboulia*) rather than obstinacy (*authadia,* cf. 1035–1038). They are soon, however, converted to "folly" (*anoias,* 1079) by the tyrannical bluster of Hermes and resolve to suffer with their friend Prometheus (1063–1070). The conversion of Teucer from despair to heroic defiance when confronted with the tyrannical threats of the Spartan king combines with other factors already discussed to invite the Athenian audience to refigure the mad defiance of Ajax as an emblem of their own many "mad" acts of daring—especially vis-à-vis Sparta.

What is least appreciated in all this is that so debased a use of democratic political ideas, in a context where no more enlightened or positive alternative is offered, tends to degrade those ideas absolutely. The democratic alternative is not simply left out, but distorted and subverted. Both in scale and content the behavior of the decently motivated Odysseus, who adroitly fawns on the Spartan tyrant, cannot constitute a viable political or social alternative.[50] His benign humanism is rightly perceived as a utopian aspiration in a world where neither the Atreidai nor Ajax finds it viable. Essentially the audience, like the chorus, is offered a choice between Ajax and the Atreidai. On the one hand is a social pyramid bound together by ties of kinship and affection, headed by a great protector in a world dominated by war. In his veins flows the blood of gods and heroes. Fully aware of his own superiority, he expects obedience from his subordinates, but despite a certain macho gruffness toward his spear-won bride, he does show his humane, paternal concern for their welfare and survival both in his reliance on the not unworthy Teucer, in his indirect reply to Tecmessa through his address to his son, and in his magnificent monologue on yielding to the pity for her that he fully acknowledges. On the other side is not so much a pyramid as a blatant binary image of masters "set over" (cf. *ephestōtōn*, 1072) their slaves (*doulōn*, 1235) where the dominant cohesive force is the naked fear (cf. 1076, 1079, 1084) of the oppressed, and where hollow snobbery about questionable lineage is the sole justification for the status of the masters. That the first is presented as Athenian and the second as Spartan easily tilts the scales.

THE DIALECTICAL STRUCTURE

The rhetorical structure of the play moves toward the validation of a tendency in fifth-century Athenian political and social institutions that may be summed up as aristocratic, militaristic, and paternalistic. The logic of this structure thus points toward an optimistic celebration of what many of Sophocles' contemporaries may have considered the actual state of Athenian political life as long as Pericles was alive. Yet the logic of the myth and the play as a whole leads toward suicide, a funeral, and an overwhelming sense of the diminution of the present order. The tension of these two logics is what I would call the dialectical structure of the play, a sustained tension between the playwright's vision of how reality ought to be and his perception of the way it in fact is. To this extent we may compare this text with the assessment by Lukács, following Marx, of the French novelist Balzac (see Lukács 1964:21–46, esp. 40). Balzac was blatantly committed to the old aristocracy, but the unfolding of his plots shows relentlessly the triumph of the bourgeoisie. On this reading there is thus both a radically partisan moment to the text and a kind of objectivity or truth.

But the dialectic of the *Ajax* is not exhausted in this relatively simple tension between a tendentious movement validating an aristocratic worldview and a movement confirming the disappearance of that view. There is a deeper, parallel dialectic structured into the delineation of the hero's intellectual progress that implies a critique and transcendence both of the aristocratic code and of the new realities that have displaced it. Yet this very transcendence remains rooted in a class-bound vision.

Ajax's defeat in the contest of the arms undermines for Ajax the fundamentally social character of the heroic imperative to be "best." Ajax's defeat confronts him with the total externality of any identity dependent upon public esteem. The depth of his perception of his own alienation is first suggested in his radical inversion of the traditional heroic imagery of light and dark:

> ἰὼ
>
> σκότος, ἐμὸν φάος,
> ἔρεβος ὦ φαεινότατον, ὡς ἐμοί,
> ἕλεσθ' ἕλεσθέ μ' οἰκήτορα,
> ἕλεσθέ μ'· οὔτε γὰρ θεῶν γένος οὔθ' ἀμερίων
> ἔτ' ἄξιος βλέπειν τίν' εἰς ὄνασιν ἀνθρώπων.

> Oh!
> Darkness, my light of salvation,
> O Night-world [of death], most dazzling bright for me,
> Take me, take me as your inhabitant,
> Take me. For no longer am I fit to look for benefit
> To the race of gods or any of the human creatures-of-a-day.
>
> (394–399)

The darkness of death is the only possible "salvation" (cf. *sesōsmenon*, 692) he can hope for in a world where he is completely cut off from positive links with either human or suprahuman forces.[51]

Ajax's first nonlyric, calmer assessment begins by exploring the breakdown of the aristocratic logic that affirms that the successful are the good and that the good produce the good. Ajax's father Telamon was great and succeeded; Ajax himself is no less great, yet failed (434). The speech explores the absoluteness of Ajax's isolation from the suprasocial order of the gods (457–458), from society at large as represented by the Greek army (458), from the very land he stands on (459), and—worst of all—from the very father whose excellence should, according to aristocratic, circular logic, legitimize his son's excellence and be in turn validated by his son's public success (462–466). In sum, all the factors—gods, family, state, and community, which Pindar normally assumes as the natural validation of aristocratic worth—are in this play recognized by the protagonist as hostile to the construction of his own subjectivity and to the preservation of any sense of self-esteem.[52]

Ajax's reemergence from his tent is not merely a dramatic surprise nor is there any practical dimension of his suicide that would necessitate deceitfulness toward his wife or followers. Not only does his expression of profound pity for his spear-won wife and child go far in answering the charge of indifference toward his *philoi,* but the rich poetry and philosophic breadth of his meditation establish his mental grandeur in the dramatic competition with Odysseus[53] and the Atreidai. Finally, his great monologue confirms on a cosmic and social level his intellectual transcendence of the simple assumptions of his own aristocratic code and, in turn, his critical negation of the forces that invalidate that code.

The very form and manner of the speech are the emblem of his lost intellectual innocence and the unbridgeable gulf between the way he thinks and the way the rest of his world thinks. This is implicit in its heavily ironic mode, the abundant use of metaphor, puns, and paradoxes, and, finally, in the haughty if kindly intentioned assumption that the listeners, Tecmessa and the chorus, cannot comprehend his double entendres. In his first monologue we have already seen Ajax's agonizing explorations of the ambiguous fit between language and reality. On the one hand, there is the grimly close fit between his own name, "Aias" (in Greek), and the cries of "ai ai" that pain has extorted from him. On the other, his father Telamon, the "man of daring and endurance," will not endure *(ou tlēsetai)* to look at his dishonored son. To return to him is a "deed not to be endured" *(ergon ou tlēton)* (Di Benedetto 1983:71). Here in the third monologue the language virtually cries out for a deconstructive reading. Ajax himself deconstructs through his self-reflective ironies all the overlapping binary oppositions that constructed his former identity: birth versus obscurity, hard versus soft, male versus female, friend versus enemy, clean versus polluted, god versus mortal, cold versus hot, bright versus dark, leader versus led, consciousness versus sleep, fixity versus movement, life versus death. The fundamental opposition is not explicitly articulated, but rather there is an unstated presupposition of his irony—namely, the opposition between word and deed, between analyzing the laws of the world and defying them through action. In the very process of standing outside his own previously unquestioning adherence to the aristocratic code, Ajax offers a withering critique of its alternative, summed up sarcastically in the virtue of "safe-think," the moderation and flexibility of those who care only for survival in day-to-day reality at whatever price.[54] The logic of suicide (Seidensticker 1982:142–143) has been raised to a new level.

The terms of Ajax's final soliloquy constitute his answers to the laws set forth in his previous monologue and to the apparent imperatives they enjoined. If all the grounds for his code have been obliterated by the realities of a "safe-think" world, Ajax will recreate them anew on a purely personal, existential basis. Systematically he restores the proper hostile status of the Trojan soil and the true hostile function of the sword of his enemy, Hector (815–820). Yet he calls attention to the slipperiness of his efforts to restore a fixed, unambiguous meaning to value terms by an ironic pun that insists on his new double-consciousness. The sword is at the same time hostile and "most kindly disposed" (822), because it will assist him in achieving the speedy death he so wishes. The Trojan land is both hostile and his nurse (863), since it has sustained his life all these years. He proceeds to invoke the will of Zeus and various other gods to participate in the validation of his own arrangements for his family, his *philoi*. His prayers culminate in a virulent, totally unrepentant curse on his enemies the Atreidai and all their supporters. To hell with *sōphrosynē*![55] His code thus reestablished, he leaps upon the sword.

If there is any progressive element in this transformation of Ajax—and many readers see none—it is surely not in the content of the values that Ajax seeks to impose by his action. It is rather the incorporation into the dramatic structure of the process by which the protagonist faces the total obliteration of the basis of his identity and by which he negates and transcends through action and through a new mode of discourse the very forces that decree his irrelevance. The figure who is validated by the society at large in the later portion of the play is no longer simply the image of a traditional, aristocratic *strategos*, but a dynamic totality who emerges triumphant from attempts to define him either as the self-evident product of a particular class (as Athena tries to do in the prologue) or as the irrelevant criminal in the lawful commonwealth (as the Atreidai claim). Sophocles represents for his audience a self-created excellence imposed on the world by action that rises phoenixlike from the ashes of his hopelessly inadequate old identity. As such, Ajax becomes both a viable measure of the pettiness of the world that could not correctly assess his worth and a potential model for the lesser man threatened with a superior force. Thus the process by which Teucer moves from self-pitying lament to a readiness to die in defense of what he believes to be right may be perceived as a process of the democratization of an aristocratic ideal.

But what are we to make of such a process? To return to Althusser, to what problematic does such an ideological tour de force attempt a response? In what sense have I historicized this play by following these structures of myth, rhetoric, and dialectical transcendence?

The dramatic development that follows Ajax from utter madness to a more and more conscious analysis of the untenability of his position at the same time affirms his creation of a new subjectivity stripped of the supports of community, family, and gods—a subjectivity that asserts its fundamental integrity in the very ferocity of the vindictive action that had initially alienated him. The contradictions between the humane openness of Odysseus and this implacable hostility of Ajax are echoed in the funeral oration attributed by Thucydides to Pericles. In both cases they represent an ideological response to the contradictory needs of the empire to project its own society as a heightened form of humane civilization at the same time that its intensified extraction of surplus wealth from the rest of Greece required a spirit of barbarous savagery toward the Other. Rather than the absolutist spirit of Ajax being dismissed as irrelevant to the humane cultivation so characteristically cited from this speech, we should recall not just the bit about loving beauty and wisdom, but also Pericles' eulogy of the dead, the chief burden of his oration. Indeed his justification for the extended disquisition on the cultural riches of Athens is to point to the different stakes the Athenians have in their contest *(agōna)* with their enemies (2.42.2–3):

> I have sung the city's praises in a mere speech, but what really honors her is the heroic achievements *(aretai)* of these men and others like them. . . . It seems to me that death *(katastrophē)* proves a man's excellence *(aretē)* by both revealing it for the first time and setting the ultimate confirmation upon it. And indeed it is just, even for those who fall short in other ways, to set up as a victory marker their heroic excellence *(andragathian)* against their enemies in behalf of the fatherland. . . . Holding vengeance *(timōrian)* against their rivals *(enantiōn)* as more desirable *(potheinoteron)* than their own lives and considering this the noblest *(kalliston)* of dangers, they chose vengeance against them *(tous men timō-reisthai)* along with the danger and let go of everything else. . . . Because in the reality of fighting they thought it better to suffer death than to survive by giving in, they escaped the shame of speech, and through action took the brunt of the assault with their bodies and in a brief moment of time *(di' elachistou kairou),* at the climax of their fortune, they passed away from the scene, not of their fear, but of their glory.
> (Thucydides 2.42 after Hornblower)

If one acknowledges the marked inter-*polis* conflict which sets Ajax as the representative of Athens against the tyrannical impositions of Spartan claims to absolute hegemony, then the usual cries that Ajax is not at all dying "in behalf of the fatherland" are misplaced. On the other hand, choosing vengeance at the price of death redeems even those who fall short in other ways. Note that the word for vengeance *(timōrian/timōreisthai)* is twice heavily emphasized as the key motive for heroic action and that consciously chosen death is precisely what proves a man's excellence *(aretē)*.

Xenophon, in his famous account of the terror that seized Athens as its citizens learned of their final defeat at Aegospotami, focuses on the way all mourned "not only for those who had died but far more still for themselves, thinking that they would suffer what they had inflicted on the Melians and those who were Spartan colonists, and the Histiaeans and the Toronians and the Aeginetans and many others of the Greeks" (Xen. *Hell.* 2.2.3–4). A bit further on in his account of their attempts to hold out against the Spartan siege, Xenophon again recounts their despair "lest they suffer what they had done—not for revenge, but out of sheer arrogance *(hubris)* they had violated *(ēdikoun)* the people in little cities for no other reason than that they were allied with the Spartans" (Xen. *Hell.* 2.2.10–11). The utopian vision of a justly hierarchical, open, and humane society was a self-serving projection of a specifically Athenian civilization bought at the price of absolute barbarity toward the Other of Athens. Sophocles' attempt to overcome this very real contradiction may strike some as finally no more successful than Athens' own efforts ultimately proved. But the complex structures of this rich play retain a haunting capacity to engage us in the very strenuousness of the effort.

Exploring such a past solution to an apparently insoluble dilemma may then, I hope, be of some value as we, the most powerful country in the world, set about forging a new world order. It would of course take far more space than I have devoted to a single Greek play to begin to offer an appropriately nuanced account of all the ways in which American imperialism differs from that of tiny Athens twenty-five hundred years ago. But I think we too in our culture need to come to grips with our deep emotional investments in our own John Waynes, Charles Bronsons, Chuck Norrises, and Clint Eastwoods—with figures whose essential brutality, moral obtuseness, and gender-based emotional blockage we are constantly invited to forgive for the little behavioral crumbs evincing their stunted potential for human feeling.[56] And why? Perhaps because we are dimly aware that, as a society, our privileges derive from the genocide of Native Americans, from the crushing of Japan, the devastation of Korea and Vietnam, and—not least—from the systematic brutal repression of the criminal element at home effected for us by our military and detective heroes. Only by confronting the cultural paradigms offered us by our own ideologues, by seeking the deepest levels on which they interpellate us as Americans do we have any hope of helping our own civilization to break the iron law articulated by Walter Benjamin: "There is no document of civilization which is not at the same time a document of barbarism."[57]

NOTES

1. I refer of course in the first instance to the much discussed article by Francis Fukuyama, "The End of History?" (Fukuyama 1989), subsequently expanded into a

book (Fukuyama 1992). There was in fact much outraged objection to his thesis from critics on the far right as well as the left (as detailed by Anderson 1992:283–284). Anderson points out that Fukuyama's formulation represents a striking reversal on many levels of a remarkable conjunction of many twentieth-century intellectual trends summed up under the rubric *Posthistoire*, a term which he amusingly declares is "a French term that exists only in German" (Anderson 1992:279). See also Halliday 1992, Milliband 1992, and Rustin 1992.

2. The phrase comes from Barthes (Barthes 1970 [1967]:154), but de Certeau's is the most recent and thorough analysis I am aware of that spells out the "ruses" of history in creating an illusion of intelligibility (de Certeau 1988:96, where he quotes Barthes with approval).

3. I should add, of course, that this seems to me a gross distortion of Derrida's own achievement, which could perhaps be summed up precisely as the critique of the history of Western philosophy, that is, as an eminently historical enterprise. The more explicitly political historical critiques of his greatest protegée, Gayatri Chakravorty Spivak, constitute a further warning that reading deconstruction as a dismissal of history is a serious misreading.

4. Foucault's definition of his task as an historian in the tradition of Nietzsche's *wirkliche Historie* (Foucault 1977:152), insofar as it entails a wholesale assault on Hegelian essentialism (cf. Foucault 1991:44–46), has much in common with Marx's attempt, especially in *The German Ideology*, to envision a historiography liberated of Hegelian a priori metaphysical assumptions. On the other hand, precisely to the extent that Foucault sees the goal of "true History" as the "systematic dissociation of identity" in terms so absolute that, in Jameson's phrase, "the doors of comprehension begin to swing closed" (Jameson 1988:151), he moves very far from the grounds on which Marx aims at a relevant intelligibility of history.

5. Heiden, for example, in his subtle analysis of the *Trachiniae*, tells us that "the insufficiency of grammar to determine the meaning of statements and consequent openness to interpretation . . . is one of the drama's chief themes" (Heiden 1989:34). I do not mean at all to impugn the validity of such a reading within its own terms, but only to mark the reemergence or persistence of, so to speak, the ethos of the old New Criticism, on which see Lentricchia 1980.

6. For some thoughtful qualifications of Culham's apparently unmediated empiricism see Gamal 1990. See also Rose 1993.

7. This is not to deny a very strong feminist current that embraces much of what is so loosely designated as postmodernism (e.g., Nicholson 1990). I do think it is fair to say that this tendency is not dominant in feminist studies of antiquity.

8. Welcker was perhaps the first to argue that the focus on Menelaus as the manipulator of votes (*Aj.* 1135) and the voice of the most strident arrogance toward the corpse of Ajax and towards his brother is due to Menelaus' status as king of Sparta and therefore reflects contemporary Athenian-Spartan political conflict, particularly over the issue of hegemony and subordination (Welcker 1845:335–340). He even sees a parallel between Ajax's duel with Hector and the isolated initiative of Athens in fighting against the Persian king (338), a point ignored by Grégoire and Orgels in their attempts to use Welcker as a warrant for linking Ajax with Alcibiades in one of the more bizarre historicizations of the play (Grégoire and Orgels 1953; Grégoire 1955). Welcker also drew

attention to a comment in Libanius (born in A.D. 314!) comparing the effect of the *Ajax* on the original audience to the impact of Phrynichus' *Capture of Miletus* (Welcker 1845: 340). Brown finds support here for the inference that "the *Ajax* had the same kind of contemporary political significance as Phrynichus' play notoriously did have" (Brown 1951:27).

9. He goes on to cite the study of the classical world as the prime example of this dilemma (Jameson 1988:151–152).

10. I attempt to spell out my assumptions in the opening chapter of *Sons of the Gods, Children of Earth* (Rose 1992:1–42). See also Rose 1993.

11. Jameson makes, for me, the key distinction: "Such an analysis [sc. a truly Marxist one] differs from the purely sociological kind in that it describes not simply the affiliation between a doctrine and a class but also the functional role of that doctrine in *class struggle*. It is an often-taught and often-forgotten lesson that ideology is designed to promote the human dignity and clear conscience of a given class at the same time that it discredits their adversaries; indeed, these two operations are one and the same" (Jameson 1971:380). Eagleton's recent historical overview of the matter is also useful and, following Althusser, places an important stress on the role of ideology in the construction of subjectivities: "It must figure as an organizing social force which actively constitutes human subjects at the roots of their lived experience and seeks to equip them with forms of value and belief relevant to their specific social tasks and the general reproduction of the social order" (Eagleton 1991:222–223). Larrain 1979 offers a very useful historical overview and analysis of ideology as well. The best example of what I would call the non- or minimally relational definition of ideology in recent classical scholarship is in Ober—despite his curious claim that his formulation has much in common with Althusser (Ober 1989:38–40). He cites various texts by M. I. Finley as warrant for his definition. This more sociological definition fails precisely to define ideology as a—not to say *the*—site of class struggle. Very much to his credit, Ober's wonderful book often does focus on sites of struggle, but his straddling of definitions with fundamentally different implications is not helpful.

12. The classic statement, relevant I believe to any exercise in ideological criticism, is as follows: "The purpose of myth is to provide a logical model capable of overcoming a contradiction (an impossible achievement if, as it happens, the contradiction is real)" (Lévi-Strauss 1967:226).

13. I yield to no one in my enthusiasm for the achievements of the sophists and their multiple relevance to tragedy—an approach revitalized for my generation, as far as I am aware, by Rosenmeyer (1955) and Segal (1962). For a daring contemporary appropriation of the sophists in many areas of intellectual endeavor see Jarratt 1991.

14. I do not mean to deny Goldhill's quite compelling emphasis on the potentially transgressive force of Greek tragedy (Goldhill 1990:114–128); like many enthusiasts of deconstructive readings (e.g., Heiden 1989) he seems to assume that the "questioning of the terms of that civic discourse" (Goldhill 1990:126) or the "undermining of a secure and stable sense of norm" (Goldhill 1990:128) is inherently free of ideology. This relentless hypostatization of tragic ambiguity recalls—mutatis mutandis—a criticism once directed by Jonathan Culler against Kristeva's celebration of semiotics' alleged capacity for perpetual autocritique: "This claim invokes most strikingly what one might call the myth of the innocence of becoming: that continual change, as an end in itself,

is a kind of freedom, and that it liberates one from the demands that could be made of any particular state of the system" (Culler 1973:480). A more relational conception of ideology might suggest that such a strategy of exploiting ambiguities is eminently suited to ideological struggle in an arena where a specifically democratic ideology might be presumed to be hegemonic.

15. Ovid's full-scale debate between Ajax and Odysseus (*Metamorphoses* 13.1–398) deploys a very full array of actions traditionally attributed to each figure and attempts to convey a sense of their opposed modes of expression. It is plausible if unprovable that Aeschylus, whose *Hoplōn Krisis* contained a debate (Jebb 1962:xx), used a wide range of this same material.

16. Without endorsing Brown's highly speculative reconstruction of the relationship between Pindar's *Nemean* 8 and Sophocles' *Ajax*, I do agree with Brown and those others who see the reference to voting in Sophocles' play a specific debt and response to Pindar's apparently original addition of this detail (Brown 1951:15 cites van der Kolf's study of myths in Pindar). See Jebb 1962:xv, which is a reprint of his earlier study (1896). Kamerbeek, while rejecting the view of Blumenthal that Pindar borrowed this detail from Sophocles, concludes cautiously "either the reverse is true or there is a common source unknown to us" (Kamerbeek 1963:5).

17. Note that this passage shares with Athena's lines the terms *kakos* (1071) and *sōphron-* (1075).

18. References to the Greek text are from Jebb 1962. All translations are my own unless otherwise noted.

19. Bradshaw 1991 has a particularly full review of what is mostly in Jebb 1962. See also Kirkwood 1965 and W. E. Brown 1965–1966. I would add one Homeric echo that none at least of the commentaries I have seen (Jebb 1962; Stanford 1963*b*; Kamerbeek 1963; de Romilly 1976) nor the previously cited treatments seem to consider worthy of mention: the picture of Ajax sweating (*Ajax* 9–10). Indeed, Kamerbeek even remarks: "Sweat streaming from his hands is not very appropriate here." I believe that an audience brought up on regular recitations of Homer would momentarily associate the image of Ajax sweating with one of his greatest moments in the *Iliad*, when in Book 16, immediately after Achilles' prayer that all the Argives save himself and Patroclus might perish, we see Ajax alone holding out, struck from every side, his left shoulder wearying from the weight of his great shield, his body bathed in sweat (cf. *Iliad* 16.97–111). The reminiscence is only at best momentary, but, if present, prepares the way for Teucer's later climactic evocation of this moment (*Ajax* 1276–1279).

20. Heath is at pains to argue that there is no departure in Odysseus' sympathy from traditional heroic values (Heath 1987:167–170); but, as Stanford long ago pointed out, Odysseus was always an "untypical" hero (Stanford 1963*a*:66–80).

21. Ostwald analyzes six political trials between the reforms of Cleisthenes and those of Ephialtes: Phrynichus, Miltiades [twice], Hipparchus, Themistocles, Cimon (Ostwald 1986:28–30). Many, of course, have focused on later trials and ostracisms, particularly that of Thucydides the son of Melisias (e.g., Bradshaw 1991:122).

22. There is an extensive debate about whether Athena is visible or invisible to the audience, e.g., Taplin 1978:185; Kitto 1986 [1939]:153; Gellie 1972:5–6; Goldhill 1986:183; Heath 1987:165–166.

23. "Friends" is of course an inadequate translation for Ajax's *philoi*, which in Greek

includes the family, social and political allies, and generally all who are supporters or dependents. Blundell makes a particularly strong case against an unrelievedly bestial Ajax on this score (Blundell 1989, esp. 72–88). Cf. Goldhill 1986:85–88.

24. Dodds notes that Herodotus often gives both a medical or physiological account of madness and the most common attribution of madness to divine visitation (Dodds 1957:65–66). His discussion of *atē* (Dodds 1957:37–41) brings out the harmony of human excess and divinely imposed delusion, particularly in Aeschylus. Simon, apropos of the *Ajax*, speaks of a somewhat different sort of double account of madness in which, on the one hand, we find the chorus and others speaking of a divine visitation and, on the other, the movement of the tragedy demonstrates that "Ajax's illness is incurable, because the illness and Ajax are one" (Simon 1978:127). Simon, like Seidensticker (1982: 105–144), seems fascinated with the parallels between the mental stages through which Ajax passes and contemporary accounts of suicidal madness. Analyses focused so centrally on Ajax's successive mental states (e.g., Goldhill 1986, which follows very closely Winnington-Ingram 1980) tend to be least interested in the political stakes of the audience in the figure of Ajax.

25. In the Melian Dialogue, for example, the Athenians suggest that the Melians change their minds and "decide on something else more sensible than their present plans" (ἄλλο τι τῶνδε σωφρονέστερον γνώσεσθε, 5.111.2–3). Cf. North 1966:109 and Knox 1961:16–17.

26. E.g., *Ajax* 30, 43, 55–61, 61–65, 95, 108–111, 219–220, 230–231, 235–242, 297–300, 308–309.

27. I do find it a mark of the overzealousness of the pietists when this claim that Troy has never seen anyone else literally "of such a sort as this" is interpreted as a categorical declaration by Ajax that he is "better" than Achilles (Winnington-Ingram 1980:14–15, where he translates *hoion*, as does Jebb, as "peer"). To claim that he was *uniquely* great (Jebb cites the parallel claim of Achilles at *Iliad* 18.105) is subtly but importantly different from claiming explicitly to be better: in effect the claim to uniqueness confirms Homer's success in conveying precisely a sense of differentiation of character from those with whom qua great hero he has generic affinities (Whitman 1958: 154–180, esp. 169–174). Any hint that Ajax underestimates the equally unique greatness of Achilles is, I believe, cancelled by Ajax's subsequent claim—again one that no reader of the *Iliad* would dispute—that Achilles himself, were he alive, would choose Ajax over Odysseus to inherit his arms (*Ajax* 442–444).

28. *Ajax* 898–899, 910, 917–919, 1003–1004, 1024–1026, 1411–1413.

29. *Ajax* 774–775, 962–965, 1221–1223, 1266–1288, 1338–1341, 1357, 1415–1417.

30. Athena's help to Achilles in killing Hector is perhaps the clearest example of that blur between human and divine responsibility so forcefully analyzed by Snell (1960:1–22), though of course much of his argument can no longer stand in its original form. Hector's death—when he becomes aware that the gods are against him and that death is inescapable and yet affirms his determination "not to perish without a struggle and without glory, / but rather after accomplishing something great to be heard of even by those that come after" (*Iliad* 22.304–305)—is the best and earliest example of a purely human heroism specifically in opposition to the will of the gods to crush him. Solon, perhaps a century later, declared, "Our city will never perish by the dispensation of Zeus and the minds of the immortal gods" and focuses on the foolish greed of the

citizens as the real danger (cf. West 4.1–22). Simonides in the early fifth century distinguishes between the impositions of the gods, or necessity, and the sort of men he considers worthy of praise: "whoever *willingly* does nothing shameful" (Simonides 542 [D. L. Page, *Poetae Melici Graeci*], esp. lines 27–30).

31. Gellrich points to the ways in which other characters in the play (Tecmessa at 950 and 954, Teucer at 1029–1033) perceive the involvement of the gods in Ajax's death as a refutation of those readers who see a valorization of Ajax's will to find some sphere of action precisely his own. It does not follow, I think, that because this will is ultimately enmeshed in factors no human could control that the only message is the fact of "irreducible ambivalence" (Gellrich 1988:263).

32. Goldhill reads Ajax's speech to his infant son (*Ajax* 545–582) in such a way as to find only a conflict with the civic ideology he so neatly elucidates in the ceremonies immediately preceding the performance of tragedies (also discussed by Zimmermann 1991:9). It seems to me that Goldhill underestimates the potential heightening of the pathos of the argument over the burial of this Athenian hero, whose orphan is before the eyes of the audience so soon after seeing actual orphans of the state—especially when the orphan on stage now appears menaced by the ruler of Sparta. Di Benedetto denies that Tecmessa is in the final tableau, where he finds an all-male family knot conducting a purely private funeral (Di Benedetto 1983:80). This does not seem to me to jibe with Teucer's invitation to Odysseus—after excluding him from the actual handling of the corpse in preparing it for burial—to bring to the ritual itself anyone he wishes from the army (*tina stratou / theleis komisdein*, 1393–1397). A funeral open to the community would normally include appropriate female mourners, as at the funerals of Patroclus and Hector.

33. The parallels are nicely underlined by Blundell, but only to the discredit of Ajax (Blundell 1989:94–95).

34. Here I find quite relevant David Rosenbloom's focus [in this volume] on Herodotus' praise of Athens as "alone" saving Greece from the Persian threat (e.g., Hdt. 7.139). See also Bradshaw 1991:114–115.

35. To the best of my knowledge this line of argument was first pursued in any detail by Bowra (1965 [1941]), followed by Whitman in his focus on Cimon (Whitman 1951: 61). I would stress the word "abstracted" in my text, since attempts to link the text with a specific *strategos* quickly founder and play too easily into the hands of readers who prefer as little politics as possible in their tragedies.

36. Stockton indeed argues that it was precisely Themistocles' policy of the "big fleet" that transformed the *strategia* into the "centrally important *archē* that it became." He suggests that even if the archonship had remained an elective office after 487/6, neither Cimon nor Pericles could have made it the "vehicle of continuing power and influence": only the successes and revenue brought in by the imperial fleet could assure that (Stockton 1991:32).

37. Ostwald is at pains to argue that there were substantially no class tensions over this issue. As long as the actual policies of Pericles aimed at the economic benefit of the *dēmos* there was no problem: "That Pericles belonged to a higher social class may have made a difference to his fellow aristocrats, but it will have made no difference to the common people" (Ostwald 1986:183–185). The evidence he cites from the "Old Oligarch" ([Xen.] *Ath. Pol.* 1.3) makes this plausible enough, but he rightly stresses that the

presumed satisfaction of the *dēmos* as well as the potential resentment of the aristocracy (underemphasized by him?) depended entirely on the control by the *dēmos* of the annual scrutiny *(euthynai)*, i.e., their ability to vote on the value of the aristocrats' performance (Ostwald 1986:42, 184). It is precisely the formal hegemony of the democracy in this whole period that explains, I believe, the highly rhetorical strategy I attribute to the play. Here Ober's generalizations about what can plausibly be expected from fourth-century orators deserve serious consideration in the analysis of tragic texts (Ober 1989: 43–45). On the other hand, the nature of our sources inevitably makes evidence of hostility or distrust from the *dēmos* harder to come by. Ober seems to me to have a more nuanced sense than Ostwald of the Athenian "mass's" awareness of the "elites among them" (Ober 1989:14 and passim).

38. See the excellent elaboration of this opposition throughout the play in Daly 1990.

39. In speaking of the Athenian associations of Ajax and his followers, I refer not only to the fact that a tenth of the Athenian population belonged to a tribe that took its name from the hero or that several prominent Athenian families traced their ancestry back to him. Davies' chart at the back of his *Athenian Propertied Families* vividly demonstrates how many of the known members of what he calls the "liturgical" class traced a connection to the Philaids, who in turn claimed descent from Ajax. Wickersham has recently reviewed the intense feud between Megara and Athens over the lines in the catalogue of ships (*Iliad* 2.557–558) which constituted Athens' only link with one of the major figures of the Trojan War as well as a warrant for their claims on Salamis. The Megarians alleged that these lines had been inserted into the text by Solon (Wickersham 1991:16–31).

40. For the term "interpellate" see Althusser 1971:170–177.

41. Ober rightly stresses the lack of any institutionalization of elite control of the executive functions of the state, but also rightly stresses that the failure of the elite on this score manifests itself after Pericles (Ober 1989:15).

42. Gardiner expresses with great vigor her towering indignation at the very idea that Sophocles could possibly wish to elicit from his audience a shred of admiration for such a blackguard as Ajax (Gardiner 1987:74–78). She accordingly effaces the problems of this haunting play by the sheer imposition of a straightforward clarity few have found in it. It is therefore not surprising that she finds in the chorus only admirable qualities, along with Errandonea (cited with approval in her note 37) she considers them "the instrument by which he [Sophocles] creates the play's dramatic unity" (Gardiner 1987: 73) and in their Athenian associations only a confirmation of "the play's obvious moral lesson" as set forth by Athena in lines 131–132 (Gardiner 1987:78). She does rightly reject Burton's odd insistence that they are not also fighting men (Gardiner 1987:52–53; Burton 1980:8), but fails to acknowledge the antiheroic character of this chorus that might inspire such a reading.

43. Ober has recently well defended the democracy against the old (indeed, as he points out, ancient) charge that it was solely a creation of imperialism (Ober 1989:23–24, following Jones 1957:3–20). He does not dispute, however, the enormous material benefits of empire in the fifth century. These are assessed somewhat differently by Meiggs (1973:255–272) and Finley (1982:41–61). See also French 1964:107–134.

44. The alternative to taking the military threat seriously is to see the play as antiwar

from start to finish, a position implicitly embraced by Gardiner (1987:71–78) and explicitly by Stanford theater director Rush Rehm (personal correspondence about his production). While I find Rehm's reading a totally justifiable twentieth-century appropriation of an ancient text, I would say that the fifth-century play confronted its audience with the contradictions of a war-based economy in terms calculated to elicit their acquiescence rather than repudiation of war as an inevitability.

45. Although, as noted earlier, this was a key factor in Welcker's pointing to a political resonance in the play (see supra n. 8), it is in fact remarkable how many readings of the play pass over the line in silence. Even Heath, whose reading has the virtue of far greater sympathy for Teucer than most critics, ignores completely this key source of audience goodwill for Teucer (1987:199–201). Tyrrell and Brown, despite the apparent political focus of their title, explore a Girardian (not to say Lacanian) psychological approach to what they posit as Ajax's fatal sense of competition with an idealized image of his father. The competition with Sparta is ignored (Tyrrell and Brown 1991: 66–72).

46. While there is little point in seeing Sparta as the innocent Other of Athenian imperialism, the mechanism of projecting the imperial nation's aggression onto the objects of that aggression is too painfully familiar in our own time to need illustration. Psychiatrist Joel Kovel has some provocative reflections on how this process operated in the conquest by Europe of the New World (Kovel 1992:49–60).

47. It has often been noted that the "word *hybris* and its cognates are used more frequently by the play for the behavior of Ajax's enemies than for Ajax's own behavior" (Gellie 1972:20).

48. Brown has, like many others, been tempted by the argument over the martial status of the bowman to seek a precise date for the play (N. O. Brown 1951:17). But the fact that the issue is already a point of ideological contention in the *Iliad* (11.368–395) means that it is available at any point thereafter as a symbolic contrast between the fully armed warrior, with the economic privilege that implies, and any sort of less heavily armed fighter.

49. Those who assume with Meier (1988:200) that the Greek army simply stands for the *polis* in general must necessarily ignore the whole dynamic in the play of inter-*polis* conflict.

50. Gellie, despite his apparent conclusion that Odysseus articulates the lessons of the play, notes some of the most striking evidence for the inherent implausibility of this character's carrying so much weight in it, for instance: "After the prologue we do not see him again for the best part of 1,200 lines" (Gellie 1972:6). He goes on to state: "The Odysseus of the prologue is a well-organized man who knows his place and will take his place on the field of battle. But when the fighting starts, we would be inclined to edge away from him and nearer to Ajax" (Gellie 1972:20).

51. For *phaos* in the Homeric sense of "help, succour, safety, salvation," see Cunliffe 1963 s.v.

52. It is this characteristic Sophoclean stripping away of divine, social, and political a priori props for the heroic identity and the move to construct a newly valid one through action that so tempted Whitman and others with the analogy of existentialism (Whitman 1982:44–65).

53. Meier's strategy, to treat this speech as owing all that is humane and sensible in

it to setting Odysseus in the heart of the drama, contains an element of truth that needs to be pushed further: Ajax is endowed here with a depth and complexity that the dramatic character Odysseus is denied, and this complexity—precisely to the extent that Ajax's rejection of Odysseus' view implies a competing truth—sets him dramatically above Odysseus.

54. Havelock (1957) and Cole (1967) long ago demonstrated the absolute centrality of the idea of survival *(sōteria)* in the anthropological speculations of the sophists as well as in their accounts of what the sophists claimed to offer their pupils. See also Rose 1992:273–278.

55. Needless to say, I do not agree with those who, like Sicherl (1977), see *sōphrosynē* as the key "lesson" of the tragedy.

56. For explorations of some of these figures that point in this critical direction see Place 1974; Winkler 1991; and Smith 1993.

57. Quoted from his "Theses on the Philosophy of History." In *Illuminations,* Walter Benjamin. Tr. Harry Zohn. New York, 1969.

REFERENCES

Althusser, Louis. 1969. *For Marx.* Trans. Ben Brewster. New York.

———. 1971. *Lenin and Philosophy and Other Essays.* New York.

Anderson, Perry. 1992. "The Ends of History." In his *A Zone of Encounter,* 279–375. London.

Barthes, Roland. 1970 [1967]. "Historical Discourse." Trans. Peter Wexler. In *Introduction to Structuralism,* Michael Lane, ed. New York.

Blundell, Mary Whitlock. 1989. *Helping Friends and Harming Enemies: A Study in Sophocles and Greek Ethics.* New York.

Bowra, Maurice. 1965 [1944]. *Sophoclean Tragedy.* Oxford.

Bradshaw, David J. 1991. "The Ajax Myth and the Polis: Old Values and New." In *Myth and the Polis,* Dora C. Pozzi and John M. Wickersham, eds. Ithaca, N.Y.

Brown, Norman O. 1951. "Pindar, Sophocles, and the Thirty Years' Peace," *TAPA* 82: 1–28.

Brown, W. Edward. 1965–1966. "Sophocles' Ajax and Homer's Hector," *CJ* 65:118–121.

Burton, R. W. B. 1980. *The Chorus in Sophocles' Tragedies.* Oxford.

Cole, Thomas. 1967. *Democritus and the Sources of Greek Anthropology.* (American Philological Association Monograph 25.)

Culham, Phyllis. 1987. "Ten Years After Pomeroy: Studies of the Image and Reality of Women in Antiquity." In *Rescuing Creusa: New Methodological Approaches to Women in Antiquity,* 9–30. (A Special Issue of *Helios* n.s. 13.)

———. 1990. "Decentering the Text: The Case of Ovid," *Helios* 17:161–170.

Culler, Jonathan. 1973. "Structure of Ideology and Ideology of Structure," *New Literary History* 4:471–482.

Cunliffe, Richard John. 1963. *A Lexicon of the Homeric Dialect.* Norman.

Daly, James. 1990. *Horizontal Resonance as a Principle of Composition in the Plays of Sophocles.* New York.

Davies, J. K. 1971. *Athenian Propertied Families 600–300 B.C.* Oxford.

Davis, Michael. 1986. "Politics and Madness." In *Greek Tragedy and Political Theory*, J. Peter Euben, ed. Berkeley.

de Certeau, Michel. 1988. *The Writing of History*. Trans. by Tom Conley. New York.

de Romilly, Jacqueline. 1976. *Sophocle 'Ajax': Edition, introduction, et commentaire*. Paris.

Derrida, Jacques. 1974. *Of Grammatology*. Trans. Gayatri Chakravorty Spivak. Baltimore and London.

———. 1978. "Structure Sign and Play in the Discourse of the Human Sciences." In *Writing and Difference*, 278–293. Trans. Alan Bass. Chicago.

Di Benedetto, Vincenzo. 1983. *Sofocle*. Florence.

Dodds, E. R. 1957 [1951]. *The Greeks and the Irrational*. Boston.

Eagleton, Terry. 1991. *Ideology: An Introduction*. London.

Finley, M. I. 1982. *Economy and Society in Ancient Greece*. Edited and with an introduction by Brent D. Shaw and Richard P. Saller. New York.

Foucault, Michel. 1977. "Nietzsche, Genealogy, History." In *Language, Counter-Memory, Practice: Selected Essays and Interviews*, Donald E. Bouchard, ed. Ithaca, N.Y.

———. 1991. *Remarks on Marx: Conversations with Duccio Trombadori*. Trans. R. James Goldstein and James Cascaito. Brooklyn, N.Y.

French. A. 1964. *The Growth of the Athenian Economy*. London.

Fukuyama, Francis. 1989. "The End of History?" *The National Interest* 16:3–18.

———. 1992. *The End of History and the Last Man*. London.

Gamal, Mary-Kay. 1990. "Reading 'Reality,'" *Helios* 17:171–174.

Gardiner, Cynthia. 1987. *The Sophoclean Chorus: A Study of Character and Function*. Iowa City.

Gellie, G. H. 1972. *Sophocles: A Reading*. Melbourne.

Gellrich, Michelle. 1988. *Tragedy and Theory: The Problem of Conflict since Aristotle*. Princeton.

Goldhill, Simon, 1986. *Reading Greek Tragedy*. Cambridge.

———. 1990. "The Great Dionysia and Civic Ideology." In *Nothing to Do with Dionysos? Athenian Drama in Its Social Context*, John J. Winkler and Froma I. Zeitlin, eds., 97–129. Princeton, N.J.

Grégoire, Henri. 1955. "La date de l'*Ajax* de Sophocle," *Bulletin de la Classe des Lettres de l'Académie Royale de Belgique* 41:187–198.

Grégoire, Henri, and Paul Orgels. 1953. "L'*Ajax* de Sophocle, Alcibiade et Sparte," *Annuaire de l'Institut de philologie et d'histoire orientale et slave* 13:653–663.

Halliday, Fred. 1992. "An Encounter with Fukuyama," *New Left Review* 193 (May/June): 89–95.

Havelock, Eric A. 1957. *The Liberal Temper in Greek Political Thought*. New Haven.

Heath, Malcolm. 1987. *The Poetics of Greek Tragedy*. Stanford.

Heiden, Bruce. 1989. *The Rhetoric of Tragedy: An Interpretation of Sophocles' 'Trachiniae'*. New York.

Jameson, Fredric. 1971. *Marxism and Form: Twentieth-Century Dialectical Theories of Literature*. Princeton.

———. 1981. *The Political Unconscious: Narrative as a Socially Symbolic Act*. Ithaca, N.Y.

———. 1988. "Marxism and Historicism." In his *The Ideologies of Theory: Essays 1971–1986*. Minneapolis.

————. 1991. *Postmodernism, or, The Cultural Logic of Late Capitalism.* Durham, N.C.

Jarratt, Susan C. 1991. *Rereading the Sophists: Classical Rhetoric Refigured.* Carbondale.

Jebb, Richard C. 1962. *Sophocles: The Plays and Fragments: Part VII. The Ajax.* Amsterdam.

Jones, A. H. M. 1957. *Athenian Democracy.* Oxford.

Kamerbeek, J. C. 1963. *The Plays of Sophocles: Commentaries: Part I. The Ajax.* Trans. H. Schreuder. Leiden.

Kirkwood, G. M. 1965. "Homer and Sophocles' 'Ajax.'" In *Classical Drama and Its Influence: Essays Presented to H. D. F. Kitto,* M. J. Anderson, ed. London.

Kitto, H. D. F. 1960. *Form and Meaning in Drama.* New York.

————. 1986 [1939]. *Greek Tragedy: A Literary Study.* London.

Knox, Bernard M. W. 1961. "The *Ajax* of Sophocles," *HSCP* 65:1–37.

————. 1964. *The Heroic Temper: Studies in Sophoclean Tragedy.* Berkeley.

Kovel, Joel. 1992. "Naming and Conquest," *Monthly Review* 44 (July/August): 49–60.

Larrain, Jorge. 1979. *The Concept of Ideology.* London.

Lentricchia, Frank. 1980. *After the New Criticism.* Chicago.

Lévi-Strauss, Claude. 1967. "The Structural Study of Myth." In his *Structural Anthropology.* Trans. Claire Jacobson and Brooke Grundfest Schoepf. Garden City, N.Y.

Linforth, I. M. 1954. "Three Scenes in Sophocles' *Ajax,*" *University of California Publications in Classical Philology* 15:1–28.

Lukács, Georg. 1964. *Studies in European Realism.* New York.

Macherey, Pierre. 1978. *A Theory of Literary Production.* Trans. Geoffrey Wall. London.

Meier, Christian. 1988. *Die politische Kunst der griechischen Tragödie.* Munich.

Meiggs, Russell. 1973. *The Athenian Empire.* Oxford.

Milliband, Ralph. 1992. "Fukuyama and the Socialist Alternative," *New Left Review* 193 (May/June): 108–113.

Nicholson, Linda J., ed. 1990. *Feminism/Postmodernism.* New York.

North, Helen. 1966. *Sophrosyne: Self-Knowledge and Self-Restraint in Greek Literature.* Ithaca, N.Y.

Ober, Josiah. 1989. *Mass and Elite in Democratic Athens: Rhetoric, Ideology, and the Power of the People.* Princeton.

Ober, Josiah, and Barry Strauss. 1990. "Drama, Political Rhetoric, and the Discourse of Athenian Democracy." In *Nothing to Do with Dionysos? Athenian Drama in Its Social Context,* John J. Winkler and Froma I. Zeitlin, eds. Princeton.

Ostwald, Martin. 1986. *From Popular Sovereignty to the Sovereignty of Law: Law, Society, and Politics in Fifth-Century Athens.* Berkeley.

Place, J. A. 1974. *The Western Films of John Ford.* Secaucus, N.J.

Podlecki, Anthony J. 1966. *The Political Background of Aeschylean Tragedy.* Ann Arbor.

Reinhardt, Karl. 1979. *Sophocles.* Trans. Hazel Harvey and David Harvey. Oxford.

Rose, Peter W. 1992. *Sons of the Gods, Children of Earth: Ideology and Literary Form in Ancient Greece.* Ithaca, N.Y.

————. 1993. "The Case for Not Ignoring Marx in the Study of Women in Antiquity." In *Feminist Theory and the Classics,* Nancy Sorkin Rabinowitz and Amy Richlin, eds. New York.

Rosenmeyer, Thomas G. 1955. "Gorgias, Aeschylus, and *Apate,*" *AJP* 76:225–260.

Rustin, Michael. 1992. "No Exit from Capitalism?" *New Left Review* 193 (May/June): 96–107.

Seale, David. 1982. *Vision and Stagecraft in Sophocles*. Chicago.

Segal, Charles. 1962. "Gorgias and the Psychology of the *Logos*," *HSCP* 66:99–155.

———. 1981. *Tragedy and Civilization: An Interpretation of Sophocles*. Cambridge, Mass.

Seidensticker, Bernd. 1982. "Die Wahl des Todes bei Sophokles." *Entretiens sur l'antiquité classique* 29. Genève.

Shumway, David R. 1989. *Michel Foucault*. Boston.

Sicherl, M. 1977. "The Tragic Issue in Sophocles' *Ajax*." In *Greek Tragedy*, T. F. Gould and C. J. Herrington, eds. (*Yale Classical Studies* 25.)

Simon, Bennett. 1978. *Mind and Madness in Ancient Greece: The Classical Roots of Modern Psychiatry*. Ithaca, N.Y.

Smith, Paul. 1993. *Clint Eastwood: A Cultural Production*. Minneapolis.

Snell, Bruno. 1960 [1953]. *The Discovery of the Mind: The Greek Origins of European Thought*. Trans. T. G. Rosenmeyer. New York.

Stanford, W. B. 1963a. *The Ulysses Theme*. Oxford.

———. 1963b. *Sophocles Ajax*. Edited with introduction, revised text, commentary, appendices, indexes, and bibliography. London.

Stockton, David. 1991. *The Classical Athenian Democracy*. Oxford.

Taplin, Oliver. 1978. *Greek Tragedy in Action*. Berkeley.

Tyrrell, Wm. Blake, and Frieda S. Brown. 1991. *Athenian Myths and Institutions: Words in Action*. New York.

van der Kolf, M. C. 1923. *Quaeritur quomodo Pindarus fabulas tractaverit quidque in eis mutarit*. (Diss. Rotterdam.)

Welcker, F. G. 1845. "Ueber den Aias des Sophokles." In *Kleine Schriften zur Griechische Literaturgeschicte*. Zweiter Theil. Bonn. (Reprinted and expanded from *Rheinishes Museum* 1829.)

Whitman, Cedric H. 1951. *Sophocles: A Study of Heroic Humanism*. Cambridge, Mass.

———. 1958. *Homer and the Heroic Tradition*. Cambridge, Mass.

———. 1982. *The Heroic Paradox: Essays on Homer, Sophocles, and Aristophanes*. Ithaca, N.Y.

Wickersham, John M. 1991. "Myth and Identity in the Archaic Polis." In *Myth and the Polis*, Dora C. Pozzi and John M. Wickersham, eds. Ithaca, N.Y.

Winkler, Marin M. 1991. "Tragic Features in John Ford's *The Searchers*." In *Classics and Cinema*, Martin M. Winkler, ed. London.

Winnington-Ingram, R. P. 1980. *Sophocles: An Interpretation*. Cambridge.

Zimmermann, Bernhard. 1991 [1986]. *Greek Tragedy: An Introduction*. Translated by Thomas Marier. Baltimore.

FOUR

MYTH, HISTORY, AND HEGEMONY IN AESCHYLUS

David Rosenbloom

Ⅰn cultures which have a history," writes Georges Duby, "all ideological systems are based on a vision of that history: a projected future in which society will be closer to perfection is built on the memory, objective or mythical, of the past."[1] Duby's insight has a particular relevance for Aeschylus' tragedy, for unlike other extant tragedies, his *Persians* and the trilogic *Oresteia* dramatize visions of the future derived from history in the sense of "the events of the past."[2] The representation of this history in tragic narrative and enactment, however, cannot replicate the events: the generic demands of tragedy impose obvious barriers to historical representation, and ideologies inform and distort tragedy's representation of history much the way they do historiography itself. One such ideology, which functions as a transparent template superimposed upon events, an inference from history, and a central element of Hellenic, particularly Athenian, communal consciousness, might be termed "the ideology of freedom." Narratives informed by this ideology feature a dual necessity: the conquest of *hubris* and the violent reversal of all forms of domination driven by the demand for freedom.

The most primitive manifestation of this ideology is perhaps the narrative of satyr drama: a chorus of satyrs falls into slavery prior to the drama, and is liberated in the course of dramatic time by an actor who avenges the *hubris* of the monster that enslaved it.[3] Aeschylean tragedy retains this simple choral plot and expands it into a vision of the structure of human action: liberation is its necessary and divinely sanctioned outcome; the drive to dominate cannot overcome the yearning for freedom. The *Choephori,* for instance, plays out a satyric pattern: Electra and a chorus of slaves are captive to Clytemnestra and Aegisthus' tyranny, and Orestes arrives to kill the hubristic monsters, liberating himself, his sister (cf. 863, 915), his *oikos,* of which the slaves are part (*Cho.* 807–811, esp. 809–810; καὶ νιν ἐλευθερίας/λαμπρὸν ἰδεῖν, 863),[4] and his city

(1046–1047: ἐλευθερώσας πᾶσαν Ἀργείων πόλιν). In the *Choephori*, the chorus members are the captives and slaves of tyrants; liberation is the transfer of their ownership from the tyrants to their rightful masters. They become slaves in a free *oikos* and *polis* (75–83; cf. *Ag.* 953, 1226). In this way, the ideology of freedom embraces its opposite, slavery, without contradiction. Likewise, the satyrs of Euripides' *Cyclops*, after their liberation, are free "to be slaves to Dionysus" (τὸ λοιπὸν Βακχίῳ δουλεύσομεν, 709).[5]

Such narratives may recognize that freedom is the precondition for domination; this contradiction, characteristic of tragedy and historiography, is more difficult to contain within the ideology of freedom. Domination is subverted and *hubris* conquered; the liberated gain power. The process threatens to repeat itself ad infinitum: the liberators become dominators and are threatened with subversion or actually subverted. Herodotus, for instance, sees freedom as a precondition for domination (5.78).[6] This contradiction is responsible for the tragic quality of the *Histories*: communities win their freedom, form empires, provoke their subjects' yearning for freedom, incur the deleterious envy of the gods, and are eventually toppled.[7] The Medes win liberation from the Assyrians (1.95.2) and inherit their realm; the Persians free themselves from the Medes (1.27.1; 3.82.5) and seize their sphere of power (1.210.2). Herodotus depicts Athens' liberation of Hellas and formation of a hegemonic league as one moment in the larger historical process: the creation of Athenian domination was also the first stage of its subversion.[8] Many have noted that the end of the *Histories* is a warning to the Athenians about the dangers of their sphere of domination.[9] The final events of the narrative, the Athenian siege of Sestos, the stoning of Artayktes' son before his eyes, Artayktes' crucifixion, and the wisdom of Cyrus on how empire is undermined by the fruits of empire, seem calculated to formulate a message to the new imperial power. A similar patterning of events is evident in Thucydides: the Athenian empire grew powerful, provoked fear in the Spartans, and compelled them to "liberate" the Hellenes.

Such a scheme informs Aeschylus' "simple" plots. The *Prometheus* dramatizes Zeus' monopolization of freedom: after subverting the Titans, he alone is free (ἐλεύθερος γὰρ οὔτις ἐστὶ πλὴν Διός, 50). His dominance is total; such figures as Kratos, Bia, and Hermes, as well as the tormented bodies of Prometheus and Io, make his tyranny visible.[10] Prometheus' prophecy implies a narrative of freedom, domination, and subversion: Zeus' rule will fall and he will know the difference between mastery and slavery (μαθήσεται/ὅσον τό τ' ἄρχειν καὶ τὸ δουλεύειν δίχα, 926–927). The trilogy does not fulfill Prometheus' boast; but the *Prometheus* presents a situation in which power estranged from foreknowledge could be subverted. Certainly the stage events display how foreknowledge deprived of power is self-frustrating. Aeschylus expresses the ideal union of power and foresight in the *Suppliants*: προμαθὶς εὐκοινόμητις ἀρχά, "May there be power with foresight, sharing well its intelligence" (*Supp.* 700).[11]

In the *Prometheus* the reversal of Zeus' power is a threat; in the *Persians* a reversal actually takes place. The Hellenes defend their freedom against the despot Xerxes (402–405), who seeks to enslave them (50, 234), reaches beyond the limits of human power, falls into the net of malicious gods and the trickery of the Greeks, and loses nearly his entire navy and infantry, particularly his best men (435–437; 441–444; cf. 728).[12] The drama suggests what Herodotus employs as the form of history: the Athenians seize a portion of the Persian empire Xerxes can no longer maintain (751–752; 864–906; cf. 583–597), gaining an analogous position of mastery and a similar vulnerability to subversion. When the chorus enumerates the areas in Thrace, the Hellespont, the Propontis, the Bosphorus, the islands, and mainland Ionia, most of which were under the hegemony of Athens at the time of the play, the message is clear: the Athenians appropriated the empire Xerxes lost in the naval battle (905–906).[13]

Accompanying the epinician of the *Persians* is a warning about the limits of domination Xerxes' failed invasion illuminated.[14] Darius' dictum in the *Persians*, "Let no one scorning his present fortune ruin his prosperity in the desire of others'" (μηδέ τις/ὑπερφρονήσας τὸν παρόντα δαίμονα/ἄλλων ἐρασθεὶς ὄλβον ἐκχέῃ μέγαν, *Pers.* 824–826), contains the basic insight that applies to both Hellene and Persian in the hegemonic struggle. To be sure, the drama intends this advice for Xerxes—but he never receives it. The Athenians institutionalized war against Persia with the aim of "avenging themselves for what they suffered by ravaging the land of the king" (πρόσχημα γὰρ ἦν ἀμύνεσθαι ὧν δῃοῦντας τὴν βασιλέως χώραν, Thuc. 1.96.1). The reality of the aim was this: to challenge Xerxes to battle by diverting troops, ships, and tribute from his first tribute district to Athens. The morality of vengeance in Aeschylus' drama offers little solace to the avowed aim of the Delian League. Even Xerxes' expedition to Hellas is framed in the conventional language of vengeance (*Pers.* 473–477). Vengeance and the justice characters invoke to support it are not immune to the law of *drama* and *pathos* that rules in Aeschylus' tragedy (*Pers.* 805–815; *Ag.* 532–533, 1564; *Cho.* 313; fr. 456; cf. Soph. fr. 229). *Hubris* blossoms into the fruit of madness, and the *polis* laments: this is a law Hellene and Persian must observe (*Pers.* 821–822).

As heir to Cyrus' and Darius' empire on the western frontier (*Pers.* 668–772; 897–906), Athens is in the position of Xerxes at the beginning of the drama. Like Xerxes, the Athenians who watched the *Persians* were the generation that "learned . . . to look to the sacred grove of the sea" (ἔμαθον . . . ἐσορᾶν πόντιον ἄλσος, 109–111).[15] The Athenian position of mastery brings a liability to the delusion of power, the "cunning deception of god" that offers a kindly look of enticement and catches Xerxes in its ineluctable net (93–110;

cf. *Ag.* 1374–1378). Athens stands in an analogous relation to Marathon and its civic past as Xerxes does to Darius and the Persian past. Each repeats and departs from the standard set at Marathon; each pursues the fruits of naval imperialism; each empties out its respective communities at Salamis, bringing the greatest defeat in its history (Xerxes' evacuation of Asia and Sousa: 117–118, 549, 718, 729, 761; greatest defeat: 759–764). Persia and Athens are parallel to the extent that the past and present of each community is marked by a division between Marathon and Salamis, between evacuating and protecting the land, between land power—and good civic order—and naval power that has a potential for destruction.[16] The *Persians* signifies Athens' transformation from Marathon to Salamis, from land to naval power, from the defense of freedom to the pursuit of domination.

Freedom is fundamental but insufficient in the absence of justice; domination either falls or is threatened with collapse. Both must be reconstructed according to a principle of preservation or salvation (σωτηρία). The driving forces of the *Oresteia*, for instance, are vengeance in the form of city-sacking and enslavement (Agamemnon), treacherous murder to gain the pleasures of revenge and to wield tyrannical power (Clytemnestra and Aegisthus), or the achievement of liberation from tyranny and vengeance for Agamemnon (Orestes, Electra, the chorus). The trilogy replaces Agamemnon's deleterious naval hegemony with the Areopagus (ἔρυμά τε χώρας καὶ πόλεως σωτήριον, *Eum.* 701), the alliance between Athens and Argos (πάλαισμ' ἄφυκτον τοῖς ἐναντίοις ἔχοις, / σωτήριόν τε καὶ δορὸς νικηφόρον, 776–777), and the cult of the Semnai Theai (τῶν βροτείων σπερμάτων σωτηρίαν, 909, among other functions). The *Eumenides* establishes a form of justice detached from war, killing, and the pleasure of vengeance and founds the Areopagus to decide cases where killing is involved. In a city that valued freedom above all, Aeschylus envisions freedom as a function of purity in the eyes of the gods (*Supp.* 416; *Eum.* 174–177; cf. Eur. *Hipp.* 1449–1450). Freedom from divine wrath and retribution is the most basic kind of security and the surest way for the city to retain its political freedom. Agamemnon's and Orestes' necessary acts of liberation—tyrannicide and matricide—do not ensure freedom (*Eum.* 340, *Cho.* 1060; cf. *Ag.* 824–828). Rather, the justice embodied in both Agamemnon's expedition and Orestes' revenge jeopardizes the freedom and security of the *polis.*

The earnest dialectical conflict between freedom and domination in Aeschylean drama situates it in both history and the evolving Athenian imagination of its own place within that history. Aeschylus' tragedy dramatizes the limits of domination in the necessity of freedom, displaying how forms of power are liable to subversion. Aeschylus formulated his tragic ideas when the ideology of freedom was in the process of negotiating new realities of power:

Athens' liberation of Hellas turned rapidly into the Athenian seizure and ex-pansion of the western frontier of Xerxes' empire.[17] The negotiation might be expressed this way: while Athens was developing and promoting a narrative form that displayed the vulnerability of the powerful to divine and human subversion of their mastery, the city was developing unprecedented forms of political and military power. Athens was free, yet the measure and guarantee of that freedom were increasingly the extent of its domination.[18] It is true, as W. R. Connor has suggested, that the City Dionysia was an occasion for cele-brating Athenian freedom and power.[19] In Aeschylus' hands, the genre places freedom and power in conflict with one another and discovers the limits of each in their opposition. In this way his tragedy formulates a message to the Athenians about the freedom and security of Athens, and the limits of the city's own domination.

Scholars have studied Aeschylus' drama in relation to Athenian democracy, seeking to determine whether the dramatist was a partisan of Themistocles, Cimon, Ephialtes, or Pericles.[20] Often this tradition bases its interpretations on one-to-one correspondences between dramatic figures and historical charac-ters.[21] Such allegories are defective: myth is formed by condensation and dramatization; it encodes more information than a single historical person or circumstance. The problem for Aeschylus, I suggest, was not democracy—the festival and the genre take this as a given. Nor can we know which *strategos*—if any—he supported. The vision of his drama implies that naval hegemony, the form of war built upon it, the power derived from it, and most of all, the delusions of conquest and justice it supports, can be deleterious to the *polis*.

Aeschylus' Athens built a fleet—the largest in Hellas—in 483/2 and manned it as a citizen body, becoming, as Thucydides observed, a naval people ($\nu\alpha\upsilon\tau\iota\kappa o\acute{\iota}$, 1.18.2). A fleet of 200 triremes was a radical innovation both in Athens and among Hellenic *poleis*. Financed in part by tribute (after 478/7) and used to maintain domination in Ionia and over the Aegean islands, such a fleet was an invention of Persia, an importation and transformation of an East-ern concept.[22] To build a fleet in Athens, Aristeides, who commanded the hop-lites of Antiochis at Marathon and after his return was the only Athenian hop-lite commander of the Persian Wars (at Psyttaleia and Plataea), was ostracized (*AP* 22.7).[23] Plato thought the construction of the fleet a "base imitation of the enemy" ($\mu\iota\mu\acute{\eta}\sigma\epsilon\iota\varsigma$ $\pi o\nu\eta\rho\alpha\varsigma$ $\mu\iota\mu\epsilon\hat{\iota}\sigma\theta\alpha\iota$ $\tau o\grave{\upsilon}\varsigma$ $\pi o\lambda\epsilon\mu\acute{\iota}o\upsilon\varsigma$, *Leg.* 705c9–d1, a reference to Minos, not Persia, but the historical situation is clear; cf. 699e1–4; Ar. *Av.* 373–378).[24] The Sicilians thought the Athenian experience of the sea was "neither ancestral nor eternal; they were more a land people, compelled by the Persians to become a naval people" (Thuc. 7.21.3). Aeschylus' Agamem-non, the "*hēgemōn* of Achaean ships" (*Ag.* 184–185), treats Troy the way Xerxes treated Athens; he allows Clytemnestra to celebrate him as a city-sacker the way "barbarians" welcome their conquerors (see below). To the extent that the fleet offered the community salvation, it created anxieties about the retention of Attic tradition, about the safety of the city, and about war as a form of cultural exchange in which the victor adopts the identity of the vanquished.

Unlike the Ionians on the Anatolian littoral and Euboea, and the Dorians in Corinth and Megara, Athens hardly colonized; the city was slow to exploit the sea.[25] And naval action was consistently a mixed blessing for Athens. Athens sent twenty pentekonters to Miletus in 498, incurring the wrath of Darius and the guilt of burning the Metroon at Sardis (Hdt. 5.102; cf. Arist. *An. Po.* 94a36–94b1). "These ships," Herodotus proclaimed, recalling the words of Homer, "were the beginning of pain for Greeks and barbarians alike" (αὗται δὲ αἱ νέες ἀρχὴ κακῶν ἐγένοντο Ἕλλησί τε καὶ βαρβάροισι, Hdt. 5.97.3; cf. *Od.* 8.81–82).[26] Miltiades took seventy ships to besiege Paros in 489: he brought pollution on himself in the temenos of Demeter Thesmophoros, and died a miserable death after a trial for "deceiving the Athenian people" (Hdt. 6.132–136; contrast his acquisition of Lemnos, 6.137–140). The defense of Athens and Hellas in 480/79 came at the cost of the destruction of Attica, the city, and the Acropolis. Naval power required a new form of war—a form for the most part avoided in Hellas prior to Athenian hegemony—[27] constant vigilance to insure that no rival fleets sailed the seas, and blockades on land and sea against island and isthmus settlements.

The fleet defended Athenian and Hellenic freedom from the Persians at Salamis; Aeschylus acknowledges this (*Pers.* 345–349, 402–405; the silence on Mykale is telling). Throughout the 470's and 460's, however, the Athenians stayed in their ships: at first to extort money from islanders and Carystans (Hdt. 8.111–112),[28] then to insure control of Xerxes' levy of troops, tribute, and ships from Asiatic and Aegean Greeks and to maintain a presence at strategic points along the land route through Thrace. The Persians could not invade if they had to fight to secure routes, ships, and rowers. The Athenians burned the ships of the Ionians (Hdt. 9.106.1), who had contributed to the Persian armada under Cambyses, served with distinction under Darius, and performed adequately for Xerxes.[29] Then they besieged Sestos over the winter of 479.[30] A year later the Hellenes gained control of the Anatolian littoral from Cyprus to Byzantion, and Athens made itself perpetual naval *hēgemōn* of the Hellenes, to the exclusion of Pausanias, Dorcis, and the Spartans.[31] Breaking Hellenic tradition, the city assessed a yearly cash tribute (φόρος) from allies that did not provide ships, a practice adapted from the Lydians and Persians who were the previous warlords in the area.[32] Under the leadership of Cimon, Athens conducted sieges against Eion (476) and Skyros (475) which ended in the enslavement of populations and the resettlement of land with Athenians.[33] Athens went to war with Carystus before besieging Naxos (between 474 and 466) and "enslaving it contrary to established usage" (Thuc. 1.98.1–4); Thasos fell next, between 465 and 463.[34] The early Delian League was concerned with the increase of Athenian power in the Aegean, often at the expense of Greeks, and conducted with an extraordinary spirit of vengeance (cf. Hdt. 9.119–120 [Artayktes]; 8.143.2–3; 144.2: ἡμέας ἀναγκαίως ἔχει τιμωρέειν ἐς τὰ μέγιστα, "we are obliged to exact revenge to the greatest extent").[35]

In the year 460/59, the Athenians inscribed 170 names of Erechtheid dead "in the war" in Egypt, Cyprus, Aegina, Megara, Phoenicia, and Halieis.[36] For Herodotus this period was a new age of iron, defined by an escalation of war and violence in the Greek world: from the time of Darius (522–486) to the time of Artaxerxes (465–425), the Hellenes experienced more pain (κακά) than in the previous twenty generations combined, both because of Persia's struggle to incorporate the Greek frontier into its empire and because of the struggle for hegemony among the principal Hellenic *poleis* (τὰ δὲ ἀπ' αὐτῶν τῶν κορυφαίων περὶ τῆς ἀρχῆς πολεμεόντων, Hdt. 6.98.2).[37]

The fleet was a source of anxiety to Aeschylus both as a citizen and as a poet. Naval power was not only foreign to the civic tradition; the tradition of poetry Aeschylus inherited expressed the highest political values in the fertility of the *chōra*: when a city is just, it "blossoms" (τέθηλε πόλις, Hes. *Op.* 227). The victory at Salamis was a necessary repudiation of this ideal; the construction of the Long Walls showed that what was a desperate expedient in 480/79 was becoming an element in the Athenian grand strategy. When the *Eumenides* enacts its paradigm of justice and golden age fertility (see below), a fleet is not part of the Athens Aeschylus envisions. Ships mark the end of the agrarian utopia that poetry needed to represent the value of political power (Hes. *Op.* 225–237, esp. 236–237: οὐδ' ἐπὶ νηῶν νίσονται, καρπὸν δὲ φέρει ζείδωρος ἄρουρα). Like Homer and Hesiod before him, Aeschylus imagines navies as a source of danger. The gods display their wrath against ships (*Od.* 12.377–419; cf. Hes. *Op.* 665–669; *Ag.* 633–669; Pind. *Pyth.* 1.72: ναυσίστονος ὕβρις). For Aeschylus, however, ships assume a new meaning as a sign of post-Salamis Athens: constant war, especially sieges and blockades requiring unprecedented investments of men, with the potential to destroy the manpower of a city. Ships that leave Persia for Hellas or Argos for Asia with the aim of conquest lose their *nostos,* shattered in horribly vivid scenes of destruction. True, Homer presented Phaeacia as the impossible society that Athens was to become, especially at festival time: a golden age sea power replete with harbors, ships, agoras, and massive fortifications (*Od.* 7.43–45). Yet the Phaeacians are neither warriors nor tradesmen—their ships' only function is to return Odysseus to Ithaca, and to incur the wrath of Poseidon, which prevents them from sailing again. The *Odyssey* enacts a closure on Phaeacian sea power: it is ephemeral, a vanishing point between two worlds. The vision of the *polis* in Archaic poetry depended upon the figure of the father-king-god for its validity: he was the talisman that promoted bounty in the land and protected the city from the wrath of the gods.[38] Civic justice is symbolized by the state of the *chōra*, which Athens abandoned in 480 and 479. The Themistocles Decree ordering the evacuation of Attica conforms to the formula: it declares the evacuation and naval defense "on behalf of the land" (ὑπὲρ τῆς χώρας, ML² 23.6), even though it authorized the destruction of the *chōra*.

In the *Oresteia* and the *Persians* Aeschylus presents the fearful vision of *poleis* ruined by the seduction of sea power and the forms of military and political domination that it makes possible.

However, naval hegemony was merely the material form of an Athenian moral hegemony. The tragedian was also the voice of Athenian moral leadership in Hellas. Aeschylus' drama seeks to transcend the material conditions of Athenian power—ships, tribute, the sea, siege—and to reconcile them with the ideology of freedom, justice, compassion, and the golden age fecundity these values bestow upon a city. His theater is a mirror of early Athenian imperialism, asserting its values while transforming them into tragedy, displaying their limits, and, in so doing, providing a moral compass for the ship of state by displaying how forms of power similar though not identical to those of Athens are vulnerable to self-delusion and ultimately to destruction.

The narrative of liberation and of the conquest of *hubris* is essential to the Athenian perception of its own history and identity.[39] Athenian history contains a legacy of citizen slavery; the earliest voice of the city, Solon, proclaims Athenian freedom: Solon "liberated the *dēmos*" (τόν τε δῆμον ἠλευθέρωσε, AP 9.1; cf. ἐλευθέρους ἔθηκα, Sol. 36.15 [West]), legally defining the free and enslaved estates of Attica, liberating citizens who had become slaves of fellow citizens, and repatriating Athenians sold into slavery abroad.[40] The Athenian community defined itself both legally and ideologically by its immunity to slavery. This official definition lodged itself in the Attic imagination and provided a basis for an identification with Dionysus and his *thiasos*: each is fundamentally resistant to enslavement and bondage.[41] The vicissitudes of history permitted this imaginary identification to blossom and to grow from a local to a Panhellenic phenomenon. Elements of Dionysiac myth are isomorphic with the central features of the Athenian identity—immunity to slavery or bondage, assertion of inclusion in the community despite forces of exclusion,[42] the destruction of the tyrant,[43] the navigation of the sea (see below). Such elements formulate a partial, conflicted, and potentially dangerous vision of the Athenian civic identity in history, for Dionysus embodies and empowers precisely what this identity excludes, represses, and defines as Other—the raw power of nature, mere phenomena without the authorizing stamp of the *polis*, madness, disguise, deception, and vengeance, women, slaves, and foreigners, especially the subjects of the despotic East.[44] The Athenian perception of itself as the liberator of Hellas and conqueror of *hubris*, as the Dionysiac hero enacting a narrative of liberation, conflicted with the realities of Athenian power and domination. In the gap between imagination and reality, the message of tragedy found its resonance.

While Athens developed tragedy as its preeminent native narrative form, it was manipulating myth in other, nontragic ways, fashioning the city as the oldest, most powerful, and most virtuous community in myth and in history. The disparity between the myths of tragedy and the myths that justified hegemony and projected civic self-identity reveals the poles between which Athenian ideology negotiated. On the one hand, civic myth formed a timeless image of the collective Athenian identity, of "being Athenians" ('Αθηναῖοι ἐόντες, Hdt. 7.161.3). At the heart of Athenian civic myth is what Herodotus refers to as the "Athenians alone" ('Αθηναῖοι μοῦνοι)[45] and the "Athenians first" ('Αθηναῖοι πρῶτοι).[46] Found often in connection with the victory at Marathon, the phrases form a network of ideas by which "Athens" can designate "Hellas" by synecdoche, and claim the essence of an idealized Hellenic tradition of valor and righteousness: being the oldest Hellenic *polis* and so having the right to rule, and exercising the right in acts of liberation and the conquest of *hubris*, the defense of suppliants, the protection of the rights of the dead, and insuring the salvation of Hellas. At one level, tragic myth presents no conflict with civic myth. It is merely a species of the myth that Athens is unique, and develops during the same period: the "Athenians alone" are not the subject of tragic *pathos*. On the contrary, Athens is the scene where tragic violence can be resolved, and tragic pain healed.[47]

It is no accident that the Athenians are the explicit subjects of history but not of tragedy. The "historical moment" of tragedy began and ended when Athens was the subject of extraordinary historical *pathos:* the Persian destruction of Attica and Athens propelled the genre to greatness and cultural dominance; the Sicilian expedition and disaster heralded its decline.[48]

From Xerxes to Alcibiades: Athenian history assumed the form of tragedy and the genre of tragedy attained its form. During this period, the Athenians experienced liberation, domination, and the subversion of their mastery. The mystique of Athenian freedom, of the city's heroic effort against the Persians, and of the process of acquiring and expanding an empire vanished as that empire dissolved. When Lysander and the Spartans dismantled the Athenian Long Walls to the accompaniment of the aulos, "believing that day inaugurated freedom for Hellas" (νομίζοντες ἐκείνην τὴν ἡμέραν τῇ Ἑλλάδι ἄρχειν τῆς ἐλευθερίας, Xen. *Hell.* 2.2.23; cf. Plut. *Lys.* 15.4), the liberator had become the tyrant and was vanquished. The festival of Dionysus Eleuthereus and the genre that expressed its meaning, tragedy, would never recover the prestige it enjoyed while Athens was the savior of Hellenic freedom. But in the lore that developed after the Sicilian expedition and the fall of Athens, tragedy continued to play a role in the discourse of freedom: recitations of Euripides' poetry kept captured Athenians from enslavement and starvation in Sicily and mariners chased by pirates gained protection inside the harbor at Syracuse if they recited tragic verse (Plut. *Nicias* 29). A Phocian's chance quotation of two lines from Euripides' *Electra* prevented Athens' total destruction (Plut. *Lys.* 15.3). A bond existed between tragedy and freedom, but the tragic moment at Athens approached the vanishing point. The mythic spectacle of others' heroic pain now contained the realization and memory of Athens' own historical suffering. Aristophanes sensed the moment slipping away when he presented the *Frogs* in 405. His Dionysus longs for Euripides and wants to return him to Athens for his own pleasure. He returns instead with Aeschylus, enjoining him to "save the city" (σῷζε πόλιν, *Ran.* 1501). It was not merely that Aeschylus warned against rearing the city-sacker and tyrant in the city (i.e., the lion cub, *Ran.* 1431b–32).[49] Nor is the unexpected shift from private pleasure to public salvation a simple matter of Aristophanic fantasy: Aeschylus' drama contains a vision of Athenian freedom and salvation, and implies that the city's rapidly expanding hegemony presented a threat to them.

"Athens," wrote Gerald Else, "became residual legatee and reinterpreter of the pan-Hellenic stock of myth for the whole Greek nation."[50] After the Persian Wars, the city began to standardize the themes of its ideology, combining myth and history in a sequence that became the backbone of the *epitaphios logos*, but was first used to justify Athenian hegemony.[51] A fixed repertory emerged: the supplications of the Argives to recover their dead from Thebes and of the Herakleidai to free themselves from the Mycenaeans, the invasion of Attica by the Amazons of Thermodon, Menestheus' leadership at Troy, and an important Athenian presence there. These complemented the tradition of Theseus' deeds and redefined Panhellenic heroism according to an Athenian model.[52] The building of the Theseion (475–470) proclaimed a new foundation not just of Athens, but of Athens in a new form, as naval *hēgemōn*.[53] The Athenians now possessed Theseus' bones as a talisman to rival those of Orestes in Sparta.[54] The Stoa Poikile (c. 460) included the battle of Athens and Sparta at Oinoe,[55] paintings of Theseus and the Athenians battling Amazons, the Battle of Marathon featuring the polemarch Callimachus and the general Miltiades attended by heroes and gods—the eponymous hero Marathon, the civic hero Theseus, the divine hero Herakles, and the goddess Athena. Also in the Stoa was a scene from the sack of Troy, the trial of Ajax for his rape of Cassandra (Paus. 1.15.2–4). History and myth appear together as equals and as bearers of the same meaning; history justified myth, and myth lent history the prestige of origins. The men of Marathon stood alongside heroes and gods of different orders— eponymous hero, civic hero, divine hero, and Athena—just as the Areopagites stand beside Athena, Apollo, the Erinyes, and Orestes in the *Eumenides*.

The legacy of heroic myth became the exclusive material for tragic drama,[56] but the validity of the heritage was not without its problems in Athens. Athenian history—its victories of liberation and vengeance over Persia—immediately bore the prestige of the mythical past, and its events functioned as paradigms for the citizen body.[57] Athens derived its social dramas from history and recast the mythical tradition in accord with them.[58] It is one of the many ironies of tragic drama at Athens that the Athenians adopted and sought to control the narration of Panhellenic myths at a time when their own historical experience revealed their inadequacy: Athens was unique in history and the tradition by itself was incapable of understanding and presenting this uniqueness unless it was reshaped according to an historical model.

The inheritance from Mycenae remained the only Panhellenically valid form of depicting the Athenian moment: Athens' victories marked the return of the *illud tempus* associated with Mycenae. But the city distinguished itself from this cycle of myths. The Athenians were heroes of a new and different order: not the "sons of the Achaeans" (υἷες Ἀχαιῶν), but the "children of the Athenians" (παῖδες Ἀθηναίων),[59] a democracy composed of anonymous heroes, a city of compassion and power, a liberator, savior, protector of the weak and the outraged, upholder of Hellenic law. As the memory of glorious ascent and destruction, Panhellenic myths were a legacy that provoked anxiety in Athenian poets. It is not merely that Athens was unimportant in Panhellenic myth and sought in its own ironic way to win a place in the heroic tradition through Menestheus son of Peteos, whom Denys Page has called "a nonentity and something of a ninny."[60] It is more: the myths portended the collapse of heroic greatness. In this perspective, the theater afforded a vehicle for expressing the contradiction between contemporary civic heroism and mythical memory.[61] In the theater, the Athenians focalized their own identities through those of the divine, heroic, and human agents of the past. Hellenic myth contains the memory of heroic *aretē* and of heroic self-destruction; the Athenian appropriation of it is both a gesture of confidence in its "unperishing glory" (ἄφθιτον κλέος, restored in ML² 26.I.1) and a collective effort to escape the destiny such glory entailed.

One of the problems the genre faced early in its evolution was how to control the degree of self-identity permitted in drama: to make the tragic *pathos* real enough to engage the emotions of the audience, but to distance the spectator far enough from it to insure the realization that it was "other" (ἀλλότριον) and not "one's own" (οἰκεῖον).[62] Pity and fear, the canonical tragic emotions, are directly analogous: to fear is to identify with the complex of *pathos* and character; to pity is to acknowledge its difference.[63] The first tragedy of which we are informed, Phrynichus' *Capture of Miletus*, was unable to attain a balance between pity and fear, self-identification with the drama and differentiation from it. The tragedy portrayed the *pathos* of Ionians that the Athenians felt they were likely to suffer: Persian retribution for breaking a pact of vassalage, revolting, and sacking Sardis. The Athenians fined Phrynichus and banned performance of his play, according to Herodotus, for "reminding the Athenians of their own suffering" (ὡς ἀναμνήσαντα οἰκήια κακά, 6.21.2).[64] This instituted a tradition that was already the norm in tragedy and epic, but that Phrynichus broke: their manifest content was an *allotrion pathos* (cf. Plato, *Resp.* 604e5–6: ἀλλοτρίου γάρ που πάθους ἡ μίμησις; 606b1: ἀλλότρια πάθη θεωροῦν).

The relation between "one's own" and "someone else's" is central to the tragic idea. After the Persian Wars, Athens developed new material bases for this relation. In 480 and 479 the Athenians evacuated Attica, leaving it to the Persians and "destroying their own" (τὰ οἰκεῖα διαφθείραντες, Thuc. 1.74.2; τὰ οἰκεῖα φθεῖραι, 6.82.4). Between 478 and 456, the city made the seizure of booty and collection of tribute a point of public policy to acquire power, prestige, and wealth and to compensate for its losses.[65] The relation between the inside and outside of the city, between *oikeia* and *allotria*, was being transformed to accommodate new forms of acquisition made possible by naval power. Inside, the Athenians fortified the city with stone walls plucked from the remnants of their temples and houses; they fortified Piraeus harbor and stockpiled silver reserves, probably on Delos, which the Persians considered inviolate (Hdt. 6.97.1–2); they requisitioned ships, men, money, and resources from their allies.[66] Open to every point of the Mediterranean by sea, Athens closed itself off by land, completing the Long Walls in 456 (Thuc. 1.107.1).[67] Tragedy flourished when relations between Athens and the external world began to be regulated by increasing degrees of physical as well as ideological openness and closure. The purest and oldest of the Hellenes, the Athenians were becoming open to external influence and contact in ways that were unprecedented ([Xen.] *AP* 7–12; Hermippus *Phormophoroi*, fr. 63 Edmonds). Autochthony, the *Tatenkatalog*, the Long Walls, and the citizenship law of 451/0 were the products of Athens' sense of uniqueness, difference, and self-identity. The fleet, the Piraeus, Panhellenic festivals, *metoikia*, democracy, and tragedy were fruits of Athenian openness.

Tragedy was the function of an increasing Athenian culture of importation: the stuff of tragedy was the suffering of others used to fashion an Athenian vision of themselves and their world. Thucydides' Pericles connects Athenian festival life with the openness of his city to imports: the magnitude of Athens brought people to its festivals and goods to its citizens from outside the community. He claims, "We use native goods with an enjoyment no more our own (μηδὲν οἰκειοτέρᾳ τῇ ἀπολαύσει) than the goods we use of others" (Thuc. 2.38.2). Pericles considered the enjoyment (ἀπόλαυσις) of others' goods a sign of Athenian greatness.

Plato applied the concept to the psychology of tragic spectatorship: it is the importation and enjoyment of "others' pains to one's own," a process that habituates spectators to treat their own suffering as they do that of others in the theater and literally to derive pleasure from the expression of their own pain. For Plato, the spectator's diversion of his own suppressed appetites for lament and anger to the spectacle of *allotria pathē* liberates those appetites. As is typical, liberation is a stage in a process that leads to domination: these appetites take control of the soul and the body politic. Socrates imagines, "I suppose that only a few bother to calculate that there has to be an enjoyment from others' pains into one's own" (λογίζεσθαι γὰρ οἶμαι ὀλίγοις τισὶν μέτεστιν ὅτι ἀπολαύειν ἀνάγκη ἀπὸ τῶν ἀλλοτρίων εἰς τὰ οἰκεῖα, *Resp.* 606b5–6). This enjoyment was the mechanism by which Plato thought tragedy became social drama: the pleasure derived from the sufferings of others insinuated itself into the minds of the audience, subverting the relation between self and other, *to oikeion* and *to allotrion*, the garrison of reason and the passions it guards, and, ultimately, between the ruler and the ruled.

Plato considered perceiving the difference between *to oikeion* and *to allotrion* fundamental to the nature of a guardian-citizen (*Resp.* 376b3–6). Tragedy relaxed the officially imposed divide between *to oikeion* and *to allotrion*, but also reinforced it. The effect was contradictory: the audience experienced an *allotrion pathos* through the eyes of characters remote in time and place who belonged to communities the Athenians often viewed as hostile. The dramatization of the *allotrion pathos* reinforced the perception that it was alien to the Athenians, but it lured the audience across generically imposed barriers to experience the *pathos* as its own. Tragedy led the audience to deliberate about its own *pathos* and hence about its freedom and salvation.[68] But it also exerted an imperceptible force for the repetition of those *allotria pathē* in Athenian life. To the extent tragedy denied or repressed history in the sense of "events of the past," it also represented history in Jameson's sense: "what hurts . . . what refuses desire and sets inexorable limits to individual as well as collective praxis, which its 'ruses' turn into grisly and ironic reversals of their overt intention."[69] Tragedy inevitably reverts to a Solonian prehistory, when Athens had no fleet, no empire, and no contradiction between its Dionysiac identity and its imperial praxis: history is the violent process of liberation, domination, and subversion. After the Persian Wars the Athenians dramatized their situation in tragedy and imagined the reality of their own potential suffering as *allotria pathē*.

We can understand the City Dionysia and the genre of tragedy as a function of Athenian institutions regulating relations between the inside and outside of the polis—slavery, *metoikia*, the family, citizenship, warfare and hegemony, the agora and economy, cult and festival. At the heart of the question, especially during the period of tragedy's ascendancy, is the Athenian fleet: it transformed how the Athenians viewed and exploited the difference between the inside and outside of their city. Ships crossed boundaries between communities, bringing profit (κέρδος), both dangerous and beneficial, "into the house" (οἴκαδε) from the outside.[70]

The City Dionysia was an appropriate occasion for a consideration of ships and the sea. The festival of Dionysus Eleuthereus marked the earliest opening of the sailing season.[71] Exekias and the poet of the *Hymn to Dionysus* (*Hymn* 8, Allen) envisioned Dionysus aboard ship: he made epiphanies and arrivals by ship.[72] The god escaped into the sea and returned safely to land, much like the Athenians at Salamis, and wine and the sea were a formulaic pair in Homer (οἴνοπα πόντον). The comedian Hermippus invokes the Muses to tell how Athens came to import products from around the world "from the time Dionysus voyaged on the wine-blue sea" (ἐξ οὗ ναυκληρεῖ Διόνυσος ἐπ᾽ οἴνοπα πόντον, fr. 63.2 Edmonds). Aristophanes presents Dionysus aboard ship reading the *Andromeda* when the longing for Euripides seizes him (Ar. *Ran.* 52–54). But his Dionysus is no oarsman, as his learning to row across the Styx reveals (197–270).

In the *Hymn to Dionysus* the god rewards the helmsman who recognizes his divinity and "makes him completely prosperous" (μιν ἔθηκε πανόλβον, 54).[73] Those who govern the ship of state must recognize Dionysus: the tyrant who refuses the god is destroyed. The City Dionysia grew to be an important festival for the display of Athenian hegemonic power and prosperity. For a *hēgemōn* to celebrate Dionysus inspired confidence in its commitment to the freedom of its allies and subjects and furthered the aims of Athenian imperialism, which claimed to preserve Hellenic freedom in the former Lydian-Persian empire.

Until the end of the Peloponnesian War the City Dionysia heralded the opening of the seas to the Athenian fleet; it was associated with the season of war. If communities did not want to do battle, they made truces at this time (e.g., Thuc. 4.118.2; 5.19.1, 23.4). The occasion also marked the season of payment—the time when assessed tribute was due at Athens. Sometime after 454 Athens made the tribute payable at the City Dionysia. We have no idea when it was due before this, but the fleet would need to secure at least partial payments and firm promises to pay prior to sailing, even if it lacked the will or means to enforce the demand.[74]

The City Dionysia deferred Athenian naval hegemony while displaying its beneficence and power. Immediately after the festival, however, Athenian hegemonic institutions went into operation: allied court cases were heard; tribute receipts were scrutinized against their assessment; triremes were launched from their sheds at the Piraeus.[75] The fact that the festival opened the season of naval activity and war made it an appendage to Athenian hegemony. Isocrates tells us that the Athenians displayed the surplus of tribute before the audience in the theater and paraded the war orphans in their panoplies, ready to avenge their fathers (*De Pace* 82–83).[76] The festival and the genre projected an ideal image of Athens and disseminated the principles of Athenian identity: autochthony; respect for strangers, suppliants, and the unburied; the risking of life for freedom and the conquest of *hubris;* and institutions based on persuasion, democracy, and justice.[77]

Festivals, as Pericles declares, gave "rest from pains to the mind" (τῶν πόνων ἀναπαύλας τῇ γνώμῃ, Thuc. 2.38.1), and created an atmosphere where "pleasure expels pain" (ἡ τέρψις τὸ λυπηρὸν ἐκπλήσσει, ibid.). But the *Oresteia* insists that its audience experience "a painful memory of pain" (μνησιπήμων πόνος, *Ag.* 180) before achieving a "release from pains" (ἀπαλλαγὴ πόνων, *Ag.* 1, 20; *Eum.* 83) and restoring the spirit of the festival occasion. At a festival where ships, the sea, freedom, and power were paramount, Aeschylus' *Oresteia* dramatized the limits, liabilities, and, we might say, the curse of Hellenic naval hegemony. Borrowing a stratagem from Pisistratus, he used the image of Athena to form a vision in which the salvation of the *polis* is a function of archaic and obsolete forms of civic life—the Areopagus, the image of justice leading to agrarian bounty, and the cult of the Semnai to insure fear and reverence—that also validates a dangerous new form embodied in the Athenian hegemonic project of glory, justice, vengeance, and aggrandizement through war.

Bernard Knox argued that Sophocles' Oedipus is more than a character: he forms by condensation and analogy Sophocles' vision of the *polis* of the Athenians.[78] This kind of vision is the legacy of Aeschylus, who presented his city and its destiny in the myths of Darius and Xerxes, Laius, Oedipus, Eteocles and Polyneices, Pelasgus and Danaus, Agamemnon, Orestes, and even Zeus and Prometheus. While Thucydides says that Athens "was becoming a democracy in name but in fact the rule of a preeminent man" (2.65.9), Aeschylus' tragedy is the reverse, "the rule of a preeminent man in name, but in fact becoming a democracy." The hero does not exist as an independent person—he embodies the collective identity of the audience. Similar condensations are evident in the figure of Menestheus in the Eion Epigram, the civic hero Theseus, the tribal hero Erechtheus who represents the entire city, and the leaders of the other nine tribes who personify their members.[79] It is crucial to perception in the theater at the time of Aeschylus that the *dēmos* see itself embodied in the hero-king and as his victim. Democracy is a form of reflexivity.

The figure of Aeschylus' Agamemnon condenses and presents in analogical form the character of Athenian naval hegemony, while the *Agamemnon* shows how such a hegemony contains the source of its own subversion. Unlike poets before or after him, Aeschylus calls Agamemnon "the elder *hēgemōn* of Achaean ships" (ἡγεμὼν ὁ πρέ-/σβυς νεῶν Ἀχαιϊκῶν, *Ag.* 184–185), the "leader of ships" (νεῶν δ᾽ ἄπαρχος, 1227), "admiral" (ναυάρχῳ, *Cho.* 723–724), "*harmost* of sailors" (Ἀγάμεμνον᾽, ἀνδρῶν ναυβατῶν ἁρμόστορα, *Eum.* 456), and "the completely feared and respected leader of ships" (τοῦ παντοσέμνου, τοῦ στρατηλάτου νεῶν, *Eum.* 637). Agamemnon and Menelaus receive an omen from Zeus as "the kings of ships" (οἰωνῶν βασιλεὺς βασιλεῦσι νεῶν . . . φανέντες, "the king of birds appear[ed] to the kings of ships," *Ag.* 114–116). The eagles hunt, sacrifice, and feast on a pregnant hare and her embryos just as the "kings of ships" sacrifice Iphigenia and destroy the wealth and life of Troy: seed and crops, cattle, property, people, and altars (*Ag.* 118–120; 122–135; 320–350; 524–537; 818–820).

Homer's Agamemnon is not a "king of ships." The concept and reality of naval hegemony do not yet exist.[80] Indeed, Athenian decrees do not specify naval commands for generals until the Sicilian expedition.[81] The *Iliad* preserves a tradition that Agamemnon is entitled "to rule all Argos and many islands" (πολλῇσι νήσοισι καὶ Ἄργει παντὶ ἀνάσσειν, *Il.* 2.108) and that he provided the most ships (100), outfitted the autochthonous Arcadians with a fleet, and sent the best army to Troy (*Il.* 2.575–577). Poets assign Panhellenic rule to Agamemnon (e.g., schol. *El.* 694–695; Eur. *IA* 414–415: ὦ Πανελλήνων ἄναξ,/ Ἀγάμεμνον), but they do not call Agamemnon's leadership a naval hegemony. Thucydides treats Agamemnon as a forebear of Athenian naval power (Thuc. 1.9) and Isocrates pleads with the Hellenes to provide another Agamemnon for a war against Persia (Isoc. *Panath.* 78), but no one goes so far as Aeschylus, in the *Agamemnon* and *Eumenides,* to link Agamemnon with ships, siege, savage violence, and vulnerability to reprisal from living and dead, gods and men.

Aeschylus compels Agamemnon to choose between the titles "father" and "naval *hēgemōn*." Choosing to be *hēgemōn* of ships, he affirms a loyalty comparable to the one the Athenians demanded from their allies. Agamemnon's decisive remarks indicate this: "How shall I become a deserter of the fleet, losing my alliance?" (πῶς λιπόναυς γένωμαι / ξυμμαχίας ἁμαρτών;, 212–213). The words λιπόναυς and ξυμμαχίας ἁμαρτών carry more weight than the multitude of words Agamemnon uses to describe his revulsion at the sacrifice of his daughter and the pollution of his "paternal hands" (1581–1582).[82] Athens invoked the term λιποστράτιον to uphold its alliance and to punish allies for leaving campaigns, using it as a pretext to strip them of fleets, walls, and independence, and to enroll them as tributary members (Thuc. 1.98.4– 99.1; 6.76.3).[83] Using the rare and specific term λιπόναυς, Agamemnon justifies his decision to sacrifice his daughter in terms that echo Athenian practices. Iphigenia is literally, as the chorus calls her, "a preliminary sacrifice of ships" (προτέλεια ναῶν, 227): she is the preliminary cost of the alliance, and of Agamemnon's hegemony over it.

The tension between paternity and alliance that leads to the sacrifice of Iphigenia is part of the larger purpose of the *Agamemnon*: to dramatize how the figure of the father-king from the tradition of Homer and Hesiod, the ruler whose justice insures the fecundity and prosperity of the people, land, and flocks, is inconsistent with the violence of a "*hēgemōn* of ships." Aeschylus inverts images of agricultural bounty to underscore the contradiction between Agamemnon and the father-king. On the homecoming, Agamemnon's fleet makes "the Aegean sea blossom with the corpses of men and bits and pieces of ships" (ἀνθοῦν πέλαγος Αἰγαῖον νεκροῖς / ἀνδρῶν Ἀχαιῶν ναυτικοῖς τ' ἐρειπίοις, 659–660; cf. Hes. *Op.* 225 of the just city: λαοὶ δ' ἀνθέουσιν ἐν αὐτῇ, "the people blossom in it"). Agamemnon is the father who sacrifices his virgin daughter (*Ag.* 218–257; 1524–1529), the ominous eagle that hunts, sacrifices, and feasts on a hare and the unborn in her womb (104–139), the leader of the Argive beast, "the savage lion" that, "leaping over the rampart, licked the blood of the tyrant to surfeit" (ὑπερθορὼν δὲ πύργον ὠμηστὴς λέων / ἅδην ἔλειξεν αἵματος τυραννικοῦ, 827–828). As the agent of Zeus' retribution, Agamemnon is a destructive farmer, "overturning the land of Troy with the mattock of Zeus who brings vengeance . . . and the seed of the entire land is entirely ruined" (Τροίαν κατασκάψαντα τοῦ δικηφόρου / Διὸς μακέλλῃ, τῇ κατείργασται πέδον / . . . καὶ σπέρμα πάσης ἐξαπόλλυται χθονός, 525–528). Agamemnon sacks Troy at the "setting of the Pleiades" (826), which inaugurates the season of plowing, when the seed sets firmly in the soil (πλειὼν δὲ κατὰ χθονὸς ἄρμενος εἴη, Hes. *Op.* 617), and when sailing is strictly out of season.[84] Two characteristics define the "*hēgemōn* of ships": he expends objects of sacred or intrinsic value to gain objects of profane or exchange value; and he destroys anything that actually grows or can be imagined to grow from the soil or in the womb. Like Ouranos and Kronos, he is the sovereign that refuses to accommodate production in his realm; like them, he also is the victim of *dolos* that removes him from power.

Aeschylus calls attention to Agamemnon's naval hegemony to dramatize it as a problem: a source of violence outside the community that activates hatred and violence within it. Aeschylus stresses Agamemnon's naval hegemony because it is essential to his vision of the hero's suffering and to the awareness he provokes in his audience, which the chorus of the *Agamemnon* calls the "painful memory of pain" (μνησιπήμων πόνος, *Ag.* 179–180). It is a commonplace in Thucydides that Aeschylus' generation acquired and handed down an empire "with toils" (μετὰ πόνων, 2.62.3) and "not without toil" (οὐκ ἀπόνως, 2.36.2). His generation won "the greatest name" (μέγιστον ὄνομα) and eternal remembrance for Athens because it "expended the most lives and efforts in war" (πλεῖστα δὲ σώματα καὶ πόνους ἀνηλωκέναι πολέμῳ, 2.64.3). The *Oresteia* offers a contemporary perspective on this πόνος and prays for a release from it (ἀπαλλαγὴ πόνων, *Ag.* 1, 20, *Eum.* 83; cf. *PV* 316, 754, 773; Isoc. *Areopag.* 16.84 takes up the theme in a similar context). The economics of πόνος—the city expends its men in exchange for glory and justice—is subject to scrutiny in the *Agamemnon*. The chorus of the play calls Ares "the gold-changer of bodies" (ὁ χρυσαμοιβὸς δ' Ἄρης σωμάτων, 438) who exchanges living men for urns stuffed ceremoniously with ashes, returned to the city, and given funereal praise (440–446). Rather than unite the city in its efforts, however, the ceremony breeds hatred and desire for vengeance against the Atreidai, whom the *dēmos* believes are fulfilling their own purposes by expending its members in war (448–457).

"The city," writes Nicole Loraux, "celebrates the citizen only because he is dead."[85] The *Agamemnon* represents this mentality of exchange as a problem. It is not simply that the elusive object of desire in war, Helen, cannot be worth the lives of the men who died to retrieve her (cf. *Ag.* 799–804, 1455–1457). Throughout the drama, rites designed to transform *ponos* into *kleos* ring false, particularly after Agamemnon's homecoming, which culminates in the carpet scene. In a fragment attributed to Aeschylus, a speaker claims, "The gods owe *kleos*, the child of *ponos*, to the one who toils" (τῷ πονοῦντι δ' ἐκ θεῶν / ὀφείλεται τέκνωμα τοῦ πόνου κλέος, fr. 315). This formula is fundamental to any faith in heroic action, but it can be fatal to the city when the costs of the *ponos* are too high, and the very burden of the *kleos* too great: "to have an excessive *kleos* is a burden indeed; a bolt of lightning is launched from the eyes of Zeus" (τὸ δ' ὑπερκόπως κλύειν / εὖ βαρύ / βάλλεται γὰρ ὄσσοις / Διόθεν κεραυνός, *Ag.* 468–470, reading with West [1990]). This is the burden of Agamemnon, and it is also the burden of hegemonic Athens.

The herald grudgingly tells of the pain of besieging Troy, describing the harshness of sleeping aboard a trireme during a naval blockade (555–557) and the soldiers' exposure to the elements during a siege that persisted season after season (558–566, an exclusively Athenian *ponos*). He seeks to suppress "the pain of pain remembered" and protests: "Why should we grieve over this? The pain has passed" (τί ταῦτα πενθεῖν δεῖ; παροίχεται πόνος, 567). "It has passed—it is not the business of the dead to rise again. For us, the remnant of the Argive army, profit is victor, and pain does not balance it on the scales" (νικᾷ τὸ κέρδος, πῆμα δ' οὐκ ἀντιρρέπει, 567–571). The herald makes explicit the calculation that justifies the sacrifice of Iphigenia, the exchange rate of Ares, and the Argive sack and destruction of Troy (ἔρως . . . πορθεῖν τὰ μὴ χρή, κέρδεσιν νικωμένους, 341–342): the dead do not have weight, do not register on the scales, and have no value in the calculation of personal and collective profit. The trilogy shows how invisible souls simmer with wrath in unseen places and are represented by the Erinyes, who have the power to avenge them (345–347; 460–467; cf. 1337–1342; Eum. 316–320).

The carpet scene dramatizes the idea that property and life exist for the sake of exchange and expenditure, and that the dead have no value.[86] Implicated in the idea is the exploitation of the sea, and the delusion of the unlimited power of exchange wealth it nourishes. While Agamemnon treads the tapestries, Clytemnestra articulates the basis for his action: "There is the sea, who will exhaust it? It nourishes an ever-renewing ooze of crimson as good as money, dye for our clothes" (ἔστιν θάλασσα, τίς δέ νιν κατασβέσει; / τρέφουσα πολλῆς πορφύρας ἰσάργυρον / κηκῖδα παγκαίνιστον, εἱμάτων βάφας, 958–960). As Clytemnestra utters these words, the "king of ships" walks on "sea," the crimson tapestries strewn along his path. The "hēgemōn of ships" never touches the soil of Argos: he arrives by chariot, treads the tapestries into his house, and dies in the bath. The carpet scene reminds us of all the lives and property expended to pay for Agamemnon's kleos and visualizes his central tendency, which the Erinyes call "eyeing profit, to dishonor the altar of justice underfoot" (μηδέ νιν / κέρδος ἰδὼν ἀθέῳ ποδὶ / λὰξ ἀτίσῃς· ποινὰ γὰρ ἐπέσται· / κύριον μένει τέλος, Eum. 540–544; cf. Ag. 382–384; Sol. 4, esp. 14–39). And it connects this tendency with his mastery of the sea.

Agamemnon acts as he has throughout the drama: exchanging wealth and life for profit, in this case, his spear-prize Cassandra. Everything about the ceremony Clytemnestra has devised to honor the sacker of Troy (905–907) contradicts the identity of a Hellene who respects the power of the dēmos (937–938): the honor should derive from the polis, not the oikos (917–918); the ceremony is "effeminate" and "barbarian" (918–920); fitting for the gods, it can only provoke divine envy (921–925). Agamemnon's fame is assured independently of the ceremony, and such a ritual of blessing is inappropriate for a living man: olbos is the honor of the dead (926–930). But Agamemnon makes the expenditure, despite his fears of divine and popular resentment. He made similar expenditures before and profited from them (933–934); his vanquished adversary would have done the same had he won (935–936); and, above all, Clytemnestra desires it (940–943). Agamemnon cannot be the gentleman Eduard Fraenkel wanted him to be: he is a political man, a man of monumental ponos, not a man of leisure. Naval hēgemōn, city-sacker, victor over the barbarian who has been seduced by the rites of the vanquished, Agamemnon is wedded to the idea that the expenditure of life and property is a form of profit and a guarantee of future power. The war in Troy incurred the wrath of the *dēmos* and the dead, and the envy of the gods; Agamemnon incurs these very same liabilities in celebrating the victory. He sacrificed Iphigenia in accord with the desire of his allies (214–217); and he treads the tapestry to satisfy the desire of Clytemnestra (940–943). To satisfy the demands of his subordinates is to invest in power: he intends the act to indebt Clytemnestra to him as part of a reciprocal exchange. He acts in accord with Clytemnestra's desire, and she must act in accord with his: to welcome and to treat kindly his concubine, the wealth he would like to import into the household in exchange for the wealth he agrees to destroy (944–955).

The ceremony dramatizes an entire history of the ambitions and practices of hegemonic power and its vulnerability to envious and seductive speech. It visualizes the mentality of exchange that justifies the killing and destruction, the repercussions of which Agamemnon as *hēgemōn* must bear: a willingness to kill is endemic in this form of power, just as it haunts the House of Atreus. In the *Oresteia* Aeschylus imagines a perspective from which the conventions of killing and the justice achieved by it offer no protection against the guilt of blood (*Ag.* 460–470; *Eum.* 367–380)—the perspective of the Semnai Theai. When Agamemnon becomes "one who murders masses" (τῶν πολυκτόνων, *Ag.* 461), his glory and reputation, his beliefs and those of his herald about the justice imposed on Paris and Troy, "disintegrating beneath the earth, wither without honor under our assaults in mourning and the malicious dance of our feet" (*Eum.* 369–371). The Erinyes mark Agamemnon as a target for reversal of fortune (*Ag.* 461–467). As tyrants Aegisthus and Clytemnestra think themselves "feared and respected" (σεμνοί, *Cho.* 975). The herald declares Agamemnon "the son of Atreus, a respected, blessed man, most deserving of honor of men now alive" (*Ag.* 530–532). Clytemnestra celebrates Agamemnon as "city-sacker" (*Ag.* 905–907; see also 461–474, 524–532, 783–787, 925). Apollo calls Agamemnon "the completely feared and respected general of ships" (*Eum.* 637). But the Erinyes alone are *semnai* (*Eum.* 383). Their feet trample what heralds, prophets, and tyrants proclaim *semnos*.

Agamemnon's fate is incorporated into a vision of punishment in Athens for transgressing the boundaries of fear and reverence the Erinyes guard. The Erinyes will punish hubristic Athenians just as they punished "the king of ships": they leap upon him and strike, and darkness, pollution, and lament descend upon his house (*Eum.* 377–380; cf. *Ag.* 1379–1380, *Cho.* 23–83, and elsewhere). The link between the violence of naval power and the Erinyes' political message is clear: they use Agamemnon's story of maritime plunder and shipwreck, of a death in which the gods not only are deaf to his prayers, but laugh at his predicament, and allow him to die "unwept, unseen," as a model for the injustice they will punish in Athens (*Eum.* 550–565; cf. *Sept.* 602–604). Their metaphor for punishment incorporates the characteristic form of Athenian power, the fleet.

The *Oresteia* invokes the Athenian memory of *ponos* to convey a message of a necessary moderation that comes even to those who reject it (καὶ παρ' ἄκοντας ἦλθε σωφρονεῖν, 180–181). In the *Eumenides*, this moderation applies to the Athenians. After the trial of Orestes, the Erinyes bid farewell to an "Attic people" that is "becoming moderate in time" (σωφρονοῦντες ἐν χρόνῳ, 1000).[87] The experience of siege warfare after the Battle of Mykale prompted Athens to compare its war against the Persians to the Trojan War.[88] The city imagined itself an important participant in the war; it claimed that its soldiers at Eion improved upon the sack of Troy, and furnished the best commander Menestheus, which gave them Homeric authority for their own command (Hdt. 7.161.3; *FGE* XL.1–6). The starting point for Aeschylus' version of the Trojan War is the Athenian imagination of its own war.[89]

The biographical tradition reports that Aeschylus left Athens in anger after he lost a bid to Simonides to commemorate the dead at Marathon (*Vit. Aesch.* 8). We may doubt this story, but there may be some truth to Aeschylus' anger over his rejection as a commemorative poet. His ideas of *nikē* and *epinikia* diverged from those of commemorative poets. After the Athenians besieged, starved, sacked, enslaved, and resettled Eion, the *dēmos* commissioned a poet to celebrate the event. Three epigrams were inscribed on herms in the Stoa of the Herms.[90] One epigram showcases the Athenian achievement at Eion:

> ἦν ἄρα κἀκεῖνοι ταλακάρδιοι, οἵ ποτε Μήδων
> παισὶν ἐπ' Ἠιόνι Στρυμόνος ἀμφὶ ῥοάς
> λιμόν τ' αἴθωνα κρυερόν τ' ἐπάγοντες "Αρηα
> πρῶτοι δυσμενέων εὗρον ἀμηχανίην.

Then these too are men stout of heart, who, bringing hot hunger and chill Ares to the sons of the Medes at Eion on the streams of the Strymon, first discovered the helplessness of their enemies.
(6–10)[91]

The Eion Epigram set the tone for the 470's and 460's in Athens: it was the people's "wage" (μίσθος, 11) to their generals for their service, and presented a model for future generations to imitate (13–14). Unlike other Athenian commemorations, the epigram does not recall the moral value of the battle—conquering *hubris*, preserving freedom, winning salvation. Styling the Athenians "first discoverers" in the field of siege operations, it remembers the siege and starvation of an enemy and the glory the Athenians derived from it. The Athenian pride in its capacity to besiege its opponents and the avowed aim of Athenian hegemony—to treat the land of the king just as he had treated Attica—suggest that Aeschylus dramatizes a breakdown between the "Hellenic" and the "barbarian" in military practices that resemble those of his own city. The herald's inflated description of Agamemnon's victory and claim to honor (524–532), particularly his proclamation that "the altars and the seats of the gods are no longer to be seen" (βωμοὶ δ' ἄιστοι καὶ θεῶν ἱδρύματα, 527),[92] recalls Darius' description of the Persian sack of Athens, in which he says that "the altars are not to be seen, and the seats of the gods have been twisted up from their foundations by the roots in disorder" (βωμοὶ δ' ἄιστοι, δαιμόνων θ' ἱδρύματα / πρόρριζα φύρδην ἐξανέστραπται βάθρων, Pers. 811–812).

Aeschylus did not so much praise as warn against *nikē*, especially siege victories. Zeus is the proper object of victory praise—this is the essence of sense (Ζῆνα δέ τις προφρόνως ἐπινίκια κλάζων / τεύξεται φρενῶν τὸ πᾶν, 174–175). The siege seeks to fulfill the "high-towered hopes" from which Zeus hurls mankind to destruction (*Supp.* 96–99: ἰάπτει δ' ἐλπίδων ἀφ' ὑψιπύργων πανώλεις βροτούς). Agamemnon and his "Argive beast" leap over the walls of Troy like a lion (*Ag.* 827–828); but Polyneices and his army epitomize the arrogance of siege warfare in the *Septem*. Capaneus' shield emblem—a naked torch-bearer scaling the ramparts and uttering the words "I shall sack the city" (πρήσω πόλιν, *Sept.* 434)—illustrates "high-towered hopes." Zeus strikes Capaneus dead with a bolt of lightning as he reaches the top of the fortifications (cf. Soph. *Ant.* 127–137; Eur. *Phoen.* 1172–1186). Capaneus's desire, like Xerxes' intention to enslave Greece (*Pers.* 820) and the Argive desire to "sack what is not right" (*Ag.* 341–342), exceeds the boundaries of human power (cf. ὁ κόμπος δ' οὐ κατ' ἄνθρωπον φρονεῖ, πύργοις δ' ἀπειλεῖ δείν', *Sept.* 425–426) and necessarily provokes violent reaction. As forms of war and of glory, as a mentality of exchange that routinely expends life and property for profit, Agamemnon's naval alliance and siege warfare contain the basis for divine and human recrimination.

We occasionally hear justifications for Agamemnon such as K. J. Dover's:[93]

Agamemnon took the course most people with Greek values and presuppositions would have felt bound to regard as dictated by honour, justice, piety and the overriding obligation to subordinate the lives of one's dependants to the common good. We must remember not only Euripides' treatment of the sacrifice of Chthonia by Erechtheus but the use Lycurgus makes of the story in addressing a jury.

Euripides debunked this interpretation of the sacrifice of Iphigenia in the *Electra:* Clytemnestra excludes Iphigenia's sacrifice from those intended to save the *polis* or to benefit the household and protect the rest of the children (Eur. *El.* 1024–1026). Erechtheus sacrificed his daughter to save the *polis* from Eumolpos and the Thracians. Agamemnon sacrificed his daughter for a different reason; his city comes under a tyranny in the process. The salvation of the *polis* has determinant features, most notably the defense of freedom. This theme is not present in the *Oresteia* until after the murder of Agamemnon, when the chorus perceives the plot to establish tyranny in Argos (*Ag.* 1354–1355; 1633–1635). The chorus harshly criticizes the king's choice both during his absence and to his face (218–227; 799–804); it does not invent a justification. In the *Agamemnon*, the explicit cost of the failure to sacrifice Iphigenia is the alliance of which Agamemnon is *hēgemōn*. There are other costs: the satisfaction of vengeance against Paris and his city for the theft of Helen and dishonor to the table of the Atreidai, the booty that accrues to the city-sacker, and the glory of military victory (cf. esp. *Cho.* 302–304; 345–363). Of these, only the last survives in the Athens of the *Eumenides.*

In the *Eumenides* Athena charges the Erinyes to "pray for those things that aim at no base victory" (ὁποῖα νίκης μὴ κακῆς ἐπίσκοπα, *Eum.* 903). This could mean, as it does in the *Septem*, a victory in which the hoplite stands his ground and fights, irrespective of fear—a form of fighting that Plato directly contrasts with marine tactics, which involve the contradictory concept of "retreat without dishonor" (Pl. *Leg.* 706c5–d1); it could also mean siege victory of the kind Agamemnon won and the Athenians commemorated at Eion. Moreover, Athena instructs the Erinyes "to suppress what is destructive madness to the land, and send what is profitable for the victory of the city" (τὸ μὲν ἀτηρὸν χώρας κατέχειν, τὸ δὲ κερδαλέον πέμπειν πόλεως ἐπὶ νίκῃ, 1007–1009).[94] Profit and victory are related to one another. In the *Agamemnon*, however, the sheer retributive destruction of life and property, the weight of booty, and the magnitude of *kleos* measure the profit of war. In the *Eumenides*, Athena enjoins the Erinyes to pray for prosperity and fertility of the kind the Hesiodic and Homeric father-king provides: fecundating effects of the wind from land, sea, and heaven; the fertility of flocks, fields, and people (921–926; 937–947, here including mines; 956–967; 980–983); the absence of civil war; and the growth of reverent citizens (904–913). The sea, associated with excessive exchange wealth, booty, and divine retribution in the *Agamemnon*, is called "marine dew" (ποντίας δρόσου, *Eum.* 904) in the *Eumenides* and invoked to contribute to the fecundity, piety, and justice of the inhabitants of Attica. These elements of Athenian bounty were inimical to the Argive siege force at Troy (*Ag.* 555–567) and combined to destroy the Argive fleet, which fled "Hades on the sea" ("Αιδην πόντιον πεφευγότες, *Ag.* 667–668). The abundance of the earth expresses the profit of war, and it is significant that, while Agamemnon returns from Troy with a concubine, Athena returns with a claim to land in the Troad that can be passed down from father to son (*Eum.* 397–402). Land is not an object of exchange and hence is not tainted with the dangers and moral ambiguity of profit.[95]

The *Eumenides* validates both the Athenian project of glory through war and what that project threatens to destroy, the yearning for justice, prosperity, and purity in the eyes of the gods. Athena insists that her citizens be just and that "war be on the outside—present in abundance—in which there will be some terrible desire for glory" (θυραῖος ἔστω πόλεμος, οὐ μόλις παρὼν / ἐν ᾧ τις ἔσται δεινὸς εὐκλείας ἔρως, *Eum.* 864–865). She will not tolerate her city's lack of honor for victory in battle (τήνδ' ἀστύνικον ἐν βροτοῖς τιμᾶν πόλιν, 913–915). It is difficult to harmonize these lines with the trilogy as a whole.[96] The year before the trilogy's presentation the city lost over 1,000 men in war, and casualties in 459/8 were heavy.[97] The bulk of the fleet was in Cyprus and Egypt while Athenians fought land battles in the Megarid and naval battles at Aegina and around the Argolid. Around the time of the drama Spartan hoplites lingered in Boeotia, uncertain of their route home, and reputedly in negotiations with the Athenians to halt the construction of the Long Walls and to dissolve the democracy (Thuc. 1.104–107).[98] The Erinyes pray that aggression be expressed outside the *polis*: "To exchange favors with a spirit that loves community, and to hate with a single mind: this is the cure (ἄκος) for many human ailments" (*Eum.* 984–997). We should emphasize the curative function of the prayer. The *Eumenides* seeks an antidote to civil war in unified public emotions and in war outside the *polis*. The drama affirms the public value of Agamemnon's *kleos*. Yet the trilogy seeks to instill the awareness that prolonged fighting outside the *polis* also breeds internal dissension and subversion. Civil war is more catastrophic than external war (cf. Hdt. 8.3.1), just as Aegisthus' and Clytemnestra's tyranny is worse than Agamemnon's excessive will to power in Troy.

Agamemnon's fate is a limiting case. He embodies a set of public values, but his story demonstrates the limits of those values. The expenditures of life Agamemnon made as *hēgemōn*, the *kleos* he purchased with them, his delusion that the sack and destruction of Troy were rooted in a single divine justice (*Ag.* 810–829)—these create the conditions for his subversion. The attainment of hegemony is based on the willingness to kill; Agamemnon's story shows how the curse provoked by such killing works itself out over time—from the struggle between Atreus and Thyestes for the scepter, to Agamemnon's sacrifice of Iphigenia and his annihilation of Troy, to Clytemnestra's and Aegisthus' murder of Agamemnon and assumption of tyranny, to Orestes' matricide and the threat of the Erinyes. Aeschylus' mythmaking appropriates the curse for

Athens to avoid the fate of Agamemnon and to profit from it by saving his heir and binding his army to the city. The Areopagus is an institution that has legal jurisdiction over killing; the cult of the Semnai Theai provides the fearful face of justice and insures fertility, growth, and the absence of plague and civil war; the alliance with Argos may prevent a Spartan army from marching through the Argolid and the Megarid to Attica and at least provide advanced notice of a march (cf., e.g., Hdt. 9.12). The trilogy seeks to harmonize war and justice by depicting the boundaries of war and killing as a form of justice.

The *Oresteia* adopts a strategy toward the Areopagus similar to the one it employs toward hegemony: it depicts an old form that both delimits and validates its new form. No doubt the Areopagus lent its prestige to Cimon when he persuaded the assembly to send 4,000 Athenian hoplites to help Sparta besiege the helots who had barricaded themselves on Mount Ithome by arguing that the city should not allow "Hellas to become lame or to neglect the city that had become a yoke-mate" (μήτε τὴν Ἑλλάδα χωλὴν μήτε πόλιν ἑτερόζυγα περιιδεῖν γεγενημένην, Ion of Chios, in Plut. *Cim.* 16.8).[99] Aeschylus hints at the language of this debate in the *Oresteia*: he calls the Atreidai "twin thrones and twin scepters from Zeus, the mighty yoke of honor of the sons of Atreus" (τιμῆς ὀχυρὸν ζεῦγος Ἀτρειδᾶν, *Ag.* 41–44). Menelaus' disappearance in the *Agamemnon* isolates Agamemnon as sole *hēgemōn*, inducing an identification between him and the audience. But Menelaus' reappearance in the *Proteus* might permit the audience to relax its view toward Sparta as its mythical king perhaps freed a chorus of satyrs from Egypt—where thousands of Athenians were fighting to help wrench it from Persian control. Using the outmoded form of Agamemnon's hegemony, the *Oresteia* validates Athenian hegemony while warning about the problems endemic to it, but it does not reject a dual hegemony in Hellas.

Ephialtes and a significant body of citizens opposed Cimon's mission and the concept of a dual hegemony in Hellas. While Cimon was in Sparta, Ephialtes prosecuted members of the Areopagus and legally removed what he claimed were the council's "acquired" (ἐπίθετα) powers, restoring it to its "ancestral" (πάτρια) condition as a murder court (*AP* 25.1; Plut. *Cim.* 15.1–2).[100] When Cimon returned from Sparta, he tried to undo these changes, but was ostracized (Plut. *Cim.* 15.3–5, 17.3; *Per.* 9.5). Ephialtes was later assassinated, exacerbating the fears of pollution and civil war in Athens the *Eumenides* expresses (858–863; 979–987). The constitutional changes probably placed ultimate judicial and legislative authority in the *dēmos* as well as oversight of magistrates before and after their tenure in office (*dokimasia* and *euthuna*). Charges lodged by "impeachment" (*eisangelia*) were tried before the Boule and *dēmos*, out of the jurisdiction of the Areopagus.[101] More important for Aeschylus, the city was free to carry a policy of expansion into the Peloponnese.

It had renounced the notion of a dual hegemony and, with it, safeguards on violence in Hellas.

The message of the *Eumenides* supports neither the democrat-imperialists nor the traditionalists in this conflict: it cuts a path between them, combining praise and warning in the manner of Solon and seeking moderation as a form of power for the city, "every middle where God bestows the power" (παντὶ μέσῳ τὸ κράτος θεὸς ὤπασεν, 529). The *Eumenides* dramatizes the ancestral (πάτριος) jurisdiction of the Areopagus as a murder court and subordinates it to the will of the warrior goddess Athena. The language of paternity in the trial scene is important in this regard: the trilogy reinstates Agamemnon in the role of father (*Cho.* 55–60; 124–163; 246–263; 483–485; 486–488) before it uses his paternity as the decisive element in his favor (κάρτα δ' εἰμι τοῦ πατρός, *Eum.* 738), making the Areopagus an institution that upholds the rights of the father, though its own vote might be taken to undermine it (734–753).[102] That this father is "the completely feared and respected leader of ships" restores compatibility to the roles of father and naval leader that the *Agamemnon* made tragically irreconcilable.

The drama adopts the language of the Areopagus' outmoded "acquired powers" to depict its middle course: this is the form in which the dominant ideology of the drama appears. The Areopagus is a council rather than a court (βουλευτήριον, 684, 704), a guardian, savior, and protector (*Eum.* 701, cited above; ἐγρήγορος φρούρημα γῆς, 706; πόλεως φρούριον, 948),[103] a body composed of "the best of my citizens" (ἀστῶν τῶν ἐμῶν τὰ βέλτατα, 487). Unlike the Areopagites whom Ephialtes prosecuted (*AP* 25.2), and Agamemnon, the Areopagus is "untouched by profit" (κερδῶν ἄθικτον, 704). Most strikingly, the *Eumenides* makes the effectiveness of the council depend upon traditional law: alteration of *polis* law is damaging. The Areopagus fulfills its function only if the assembly does not change the laws of the city, polluting them with "bad influxes and with muck" (693–695). This is hardly encouragement of democratic *nomoi*.[104] Law should be internalized by fear and reverence rather than written (cf. the contempt for written law in *Supp.* 940–949; divine law is written: *Supp.* 707–709; cf. fr. 282.20). The *Eumenides* endorses a tradition that the reforms doomed to obsolescence: obedience to the laws (θέσμια) of the Erinyes, which later became the "unwritten laws" (respect for parents, strangers, and gods, 490–565; cf. *Supp.* 708).[105] The institution (θεσμός) of the Areopagus (484, 615; cf. 571) is a repository for the "fear and reverence" of citizens and a guardian against injustice in Athens (683–711). Aeschylus commands a language to describe democracy: this requires the word *dēmos* and its cognates (*Supp.* 699, 943). The word *dēmos* does not appear in the *Eumenides*. The words λεώς and στρατός (556, 569, 638, 668, 683, 762, 775, 889) designate the Athenians, as do honorific titles such as "the children of Kranaos."[106] Agamemnon is twice praised as a leader of sailors (456, 637), but there are no sailors, ships, siege armies, or "kings of ships" in the Athens of the *Eumenides*.[107]

An anecdote may serve as a conclusion: in the year 468, a young Sophocles, who was said to have stripped and anointed himself with oil to sing epinician odes while the sailors who fought at Salamis lounged at their victory monument (*Vit. Soph.* 3), competed for the first time against Aeschylus, veteran of Marathon and composer of his own epinician on Salamis, the *Persians*. There was a nervous energy in the theater, and the archon for the year, Apsephion, thought the crowd might get out of hand. When the ten generals led by Cimon entered the theater to make their customary libations before the contest, Apsephion would not let them depart: he insisted that they act as judges to insure order and fairness in the determination of the victory and administered the oath to them. After watching the play, the generals proclaimed Sophocles the winner. Aeschylus, the story goes, stormed off to Sicily (*Plut. Cim.* 7–8). That the generals preferred Sophocles to Aeschylus may indicate more than their aesthetic preferences. I hope I have suggested why.

NOTES

1. Duby 1974/1985:154.

2. For the meaning of "history" as "the events of the past," see Ehrenberg 1954:12.

3. Scholars have recently restored faith in Aristotle's contention that tragedy derived from an undifferentiated satyr genre (ἐκ τοῦ σατυρικοῦ, *Poet.* 1449a20). See Seaford 1976:209–221, 1984:10–11; Nagy 1990:385. For the plot of captivity and liberation, see Sutton 1980:145–148; Seaford 1984:43. Cf. Seaford 1981:272 with n. 2: "the myth of the captivity and liberation of the *thiasos* was associated with the origins of tragedy." Whether Pratinas' fragment is satyr genre (Seaford 1977:81–94) or dithyramb (*DTC*[2] 20), it poses as an attempt to stop *hubris* (*PMG* 708.2). Cf. Bacchyl. 15.57–63.

4. I take *oikos* as the referent of νῦν. Garvie (1986:265) prefers Orestes.

5. The *Suppliants* and *Septem* also play on a satyric pattern of captivity, liberation, and the conquest of *hubris*. Space does not permit a discussion of the details.

6. Cf. de Romilly 1947/1964:80, with special application to Thucydides, "the act of ruling was really considered as the perfect expression of both internal and external freedom, and, in fact, as a superior freedom." De Romilly notes that the conception is widespread in "the ancient world" (127 n. 1); cf. 84–86 and Forde 1989:39–40.

7. For Fornara 1971:78, "it is no understatement to say that for Herodotus this was an immutable law of history." Herodotus' historical vision is therefore the precursor of Polyb. *Hist.* 1.2; Arr. *Anab.* 2.6.7.; *Dion. Hal. Ant. Rom.* 1.2–3; Souda 4289, s.v. Ἀσσύριοι.

8. Cf. Meiggs 1972:376: "When he considered the Athenian empire we may guess that the question uppermost in his mind was: 'How will it end?'"

9. For the Sestos episode, see Redfield 1985:115; Konstan 1987:72; Boedeker 1988:

30–48. For the *Histories* as a warning to Athens, see Fornara 1971:75–93; Wood 1972: 193; Nagy 1990:308.

10. For the connection between tyranny and bodily mutilation, see Hartog 1988:332.

11. All translations in this paper are my own.

12. A recurring problem for the Hellenes, even for democratic Athens: Thuc. 3.98; 4.34–41.

13. This is a controversial point. See *ATL* 3.207. For the view that the catalogue is a "geographical extravaganza of the kind beloved by Aeschylus and his audience," see Robertson 1980a:90–91, n. 47. Like the map shown to Cleomenes (Hdt. 5.49.5–8) and the maps of Sicily and the African coastline Athenians sketched before the invasion of Sicily (Plut. *Nicias* 12; *Alc.* 17), "geographical extravaganzas" visualize a sphere of dominion. I agree with *ATL* 3.194–225; Blackman 1969:179–183; Meiggs 1972:50–67; Balcer 1984:331–335; and others in believing that the membership of the Delian League was originally large.

14. Nagy 1990:14 and passim illuminates how the logic of praise contains an implicit warning.

15. Reading with Page 1972; West 1990 athetizes ἐσορᾶν.

16. Darius' fighting is confined to archery, infantry, cavalry, and siege: *Pers.* 102–107; 244; 556; 857–862; 901–903. He is the harmless "father," whose soldiers return from battle and under whom Persia enjoyed good civic order: 555–556; 652–657; 662–671; 852–856; 861–862; 864–866. Ships share responsibility with Xerxes for the disaster (550–562) in contrast to Darius' successful leadership of archers (555–557). For the "spiritual problem" of "Athenian thalassocracy" in the *Persians*, see Momigliano 1944/1960:58.

17. See Badian 1987/1993:1–72, who argues that the "Peace of Kallias" should be dated in the 460's, after the Battle of the Eurymedon (466 B.C.).

18. Galpin 1983/1984:esp. 108–109, whose conclusion, however, is rejected by Ober 1989:23–24.

19. Connor 1989:7–32.

20. Modern scholarship locates Aeschylus either on the left of the democratic spectrum (e.g., Forrest 1960:221–241 and Podlecki 1966, who consider Aeschylus to be allied with Themistocles and Ephialtes; the tradition is venerable—cf. Themistocles' letter to Aeschylus [1 Hercher]); its center (e.g., Thomson 1945:309; Dodds 1960/1973:49–50; Dover 1957/1987:161–175; Meier 1980/1990:114; Rhodes 1981:312); or its right (e.g., Müller 1853:71–81).

21. For the tradition, see Harmon 1920:12–25; Davison 1949:66–93, 1966:93–107; Post 1950:49–52; Stössl 1952:113–139. Cole (1977:99–111) offers a complex version of the allegorical tradition, claiming that Agamemnon and Orestes figure two sides of Cimon, and that the *Oresteia* argues that Cimon should be recalled from ostracism and internecine violence turned outward.

22. For the construction of the Persian fleet and regularization of tribute payments to finance it see Wallinga 1987:47–77; cf. Ferrill 1985:85–89.

23. For the building of the Athenian fleet (probably 100 ships), see Hdt. 7.144.1 (200 ships); Thuc. 1.14.3; *AP* 22.7 (100 ships); Plut. *Them.* 4.2 (100 ships). Some version of Thuc. 1.14.3 must be correct, as opposed to Plut. *Them.* 4.2: both Persia and Aegina were behind the decision to build.

24. For Minos as the mythical embodiment of "the form assumed by Athenian imperialism," see de Romilly 1947/1963:67–68.

25. For the belatedness of Athenian naval power, see Haas 1985:29–46.

26. Haas (1985:45) has seen that these ships were pentekonters and not triremes. Athens borrowed ships of war from Corinth in the 490's and 480's to fight Aegina (Hdt. 6.89; Thuc. 1.41.2). It is unlikely the Athenians would send 4,000 men, perhaps half of its available manpower, on this mission.

27. Hdt. 7.9a2; *HCT* 1.10–15; Hanson 1989:3–39.

28. Cf. *ATL* 3.185: "Such was the unfortunate precedent for the later collection of tribute."

29. See Wallinga 1987:47–77. The Athenians remembered this (Thuc. 6.82.3–4).

30. Hdt. 9.116–120; Thuc. 1.89.2; Diod. Sic. 11.37.4–5. Sestos was a supremely difficult place to besiege: Xen. *Hell.* 4.8.5.

31. Hdt. 8.3.2; Thuc. 1.94–95, 128–135; Diod. Sic. 1.44–46. For Pausanias, see, e.g., Fornara 1966:257–271; Lang 1967:79–85; Rhodes 1970:387–400; Westlake 1977/1989: 1–18.

32. To be tributary is to be "enslaved": Hdt. 1.6.2–3; 7.108. The first district was assessed at 400 Babylonian talents (= 466 silver talents) (Hdt. 3.90.1). Aristeides' assessment was 460 talents (Thuc. 1.96.2). I agree with *ATL* 3.234; Balcer 1984:204–205; and others in thinking that Athens derived the figure from Artaphrenes' assessment. The classic statement to the contrary is Murray 1966:142–156; Murray 1988:489 is more tentative. Ehrenberg 1960:115 captured the spirit of the problem: "the mere fact of a *phoros* was felt as an infringement of autonomy." Cf. also Robertson 1980a:65. In the Greek *polis*, tax and tribute are forms of subordination and communication of status in which the payer marks his inferiority to the payee; cf. Whitehead 1977:76. It is worth noting that Mycenaean *e-re-u-te-ro* (ἐλευθερ-) seems to mean "free from tax or tribute." See Morpugo 1963, s.v. *e-re-u-te-ra;* Ventris and Chadwick 1972:298, 310, 469.

33. The fall of Eion: Thuc. 1.98.1; colonization: Plut. *Cim.* 7.3; date: schol. Aeschin. 2.34; *ATL* 3.158–160; *HCT* 1.394; Steinbrecher 1985:37–38. Diod. Sic. 11.60.2 dates the fall to 470/69; Smart 1967:136–138 dates likewise. Skyros: Thuc. 1.98.2; Plut. *Thes.* 36.1–4; *Cim.* 8.5–7; Diod. Sic. 11.60.3. Steinbrecher 1985:39 dates it to 476/5; cf. *HCT* 1.399; Podlecki 1971:141–143 dates it to *c.* 470; Levy 1976:277–279 to 469/8, the "first excess" of the league, followed by Naxos' revolt.

34. War with Thasos: Thuc. 1.100.2–101.3; Plut. *Cim.* 14.2; Diod. Sic. 11.70.1; Nepos *Cimon* 2.5. *ATL* 3.258 follows Thucydides and sees the war as a bid for Thasos' markets and mines in Thrace and part of the effort to colonize the "Nine Ways." Balcer (1984: 368, 371) follows Diod. Sic. 11.70.3, dating "the processes of Athenian imperialism" to this war. Cf. Meiggs 1972:84–86.

35. Meiggs 1972:42–108; *ATL* 3.187–264; Steinbrecher 1985:51–115; Rhodes 1985 and 1992:34–61 accept Thucydides' belief that Athenian hegemony began as an instrument of liberation and later became a form of suppression. The Delian League was a force for both from its origin and was modeled rather more on Persian imperialism than most have been prepared to admit.

36. ML² 33; cf. *SEG* XXXIV 45. As Lewis (1992:113, n. 57) suggests, "the total surely ran well into four figures" for the year. Cf. *AP* 26.1.

37. Cf. Thuc. 1.23.1–2; for the *topos,* Cobet 1986:11.

38. For the ideal: Hes. *Op.* 225–237; *Od.* 19.107–114; Plato *Resp.* 363a5–c2. See Eliade 1949/1974:128–129; Detienne 1973:298–300; Vidal-Naquet 1973:271, 283–285; Vernant 1965/1983:140–141.

39. Liberation: Solon fr. 36.7 (West), 36.15; *PMG* 893–896. Liberation and salvation of Hellas: ML² 23.15–16, 26.I.4; cf. Aesch. *Pers.* 242, 402–404; Pind. fr. 77 (Snell); Hdt. 7.139.5, 144.2; Thuc. 1.73.4–74.4; West 1970:271–282. Conquest of *hubris*: Hdt. 5.77.4 (= ML² 15a1, b3); Bacchyl. 17.39–41, 18.15–30; Hdt. 8.3.2; 9.27.2.

40. See Manville 1990:132, 183; Ober 1989:62.

41. For the representation of the *thiasos* in Attic vase painting and the proliferation of scenes showing the return of Hephaestus after the reforms of Solon (*c.* 580–570), see Schöne 1987:18–47; Carpenter 1991:13–16. That it is *hubris* to enslave or imprison Dionysus or his *thiasos* is a commonplace: Eur. *Bacch.* 516–518; cf. 374–375, 555; *H. H. Dion.* 7.12–14; Eur. *Bacch.* 443–450, 499, 516–518, 613, 616–617. For Dionysus as liberator, see Connor 1989:18–19; for festivals of liberation, Connor 1985:96–99. For the relationship among Dionysus, the *thiasos*, and the *polis*, see Seaford 1993:134, n. 88.

42. For Dionysus and the myths of his exclusion from the *polis*, see Kerenyi 1976: 129–188. For the threat of exclusion at the heart of Cleisthenes' reforms, see Manville 1990:198: "the reforms were (in the immediate context) a response to the aristocratically motivated *diapsēphismos* of 510/9" (cf. 206). For accounts of the mechanism, causes, agents, and victims of the *diapsēphismos*, see Manville 1990:173–185, with bibliography. Arist. *Pol.* 1275b34–39 claims that Cleisthenes "enrolled many strangers and slave-metics into the tribes" (πολλοὺς γὰρ ἐφυλέτευσε ξένους καὶ δούλους μετοίκους).

43. For the Athenian heroic image of the tyrant slayers see Taylor 1981; for an interpretation of its political significance, see Podlecki 1966b:129–141.

44. Cf. Burkert 1977/1985:165, "it is in this inversion [sc. of the normal order of the *polis*] that Dionysos fulfils his true nature." See Hendrichs 1984:205–239; Segal 1982: esp. 7–26.

45. E.g., Hdt. 7.10β1; 7.161.3; 8.44.1; note the irony of 8.62.2; 8.140β4; 9.27.2; 9.27.5–6 (Marathon): μοῦνοι Ἑλλήνων δὴ μουνομαχήσαντες τῷ Πέρσῃ . . . ἀπὸ τούτου μούνου τοῦ ἔργου. Cf. Thuc. 1.73.4; 2.40.5; 2.41.2–3; Lys. 2.20, 57; [Dem.] 60.4, 9, 11; Lycurg. *Leoc.* 70; Loraux 1973:20–21, 1981/1986:158–159; de Romilly 1947/1963:245.

46. Hdt. 1.60.3; 2.51.1, 4; 5.78; 6.109.3, 109.6, 112.3; cf. 8.11.2, 8.21.2, 9.28.6. For the μόνος-πρῶτος *topos*, Lys. 2.18; Pl. *Menex.* 237e7–238a3; cf. Arist. *Rh.* 1368a10–11; Walters 1980:3–4.

47. Zeitlin 1986/1990:132.

48. For the term "historical moment" of tragedy, see Vernant 1968/1988:23–28. Connor (1989:25–32) argues that the City Dionysia and tragic performances were instituted after Cleisthenes' reforms; this is an attractive hypothesis and may be correct. Cf. West 1989:251–254. My view is that whatever form it assumed before Aeschylus, tragedy was a major genre only after the Persian Wars, when the Athenian civic identity was projected in fixed, heroic narratives and the genre adopted epic myth as its material, both dramatizing and distinguishing the Athenian identity on stage. Else (1964:32) believes the genre was "not completely there in 472 when Aeschylus wrote the *Persians*." For the Persian Wars as critical in the evolution of tragedy, see Knox 1978:48. For a sketch of tragedy in decline, see Lesky 1972/1983:394–405.

49. For the *ainos* of *Ag.* 717–736, "as a reference not only to various characters of

the *Oresteia*, but even to the audience itself as the embodiment of the Athenian empire," see Nagy 1990:312.

50. Else 1964:38.

51. For the *Tatenkatalog* of mythical and historical exploits that justified Athenian hegemony and arose shortly after the Persian Wars, see Kierdorf 1966, esp. 89–97; Thomas 1989:212–213. For Athenian civic ideology and public art, see Castriota 1992, esp. 33–133.

52. Argive Seven: Aesch. *Eleusinioi* (475–470?—so Hauvette 1898:159–178). Cf. Plut. *Thes.* 29.4; Hdt. 9.27.3. Herakleidai: Aesch. *Herakleidai* (*TrGF* 3.190–193); Hdt. 9.27.2. Amazons of Thermodon: Aesch. *Eum.* 685–690; cf. *PV* 415–416, 721–727; Hdt. 9.27.4. Amazons on the Athenian treasury at Delphi: Boardman 1982:1–28; Dinsmoor 1946:111–113; Tyrell 1984:7. Trojan War and Menestheus: Eion Epigram, Plut. *Cim.* 7.4– 5 (= Aeschin. *Ctes.* 184–185); *FGE* XL; Aesch. *Eum.* 397–402; Hdt. 7.161.3, 9.27.4. Cimon returned Theseus' bones to Athens from Skyros, probably *c.* 475 (Plut. *Cim.* 8.3–6) and constructed the Theseion to house them. For an historical reading of Bacchyl. 17 and 18 see Barron 1980:1–8; for the paintings of the Theseion, see Paus. 1.17.2–3; Barron 1972: 20–45. For Theseus, see Connor 1970:143–174. For the Stoa Poikile, see Meritt 1970: 233–264; Shear 1984:5–19; Castriota 1992:76–89.

53. Cf. Meiggs 1972:69; Barron 1980:2.

54. The Spartan recovery of Orestes' bones from Tegea and appropriation of Agamemnon's line: Hdt. 1.67.1–68.6, 7.134, 159.1; Adshead 1986:29–30; Pind. *Pyth.* 11.16, 31– 32; Paus. 3.19.6; schol. Eur. *Or.* 46; Bowra 1934:115–119.

55. Or, as Francis and Vickers (1985:99–113) argue, the mustering of the Plataeans and Athenians at the village of Oenoe in Attica before the Battle of Marathon.

56. Wilamowitz (1907:93) saw Aeschylus' introduction of dialogue and heroic myth as the origin of drama and tragedy respectively. Herington (1985:138) sees tragedy as we know it in the use of Homeric techniques to dramatize myth, a step he dates to the period 499–472. For another view, see Lloyd-Jones 1966/1990:225–227, 231–232.

57. Cf. Herington 1985:129; for a slightly different view, see Hall 1989:65–70.

58. For "social drama," see Turner 1982:61–87, esp. 72–73. Cf. Ober and Strauss 1990:245–246; Pozzi and Wickersham 1991:2.

59. For παῖδες Ἀθηναίων, see Hdt. 5.77.2 (= *FGE* III.693, *c.* 506); ML² 18.5 *c.* 490; Plut. *Them.* 8.4 (= *FGE* XXIV.781, *c.* 480); *FGE* XVIII.754; Pind. fr. 77. The Hellenes at Salamis are assimilated to the form in Aeschylus, παῖδες Ἑλλήνων, *Pers.* 402; cf. Pind. *Isth.* 3/4.54b; fr. 118; Bacchyl. 8.11 [restored]. The hippeis at Tanagra, however, are called κοῦροι Ἀθηναίων (*FGE* XLIX.889).

60. Page 1959:146 with n. 79, pp. 173–175; cf. Kirk 1985:179–180, 205–207.

61. Cf. Hermassi (1977:23), who neglects the fact that tragedy was an exhibition of *allotria pathē*.

62. Cf. Segal 1962:132.

63. It is impossible to feel pity for one's *oikeioi*. We can pity *alloi* or *heteroi*, "others": Arist. *Rh.* 1386a17–23; cf. Hdt. 3.14.9–10. What we fear for ourselves or our *oikeioi* is pitiable when it happens to others: *Rh.* 1382b26; 1386a28–29. Fear requires the perception of similarity: φόβος δὲ περὶ τὸν ὅμοιον, Arist. *Poet.* 1453a5–6. For περί here, see Belfiore 1992:231; otherwise Else 1957:372. For fear as an "ego-centric" emotion, see Heath 1987:11.

64. For different views of the play and event, see Marx 1928:337–360; Freymuth 1955:51–69; Lloyd-Jones 1966/1990:225–237; Roisman 1988:15–23.

65. For booty as central to the activities of the Delian League, see Pritchett 1971:61–67; Sealey 1966:233–253. The Persians probably knocked out Athenian mines. See Starr 1970:17.

66. For the stockpiling of silver reserves, see Robertson 1980a:65, 1980b:112–119; French 1972:19; ATL 3.238. Meiggs 1972:65 is not compelling.

67. For the date and significance of the Long Walls, see Fornara and Samons 1991: 129–132.

68. Cf. Salkever 1986:295, n. 50; Belfiore 1992:229.

69. Jameson 1981:102.

70. οἴκαδε κέρδος ἄρηαι, Hes. Op. 632, cf. 673; Solon 13.44, οἴκαδε κέρδος ἄγειν; cf. Od. 8.160–164.

71. Theophr. Char. 3.3; DFA² 58–59. The alternate tradition is the Panathenaia: Arist. Gen. An. 724b2. Hes. Op. 663–688 endorses a season between June and August, i.e., what becomes the Panathenaic tradition, and rejects sailing even in late April. From this perspective, Athenian Elaphebolion was far too early for anyone to take to the sea.

72. The ship-cart processions are problematic. DFA² 12 with nn. 12–13 associates them with the Anthesteria, but acknowledges these scenes may be independent of a particular festival. Kerenyi (1976:172) seems to think that the ship scene represents Dionysus' arrival to Eleuther and was part of the procession of the City Dionysia.

73. For Dionysus as navigator see Daraki 1985:31–44.

74. For collection of the tribute, presumably 454 and later (though not necessarily), see Pritchett 1969:17–21; Robertson 1980b:112–119; Ar. Ach. 505–506 with schol. to 504; Eupolis fr. 240 [Kock]; Isoc. De Pace 82; ML² 46.19. Late payments arrive after the Dionysia: ML² 50.

75. The assembly convened after the Dionysia, and the Hellenotamiai reported on the receipts: ML² 46.18–22 (c. 447); 68.12–15 (426).

76. See Goldhill 1987/1990:97–129.

77. In general, see Hall 1989:160–200; more specifically, Zuntz 1955:11. For praise of Athens in tragedy, see Butts 1942:9–175. For persuasion see Buxton 1982:10–18.

78. Knox 1957:53–106.

79. Menestheus personifies the Athenian warrior: FGE LX.1–6; cf. Hdt. 7.161.3. Cf. Parker 1987:187: "Attic mythology is therefore a distinctive 'political mythology,' through which the Athenians forged a sense of their identity as a people." The most detailed verbal example of the logic of condensation is [Dem.] 50.27–31, where the name of each tribal archēgos personifies the character of each tribe. Plato and Aristotle assume that characteristics such as justice and happiness are attributes of the city and citizens (e.g., Plato, Resp. 368e2–369a3; Arist. Pol. 1324a5–13). For the principle in Herodotus, see Cobet 1986:16.

80. None of Homer's titles for Agamemnon includes the specifics of his military command. See Furtwängler in Roscher, s.v. Agamemnon.

81. For official Athenian terminology, see Jordan 1975:117, 121, with sources.

82. See Winnington-Ingram 1983:82–83. My interpretation is compatible with Fraenkel 1950:123.

83. For the meaning of the term, see *HCT* 1.283. Dover (1977/1987:159) points out that diction of *Ag.* 212–213 lends Agamemnon's decision a contemporary flavor.

84. For πλειών (seed) see West 1978:312–313; for the Pleiades see his note to line 619.

85. Loraux 1981/1986:99; for the idea of death in the *epitaphios*, see 98–118.

86. See most recently Crane (1993:117–136), who argues that the scene represents both Agamemnon's lack of aristocratic *megaloprepeia*, and democratic suspicions of the rich and powerful.

87. Reading χρόνῳ at *Eum.* 1000 with the MSS; Page 1972; and Sommerstein 1989. West (1990) accepts Heerweden's emendation of κόρῳ.

88. See Barron 1980:4 for the tendency; cf. Castriota 1992:86.

89. See Leahy 1974:5.

90. For the Stoa, see *Agora* 94–96; Shear 1984:40–43. Woodhead (1981:188) describes it as "the favorite assembly-place of the young cavalrymen, the well-to-do hippeis, and of the phylarchs who commanded and trained them."

91. The text is that of *FGE* XL. For the arrangement of the verses adopted, and the probable date of composition, see Jacoby 1945:187–193; Gomme 1948:5–7. Wade-Gery (1933:94) accepts the text of Plut. *Cim.* 7.4–6 and Aeschin. *Ctes.* 184–185 and argues (p. 74) for a date of composition after the Battle of the Eurymedon.

92. West (1990) thinks *Ag.* 527 should be deleted; Fraenkel (1950:266–267) condemns it. His justification, that "no reference to Agamemnon can be found in lines 338–43" (p. 267, n. 2), is probably mistaken; his uncritical view of Agamemnon is open to challenge. Denniston and Page (1957) offer an adequate defense of the lines.

93. Dover 1973/1987:145–146.

94. Reading the MS χώρας κατέχειν. Sommerstein (1989:274) compares *Pers.* 220–223.

95. Finley 1973:118; 1981:71; Osborne 1985:47–63; E. M. Wood 1988:81–125.

96. See Dodds 1960/1973:51–52 and Sommerstein 1989:251 for the view that *Eum.* 858–866 were late insertions to the scene. Taplin (1977:401, n. 1) rejects them.

97. Lewis 1992:133, n. 47.

98. For a date in 458 see Lewis 1992:112–113; dating these events in relation to the drama is impossible. The point is that the city was at war on a number of fronts.

99. 4,000 hoplites: Ar. *Lys.* 1143–1144. Cf. Thuc. 1.102.1; Plut. *Cim.* 16.8; Diod. Sic. 11.64.2; Meiggs 1972:87–91; *HCT* 1.300–302, 411 n. 1; Cole 1974:369–385.

100. Meiggs (1972:89 n. 3) is justified in making Cimon's absence a condition for the reform of the Areopagus. Hansen (1991:37, 126) links the reforms of both 462 and 411 to the absence of a significant portion of the voting population. See also Rhodes 1992b:69.

101. See Rhodes 1992b:71–74.

102. See Winnington-Ingram 1983:101–131; Goldhill 1984:99–207.

103. The Areopagus must have exercised some kind of "guardianship" of the laws (*AP* 3.6, 4.4, 8.4, 25.2) that was taken away by the reform. See Cawkwell 1988:1–12; Rhodes 1992b:72.

104. The edict of the Argive assembly in the *Suppliants* likewise validates an ancestral law (θέσμιον). The institutional arrangements and procedure are democratic, but the substance is the law of Hellas which Athens as *hēgemōn* took for itself to protect. The

vote of the *dēmos* is a decree that should not be written; it is written among the laws of the gods (*Supp.* 600–601; 701–709; 739–740; 942–949).

105. Cf. Ehrenberg 1954:167–172.

106. For the difference between λαός and δῆμος, see Donlan 1989:22.

107. Likewise, the citizens of Pelasgos' Argos are zeugiteis and hippeis (180–183); cf. γάμοροι (613) and the repeated use of ἐγχώριος to refer to citizens: 517, 492, 600. Argos lacks harbor and port (763–770). The only sailors there are Egyptians: Danaos is a "ship-owner" (ναύκληρος, 177) and "sailor" (ναυτής, 503); the sons of Aigyptos comprise a "navy" (ναυτικός στρατός, 764).

REFERENCES

Adshead, K. 1986. *The Politics of the Archaic Peloponnese.* London.

Agora = Homer A. Thompson and Richard E. Wycherley. *The Agora of Athens.* Vol. 14. Princeton 1972.

Allen, Thomas W. 1946. *Homeri Opera,* Tomus V. Oxford.

AP = AΘHNAIΩN ΠOΛITEIA. Mortimer Chambers, ed. Leipzig 1986.

ATL = Benjamin D. Meritt, Henry T. Wade-Gery, and Malcolm F. McGregor, eds. *The Athenian Tribute Lists.* Cambridge, Mass. Vol. 3: Princeton 1939–1953.

Badian, Ernst. 1987/1993. "The Peace of Kallias." In his *From Plataea to Potidaea: Studies in the History and Historiography of the Pentecontaetia.* Baltimore and London. (Originally published in *JHS* 107:1–39.)

Balcer, Jack M. 1984. *Sparda by the Bitter Sea: Imperial Interaction in Western Anatolia.* (Brown Judaic Studies 52.) Chico, Cal.

Barron, John P. 1972. "New Light on Old Walls: The Murals of the Theseion," *JHS* 92: 35–49.

———. 1980. "Bakchylides, Theseus, and a Wooly Cloak," *BICS* 27:1–8.

Belfiore, Elizabeth. 1992. *Tragic Pleasures: Aristotle on Plot and Emotion.* Princeton.

Blackman, David. 1969. "The Athenian Navy and Allied Naval Contributions in the Pentecontaetia," *GRBS* 10:179–216.

Boardman, John. 1982. "Herakles, Theseus, and the Amazons." In *The Eye of Greece,* Donna Kurtz and Brian A. Sparkes, eds., 1–28. Cambridge.

Boedeker, Deborah. 1988. "Protesilaos and the End of Herodotos' *Histories,*" *CA* 7: 30–48.

Bowra, Maurice. 1934. "Stesichorus in the Peloponnese," *CQ* 28:115–119.

Burkert, Walter. 1977/1985. *Greek Religion.* Trans. J. Raffan. Cambridge, Mass.

Butts, H. R. 1942. *The Glorification of Athens in Greek Drama.* (Iowa Studies in Classical Philology 11.) Ann Arbor.

Buxton, R. G. A. 1982. *Persuasion in Greek Tragedy: A Study of Peitho.* Cambridge.

*CAH*² 4. John Boardman, Nicholas G. L. Hammond, David M. Lewis, and Martin Ostwald, eds., *The Cambridge Ancient History, Volume IV: Persia, Greece, and the Western Mediterranean c. 525–479.* 2nd ed. Cambridge 1988.

*CAH*² 5. David M. Lewis, John Boardman, J. K. Davies, and Martin Ostwald, eds., *The Cambridge Ancient History, Volume V: The Fifth Century.* 2nd ed. Cambridge 1992.

Carpenter, Thomas H. 1991. *Art and Myth in Ancient Greece.* London.

Castriota, David. 1992. *Myth, Ethos, and Actuality: Official Art in Fifth-Century Athens*. London.

Cawkwell, George. 1988. "ΝΟΜΟΦΥΛΑΚΙΑ and the Areopagus," *JHS* 108:1–12.

Cobet, J. 1986. "Herodotus and Thucydides on War." In *Past Perspectives: Studies in Greek and Roman History Writing*, I. S. Moxon, J. D. Smart, and A. J. Woodman, eds., 1–18. Cambridge.

Cole, John R. 1974. "Cimon's Dismissal, Ephialtes' Revolution, and the Peloponnesian Wars," *GRBS* 15:369–385.

———. 1977. "The *Oresteia* and Cimon," *HSCP* 81:99–111.

Connor, W. Robert. 1970. "Theseus in Classical Athens." In *The Quest for Theseus*, A. G. Ward, ed., 143–174. London.

———. 1985. "The Razing of the House in Greek Society," *TAPA* 115:79–102.

———. 1989. "City Dionysia and Athenian Democracy," *CM* 40:7–32.

Crane, Gregory. 1993. "Politics of Consumption and Generosity in the Carpet Scene of the *Agamemnon*," *CP* 88:117–133.

Daraki, Maria. 1985. *Dionysos*. Paris.

Davison, John A. 1949. "The Date of the *Prometheia*," *TAPA* 80:66–93.

———. 1966. "Aeschylus and Athenian Politics, 472–456 B.C." In Ehrenberg 1966: 93–107.

Denniston, John and Denys Page, eds. 1957. *Aeschylus Agamemnon*. Oxford.

de Romilly, Jacqueline. 1947/1963. *Thucydides and Athenian Imperialism*. Trans. P. Thody. Oxford. (Originally published as *Thucydides et l'imperialisme athénien—La pensée de l'historien et la genèse de l'oeuvre*. Paris.)

Detienne, Marcel. 1973. "L'olivier: Un mythe politico-religieux." In *Problèmes de la terre en Grèce ancienne*, M. Finley, ed., 293–306. Paris.

DFA[2] A. Pickard-Cambridge. *The Dramatic Festivals of Athens*. Oxford 1968. 2nd ed. revised by J. Gould and D. M. Lewis.

Dinsmoor, William B. 1946. "Athenian Treasury as Dated by Its Ornament," *AJA* 50: 111–113.

Dodds, Eric R. 1960/1973. "Morals and Politics and the *Oresteia*." In his *The Ancient Concept of Progress*, 45–63. Oxford. (First published in *PCPS* 186:19–31.)

Donlan, Walter. 1989. "The Pre-State Community in Ancient Greece," *SO* 64:5–29.

Dover, K. J. 1957/1987. "The Political Aspect of Aeschylus' *Eumenides*." In Dover 1987: 161–175. (Originally published in *JHS* 77:230–237.)

———. 1973/1987. "Some Neglected Aspects of Agamemnon's Dilemma." In Dover 1987:135–150. (Originally published in *JHS* 93:58–69.)

———. 1977/1987. "I tessuti rossi dell' *Agamemnone*," *Dionisio* 48:55–69. (Reprinted in English in Dover 1987:151–159.)

———. 1987. *Greek and the Greeks*. Oxford.

DTC[2] = *Dithyramb, Tragedy, and Comedy*. 2nd edition revised by T. B. L. Webster. Oxford 1962.

Duby, Georges. 1974/1985. "Ideologies in Social History." In *Constructing the Past: Essays in Historical Methodology*, Jacques Le Goff and Pierre Nora, eds. Eng. trans. Cambridge.

Edmonds, John Maxwell. 1957. *The Fragments of Attic Comedy*, vol. 1. Leiden.

Ehrenberg, Victor. 1954. *Sophocles and Pericles*. Oxford.

————. 1960. *The Greek State*. New York.

————. 1966. *Ancient Society and Institutions*. Studies Presented to Victor Ehrenberg on his 75th Birthday. Oxford.

Eliade, Mircea. 1948/1974. *The Myth of the Eternal Return*. Trans. Willard R. Trask. (Bollingen Series XLVI.) Princeton. (Originally published as *Le Mythe de l'éternel retour: Archétypes et répétition*. Paris.)

Else, Gerald. 1964. *The Origin and Form of Early Tragedy*. New York.

————. 1967. *Aristotle's Poetics: The Argument*. Cambridge, Mass.

Euben, J. Peter, ed. 1986. *Greek Tragedy and Political Theory*. Berkeley and Los Angeles.

Ferrill, Arthur. 1985. *The Origins of War*. London.

FGE = D. Page, ed., with R. D. Dawe and J. Diggle *Further Greek Epigrams*. Cambridge. 1981.

FGrH F. Jacoby. *Die Fragmente der griechischen Historiker*. Berlin 1923–1958.

Finley, M. I. 1973. *The Ancient Economy*. Berkeley and Los Angeles.

————. 1981. B. Shaw and R. Saller, eds. *Economy and Society in Ancient Greece*. London.

Forde, Steven. 1989. *The Ambition to Rule: Alcibiades and the Politics of Imperialism in Thucydides*. Ithaca and London.

Fornara, Charles W. 1966. "Aspects of Pausanias," *Historia* 15:257–271.

————. 1971. *Herodotus: An Interpretive Essay*. Oxford.

Fornara, Charles W. and Lorne Samons. 1991. *Athens from Cleisthenes to Pericles*. Berkeley and Los Angeles.

Forrest, William G. 1960. "Themistocles and Argos," *CQ* 10:221–241.

Fraenkel, Edouard. 1950. *Aeschylus: Agamemnon*. 3 vols. Oxford.

Francis, E. D., and M. Vickers. 1985. "The Oenoe Painting in the Stoa Poikile and Herodotus' Account of Marathon," *BSA* 99–113.

French, A. 1972. "The Tribute of the Allies," *Historia* 21:1–20.

Freymuth, G. 1955. "Zur ΜΙΛΗΤΟΥ ΑΛΩΣΙΣ des Phrynichos," *Philologus* 99: 51–69.

Galpin, Timothy. 1983/1984. "The Democratic Roots of Athenian Imperialism in the Fifth Century B.C.," *CJ* 79:100–109.

Garvie, Alfred F., ed. 1986. *Aeschylus Choephoroe*. Oxford.

Goldhill, Simon. 1987/1990. "The Great Dionysia and Civic Ideology." In Winkler and Zeitlin 1990:97–129. (Originally published in *JHS* 107:58–76.)

Gomme, A. W. 1948. "The Eion Epigram," *CR* 62:5–7.

Haas, Christopher J. 1985. "Athenian Naval Power Before Themistokles," *Historia* 34: 29–46.

Hall, Edith. 1989. *Inventing the Barbarian: Greek Self-Definition through Tragedy*. Oxford.

Hansen, Mogens. 1991. *The Athenian Democracy in the Age of Demosthenes*. Oxford and Cambridge.

Hanson, Victor Davis. 1989. *The Western Way of War*. New York.

Harmon, E. G. 1920. *The Prometheus Bound of Aeschylus*. London.

Hartog, François. 1988. *The Mirror of Herodotus: The Representation of the Other in the Writing of Greek History*. Trans. J. Lloyd. Berkeley and Los Angeles.

Hauvette, A. 1898. "Les *Eleusiniens* d'Eschyle et l'institution du discours funèbre à Athènes." In *Mélanges Henri Weil*. Paris:159–178.

HCT 1 Alfred W. Gomme, ed. *An Historical Commentary on Thucydides*. Oxford 1945.

Heath, Malcolm. 1987. *The Poetics of Greek Tragedy*. Stanford.

Henrichs, Albert. 1984. "Loss of Self, Suffering, Violence: The Modern View of Dionysus from Nietzsche to Girard," *HSCP* 88:205–239.

Hercher, Rudolf. 1873. *Epistolographi Graeci*. Paris.

Herington, C. John. 1985. *Poetry into Drama: Early Greek Tragedy and the Greek Poetic Tradition*. (Sather Classical Lectures vol. 49.) Berkeley and London.

Hermassi, Karen. 1977. *Polity and Theater in Historical Perspective*. Berkeley and Los Angeles.

Jacoby, Felix. 1945. "Some Athenian Epigrams from the Persian Wars," *Hesperia* 14:157–211.

Jameson, Fredric. 1981. *The Political Unconscious: Narrative as a Socially Symbolic Act*. Ithaca, N.Y.

Jordan, Borimir. 1975. *The Athenian Navy in the Classical Period*. (University of California Publications in Classical Studies 13.) Berkeley and Los Angeles.

Kerenyi, Carl. 1976. *Dionysos: Archetypal Image of Indestructible Life*. (Bollingen Series 65.2.) Princeton.

Kierdorf, William. 1966. *Erlebnis und Darstellung der Perserkriege*. (*Hypomnemata* Heft 16.) Göttingen.

Kirk, G. S. 1985. *The Iliad: A Commentary*. Vol. 1: Books 1–4. Cambridge.

Knox, Bernard M. W. 1957. *Oedipus at Thebes*. London and New Haven.

———. 1978. "Literature." In *Athens Comes of Age: From Solon to Salamis*. Princeton.

Konstan, David. 1987. "Persians, Greeks and Empire," *Arethusa* 20:59–73.

Lang, Mabel. 1967. "Scapegoat Pausanias," *CJ* 63:79–85.

Leahy, D. M. 1974. "The Representation of the Trojan War in Aeschylus' *Agamemnon*," *AJP* 95:1–23.

Lesky, Albin. 1972/1983. *Greek Tragic Poetry*. Trans. M. Dillon. New Haven and London. (Originally published as *Die tragische Dichtung der Hellenen*. Göttingen.)

Levy, E. 1976. *Athènes devant la défaite de 404: Histoire de une crise idéologique*. (Bibliothèque des écoles françaises d' Athènes et de Rome. fasc. 225.) Paris.

Lewis, David M. 1992. "Mainland Greece, 479–451 B.C." In *CAH*² 5:96–120.

Lloyd-Jones, Hugh. 1966/1990. "Problems of Early Greek Tragedy: Pratinas and Phrynichus." In *The Academic Papers of Hugh Lloyd-Jones: Greek Epic, Lyric, and Tragedy*, 225–237. Oxford. (Originally published in *Estudios sobre la tragedia griega*, 11–33. Cuadernos de la Fundacíon Pastor 13. 1966. Madrid.)

Loraux, Nicole. 1973. "'Marathon' ou l'histoire idéologique," *REA* 75:13–42.

———. 1981/1986. *The Invention of Athens: The Funeral Oration in the Classical City*. Trans. A. Sheridan. Cambridge, Mass. (Originally published as *L'Invention d'Athènes*. Paris.)

Manville, P. Brooke. 1990. *The Origins of Athenian Citizenship*. Princeton.

Marx, Friedrich. 1928. "Der Tragiker Phrynichus," *RhM* 77:337–360.

Meier, Christian. 1980/1990. *The Greek Discovery of Politics*. Cambridge, Mass. (Originally published as *Die Entstehung des Politischen bei den Griechen*. Frankfurt am Main.)

Meiggs, Russell. 1972. *The Athenian Empire*. Oxford.

Meritt, Lucy. 1970. "The Stoa Poikile," *Hesperia* 39:233–264.

ML² Russell Meiggs and David M. Lewis, eds. *A Selection of Greek Historical Inscriptions*. 2nd ed. Oxford 1988.

Momigliano, Arnoldo. 1944/1960. "Sea Power in Greek Thought." In *Secondo contributo alla storia degli studi classica*. Rome. (Originally appeared in *CR* 58:1–7.)

Morpugo, Anna. 1963. *Mycenaeae Graecitatis Lexicon*. (*Incunabula Graeca* 3.) Rome.

Müller, Karl O. 1853. *Dissertations on the Eumenides of Aeschylus*. 2nd ed. London and Cambridge.

Murray, Oswyn. 1966. "Ο ΑΡΧΑΙΟΣ ΔΑΣΜΟΣ," *Historia* 15:142–156.

———. 1988. "The Ionian Revolt." In *CAH*² 461–490.

Nagy, Gregory. 1990. *Pindar's Homer: The Lyric Possession of an Epic Past*. Baltimore and London.

Ober, Josiah. 1989. *Mass and Elite in Democratic Athens*. Princeton.

Ober, Josiah, and Barry Strauss. 1990. "Drama, Political Rhetoric, and the Discourse of Athenian Democracy." In Winkler and Zeitlin 1990:237–270.

Osborne, Robin. 1985. *Demos: The Discovery of Classical Attika*. Cambridge.

Page, Denys. 1959. *History and the Homeric Iliad*. (Sather Classical Lectures vol. 31.) Berkeley and Los Angeles.

Page, D., ed. 1972. *Aeschyli Septem quae Supersunt Tragoediae*. Oxford.

Parker, Robert. 1987. "Myths of Early Athens." In *Interpretations of Greek Mythology*, J. Bremmer, ed., 187–214. London.

PMG = Denys Page, ed. *Poetae Melici Graeci*. Oxford 1962.

Podlecki, Anthony. 1966a. *The Political Background of Aeschylean Drama*. Ann Arbor.

———. 1966b. "The Political Significance of the Athenian 'Tyrannicide Cult,'" *Historia* 15:129–141.

———. 1971. "Cimon, Skyros, and Theseus' Bones," *JHS* 91:141–143.

Post, L. A. 1950. "The Seven against Thebes as Propaganda for Pericles," *CW* 44:49–52.

Pozzi, Dora, and John Wickersham, eds. *Myth and the Polis*. Ithaca.

Pritchett, W. Kenneth. 1969. "The Transfer of the Delian Treasury," *Historia* 18:17–21.

———. 1971. *The Greek State at War*. Vol 1. Berkeley and Los Angeles.

Redfield, James. 1985. "Herodotus the Tourist," *CP* 80:97–118.

Rhodes, Peter J. 1970. "Thucydides on Pausanias and Themistocles," *Historia* 19:387–400.

———. 1981. *A Commentary on the Aristotelian Athenaion Politeia*. Oxford.

———. 1985. *The Athenian Empire*. (*Greece and Rome* New Surveys in the Classics vol. 17.) Oxford.

———. 1992a. "The Delian League to 449 B.C." In *CAH*² 5.34–61.

———. 1992b. "The Athenian Revolution." In *CAH*² 5.62–95.

Robertson, Noel D. 1980a. "The True Nature of the Delian League, 478–461 B.C.," *AJAH* 5:64–96.

———. 1980b. "The True Nature of the Delian League, 478–461 B.C. Continued" *AJAH* 5:110–133.

Roisman, Joseph. 1988. "On Phrynichus' *Sack of Miletos* and the *Phoinissai*," *Eranos* 86:15–23.

Roscher = W. H. Roscher, ed. *Ausfürliches Lexicon der Griechischen und Römischen Mythologie*. Leipzig, 1894–1937.

————. 1993. "Dionysus as Destroyer of the Household: Homer, Tragedy, and the Polis." In *Masks of Dionysus*, Thomas H. Carpenter and Christopher Faraone, eds., 115–146. Ithaca and London.

Salkever, Stephen. 1986. "Tragedy and the Education of the *Dēmos*: Aristotle's Response to Plato." In Euben 1986:274–303.

Schöne, A. 1987. *Der Thiasos*. Göteborg.

Seaford, Richard. 1976. "On the Origins of Satyric Drama," *Maia* 28:209–221.

————. 1977. "The 'Hypochorema' of Pratinas," *Maia* 29:81–94.

————. 1981. "Dionysiac Drama and the Mysteries," *CQ* 31:252–275.

————. 1984. *Euripides' Cyclops*. Oxford.

Sealey, Raphael. 1966. "The Origin of the Delian League." In Ehrenberg 1966:233–255.

SEG = *Supplementum Epigraphicum Graecum*. Leiden, 1923–.

Segal, Charles P. 1962. "Gorgias and the Psychology of the Logos," *HSCP* 65:99–155.

————. 1982. *Dionysiac Poetics and Euripides' Bacchae*. Princeton.

Shear, T. Leslie Jr. 1984. "The Athenian Agora: Excavations of 1980–1982," *Hesperia* 53:1–57.

Smart, J. D. 1967. "Kimon's Capture of Eion," *JHS* 87:136–138.

Sommerstein, Alan H., ed. 1989. *Aeschylus Eumenides*. Cambridge.

Starr, Chester G. 1970. *Athenian Coinage 480–449 B.C.* Oxford.

Steinbrecher, M. 1985. *Der delisch-attische Seebund und die athenisch-spartanischen Beziehungen in der kimonishen Ära*. Palingenesia. (Monographien und Texte Band 21.) Wiesbaden and Stuttgart.

Stössl, Franz. 1952. "Aeschylus as a Political Thinker," *AJP* 73:113–139.

Sutton, Dana. 1980. *The Greek Satyr Play*. (Beiträge zur klassischen Philologie, Heft 90.) Meisenheim am Glan.

Taplin, Oliver. 1977. *The Stagecraft of Aeschylus*. Oxford.

Taylor, Michael W. 1981. *The Tyrant Slayers: The Heroic Image in the Fifth Century B.C. Athenian Art and Politics*. New York.

Thomas, Rosalind. 1989. *Oral Tradition and Written Record in Classical Athens*. Cambridge.

Thomson, George. 1945. *Aeschylus and Athens*. 2nd ed. New York.

TrGF 3 Stefan Radt, ed. *Tragicorum Graecorum Fragmenta*. Vol. 3. *Aeschylus*. Göttingen 1985.

Turner, Victor. 1982. *From Ritual to Theater: The Human Seriousness of Play*. New York.

Tyrrell, W. Blake. 1984. *Amazons: A Study in Athenian Mythmaking*. Baltimore and London.

Ventris, Michael, and John Chadwick. 1972. *Documents in Mycenaean Greek*. 2nd ed. Cambridge.

Vernant, Jean-Pierre. 1965/1983. "Hestia-Hermes: The Religious Expression of Space and Movement in Ancient Greece." In *Myth and Thought among the Greeks*. London. (Originally published as *Mythe et pensée chez les Grecs*. Paris.) The article first appeared in *Revue Française d' Anthropologie* 3 (1963): 12–50.

————. 1968/1988. "The Historical Moment of Tragedy in Greece: Some of the Social and Psychological Conditions." In Vernant/Detienne 1972/1988:23–28. (Originally published in *Antiquitas graeco-romana ac tempora nostra*, 246–250. Prague.)

Vernant and Vidal-Naquet. 1972/1988. Jean-Pierre Vernant and Pierre Vidal-Naquet. *Myth and Tragedy in Ancient Greece.* Trans. Janet Lloyd. New York. (Originally published as *Mythe et tragédie en Grèce ancienne.* Paris.)

Vidal-Naquet, Pierre. 1973. "Terre et sacrifice dans l' *Odyssée.*" In *Problèmes de la terre en Grèce ancienne,* M. I. Finley, ed., 269–292. Paris. (Reprinted in *The Black Hunter: Forms of Thought and Forms of Society in the Greek World.* Trans. Andrew Szegedy-Maszak. Baltimore and London 1986:15–38.)

Wade-Gery, Henry T. 1933. "Classical Epigrams and Epitaphs," *JHS* 53:71–104.

Wallinga, H. T. 1987. "The Ancient Persian Navy and its Predecessors." In *Achaemenid History I: Sources, Structures, and Synthesis,* H. Sancisi-Weerdenberg, ed., 47–77. Leiden.

Walters, K. R. 1980. "Rhetoric as Ritual: The Semiotics of the Attic Funeral Oration," *Florelegium* 2:1–27.

West, Martin L. 1972. *Iambi et Elegi Graeci,* vol. 2. Oxford.

———. 1978. *Hesiod's Works and Days.* Oxford.

———. 1989. "The Early Chronology of Attic Tragedy," *CQ* 39:251–254.

———. 1990. *Aeschylus Tragoediae.* Stuttgart.

West, William C. III. 1970. "The Saviors of Greece," *GRBS* 11:271–282.

Westlake, Henry D. 1977/1989. "Thucydides on Pausanias and Themistocles—A Written Source." In *Studies in Thucydides and Greek History,* 1–18. Bristol. (Originally published in *CQ* 27:95–110.)

Whitehead, David. 1977. *The Ideology of the Athenian Metic.* Cambridge.

Wilamowitz, Ulrich von. 1907. *Einleitung in die Griechische Tragödie.* Berlin.

Winkler, John W., and Froma I. Zeitlin, eds. 1990. *Nothing to Do with Dionysos? Athenian Drama in Its Social Context.* Princeton.

Winnington-Ingram, R. P. 1983. *Studies in Aeschylus.* Cambridge.

Wood, Ellen. 1988. *Peasant-Citizen and Slave: The Foundations of Athenian Democracy.* London and New York.

Wood, Henry. 1972. *The Histories of Herodotus: An Analysis of the Formal Structure.* Paris and The Hague.

Woodhead, A. G. 1981. "The Founding Fathers of the Delian Confederacy." In *Classical Contributions: Studies in Honour of Malcolm Francis McGregor,* 179–190. New York.

Zeitlin, Froma I. 1986/1990. "Thebes: Theater of Self and Society in Athenian Drama." In Winkler and Zeitlin 1990:130–167. (Published also in Euben 1986:101–141.)

Zuntz, Gunther. 1955. *The Political Plays of Euripides.* Manchester.

FIVE

TRAGEDY AND DEMOCRATIC IDEOLOGY

The Case of Sophocles' Antigone

Helene Foley

Sophocles' *Antigone* has always held a special attraction, especially in recent times, for those who want to interpret tragedy in and through its historical context. The issues raised concerning the burial of traitors in both Athens and dramatic Thebes have proved particularly tempting in this respect. Recent work in classics has undoubtedly paved the way for a more sophisticated use of history in the study of tragedy. Gone are the days when we simply read Oedipus as Pericles, for example, and date the *Oedipus Tyrannus* accordingly; indeed, assuming a direct relation between the play and a specific historical event such as the Athenian plague makes the play more puzzling and, by narrowing its focus, less interesting. Both the recent interest in social history in the field as a whole and the work of the French cultural historians Vernant, Detienne, Vidal-Naquet, Loraux, and their colleagues in Paris have laid the groundwork for this effort by bringing together historical and literary sources with a sophisticated use of anthropological theory. In addition, contemporary literary theory and criticism, by simultaneously enhancing our sensitivity to the multiple codes operating in ancient literary texts and increasing our appreciation for their density, ambiguity, and refusal of easy closure, have raised questions that make historical criticism of tragedy even more treacherous than before.

One fruitful line of historical criticism deployed with considerable success by Nicole Loraux, for example,[1] has involved interpreting tragedy not in relation to specific historical persons and events, but in light of democratic ideology as expressed through such media as the Attic funerary oration. Yet this valuable approach has its own pitfalls. In this essay I would like to begin by looking at two recent ambitious and, I would say, representative arguments about the *Antigone* that selectively deploy a knowledge of democratic ideology to arrive at diametrically opposed conclusions about the play, one appearing in a series of articles by Christiane Sourvinou-Inwood, and the other in a brief article by Larry Bennett and Blake Tyrrell.[2] This examination will, I hope, both affirm the importance of interpreting tragedy in its cultural context and reveal the caution that must be exercised when we are confronted not only with a cultural system that prided itself on being open to public exchange of ideas and differences of opinion but also with a literary form such as drama, which unfolds as a complex dialogue that refuses to be bound in any direct fashion by the discourses of the agora.

Sourvinou-Inwood aims to interpret the *Antigone* by reconstructing "cultural assumptions, by means of which meaning was created, and [to] try to read through perceptual filters created by those assumptions."[3] In other words, she aims to block the preconceptions that a twentieth-century reader would bring to the text, by recovering the mind set of a fifth-century audience viewing the play in the 440's B.C. This contemporary audience is treated in her analysis as an undifferentiated collectivity; it is a group of male citizens who interpret tragedy in light of a unified cultural ideology. Despite the fact that Sourvinou-Inwood acknowledges the polysemic, ambiguous, and multivocalic nature of Greek drama itself,[4] the text of the *Antigone* is assumed to be accessible to this kind of unilateral interpretation. What Sourvinou-Inwood's articles collectively argue is that by the standards of Attic ideology the play characterizes Antigone as a "bad woman," whereas Creon throughout much of the play represents and adopts the interests of the Athenian *polis*. Supporters of Creon have always shown a tendency to have recourse to historical sources external to the text, in part because at the very least the concluding scenes seem to make mincemeat of their hero; Sourvinou-Inwood's position is in many respects a sophisticated and carefully argued version of that taken by a number of earlier critics. "My point is," William Calder argued bluntly some years earlier, "that to side with Antigone is a cultural anachronism."[5]

Bennett and Tyrrell, on the other hand, employ a strategy of reading based on a 1986 *Arethusa* article by Peter Rabinowitz. Authors, Rabinowitz argues, "imagine presumed audiences for their texts. Since textual decisions are consequently made with the authorial audience in mind, the actual readers must come to share its characteristics as they read if they are to understand the text as the author wished."[6] In this case, it should be noted that the authors make no attempt to account for recent criticism that asserts the difficulty of establishing authorial intention and the author's inability to control his or her text. By examining Antigone's words and actions in the light of the topoi of Greek funerary orations, Sophocles' Antigone becomes in Bennett and Tyrrell's analysis a champion of democratic ideology, whereas Creon is or soon becomes a tyrant, an embodiment of the impious anti-Athens that is Thebes on the Attic stage.[7] "Antigone acts correctly because she does not defy Creon, leader of Athens, but Creon, the totalitarian ruler of impious Thebes."[8]

Let us now look at each of these arguments in more detail. I shall use the far shorter article of Bennett and Tyrrell primarily to query the more detailed efforts of Sourvinou-Inwood in her series of articles. For Sourvinou-Inwood, our first impression of Antigone is negative, because we are presented with two young women outside the house and conspiring in the dark, a situation that would have been viewed as inappropriate and dangerous in an Attic context. Because the scene relies on and makes verbal references to democratic topoi on the place of women as well as to democratic terminology, the audience would have judged this scene not by the standards of its setting in heroic Thebes, but by contemporary ones.[9] In Sourvinou-Inwood's view, Antigone's actions are repeatedly subversive (to use her term) of the ideology of the contemporary *polis*.[10] It is true that Attic women did play an important role in the early phases of the burial ritual, such as washing and lamenting the body, but they did this, in the case of private citizens, inside the house; both the burial of war dead and the physical covering of the corpse with earth were a male affair on which Antigone is illegitimately encroaching.[11] Furthermore, the *polis* regulated all funerary behavior in Athens, especially that of women. It was Antigone's duty here as elsewhere to obey Creon as ruler and guardian, and it was Creon's, not Antigone's, prerogative to perform the burial. Here Sourvinou-Inwood provocatively challenges the commonly held assumption that Antigone is in any simple sense pursuing a traditional female duty in burying Polynices.

Later, Antigone engages in more perverse behavior. In her infamous speech at 904ff., she defends burying her brother, but argues that she would not have acted to bury a husband or son.[12] Yet, Sourvinou-Inwood argues, an Athenian woman's first duty was to produce children. She must ultimately be loyal not to her natal family but to her marital family. Antigone, in an argument that Aristotle himself characterized as *apiston* (unpersuasive), rejects these responsibilities.[13] Antigone's intense devotion to her dead brother is yet another sign of her membership in a perverted family, and her unwillingness to act for a hypothetical son in the same speech makes her a symbolic bad mother.[14] Finally, Antigone's championing of the unwritten laws is reasonable (and ultimately, and from the audience's point of view, surprisingly right), but her claim to authority to contest the will of the *polis* is not.[15] How can she know better than the *polis*, represented by Creon, when the audience's own *polis* did in fact deny burial to traitors and some others? Indeed, Sourvinou-Inwood stresses, both Ismene and Antigone say that she is acting *biai politon* (79; 907). Hence Antigone is appropriately punished by a bad death—she dies a suicide, unmarried and unmourned.[16] Overall, what Antigone evokes is the dangerous tragic scenario of woman in control or out of control—the two amount to the same thing—and the play's repeated references to Dionysus underline this point.[17] Ismene, by contrast, at least until she too falls victim to the family *atē* (blindness leading to disaster), exemplifies the "correct modality of female response."[18]

Sourvinou-Inwood's Creon, by contrast, embodies standard Attic attitudes.[19] Men were supposed to control women, and sons were supposed to obey and defer to fathers. Demosthenes' approving quotation of parts of Creon's first speech confirms that it conformed with contemporary ideology (19.247 on *Ant.* 175–190). *Strategoi* (generals), like Creon, were expected to pronounce decrees or *kerygmata* in emergencies, and Antigone's use of these terms in the first scene evokes this democratic context.[20] The *polis*, like Creon, did exercise authority over the living and the dead, and could be both very harsh to those who failed it, like the generals at Arginousai, and suspicious of conspiracy.[21] Hence there is nothing out of the way in Creon's suspicion of the guard in what is in any case a light and almost comic scene.[22] Above all, Creon exemplifies democratic patriotism and the necessity of a commonly shared ideology. Obedience to the *polis* and its laws—just or unjust—was an important part of democratic ideology, even if it meant sacrificing family to city. Witness the loyalty required in the Athenian ephebic oath (echoed at *Ant.* 663–671). Finally, Haemon's defense of Antigone fails to reply to Creon's critical concerns about anarchy and obedience to the laws.[23]

How, then, does Sourvinou-Inwood's argument account for what happens to Creon in the final scenes of the play? In her view Creon makes an error that could not have been anticipated. Nor could the audience have known that Creon made a mistake until Tiresias arrived on stage.[24] Creon's problem was not in denying burial to the traitor Polynices, but in the specific form of his punishments. He buried a living person, Antigone, and kept in the upper world someone who belonged to the gods below. Contemporary Attic punishments of traitors involved casting the body outside the city's borders, throwing them below into pits and gorges, or casting them into the sea. Creon, on the other hand, left the body exposed and created pollution. In the play as a whole, then, Sophocles suggests that *polis* discourse might unwittingly offend the gods. But in this he was not being subversive. Both Sophocles' offices in Athens and the success of his plays make this clear.[25] There is even a story that Sophocles was elected general as a result of the success of *Antigone* (Radt, *Tragicorum Graecorum Fragmenta* 4.45T. no. 25). Here is how Sourvinou-Inwood finally summarizes her interpretation: "On my reading, the tragedy places on the one side the polis, with all its positive connotations in the eyes of the Athenians of the late 440s, and on the other a woman, acting out of place and subverting the polis order in defence of the cause of a traitor and aspiring sacrileger—both being the offspring of a terrible incestuous union of a patricide with his mother, and the children of a doomed house. Despite all this, the play is saying that the cause was *right,* and the *polis* was in the *wrong.* Understanding the will of the gods is not easy" (my italics).[26]

Sourvinou-Inwood's argument as a whole requires our accepting the operation of what she calls zooming and distancing techniques.[27] That is, tragedy alternately brings the action close to the realities of the contemporary *polis,* when its characters raise issues of contemporary concern like burying traitors and the proper place of women, and distances the action from its audience, by setting the play in heroic Thebes and making Creon a sole ruler, or by staging the play's debate as a quarrel among members of a ruling elite.[28] The precise ways in which a poet (or, one might add, the critic) controls this anachronistic camera or by which an audience knows how to recognize when it has moved close or far are not adequately explained—although I do not mean in raising this point to trivialize the problem of deciding when an audience would apply contemporary standards to the action of a play and when its response would be conditioned by dramatic convention (or both). In Sourvinou-Inwood's view the use of democratic terminology (which Bennett and Tyrrell also find in the language of Antigone) evokes a contemporary frame of judgment; the predictable nature and implications of father-son quarrels, for example, also create a schema by which the audience will judge Haemon negatively in his interaction with Creon.[29] Yet when both zooming and distancing are used on one character or when two contemporary topoi appear in combination it is by no means as clear as Sourvinou-Inwood implies how the audience will weigh the combination. For example, Antigone is distanced as heroic Theban princess[30] and judged by contemporary standards as generalized (Attic) woman; her language about the unwritten laws appears joined with civic disobedience. Rejecting the possibility that the *polis* could be divided over Antigone's behavior, Sourvinou-Inwood cites the choral disapproval of her disobedience, but not their praise of her noble death (836–839) and their tears over the loss of the last member of the House of Labdacus (801–805).[31] Her technique becomes particularly problematic when she refuses, until the scene with Haemon, to judge Creon by certain topoi of the tragic stage, whereby he becomes a representative of a dramatic anti-Athens who increasingly demonstrates all the qualities of a stage tyrant or a sole ruler.[32]

On the level of detail, Sourvinou-Inwood, despite a critical stance that stresses the multivocality of tragedy, also requires us to dismiss those elements in the text that apparently create a complex dialectic between points of view or even within one position in the play. Her most desperate contention is that Haemon's claim that the citizens praise Antigone for her act and think her worthy of honor (732–733) is unreliable; how, she argues, are we to believe a character who is clearly lying when he says that he cares for Creon and the gods, and not Antigone, and apparently threatens his father's life?[33] Yet the chorus finds merit in Haemon's argument as well as in Creon's (724–725). And why should we not, by these same standards, argue that Creon's original stance is undermined as he attempts to adhere to it in the face of stated political opposition in this scene? Furthermore, if Creon simply made a technical mistake in the way he denied burial to Polynices, how can we explain that on Tiresias' instructions Polynices does receive full burial in Thebes at the end? Indeed, the complete and honorable burial finally accorded to Polynices seems to make it difficult to argue that an historical knowledge of the technicalities concerning the burial of Attic traitors, or more accurately, to use the language of the play, the burial of enemies, is really essential to understanding the play and Creon's disaster.[34] Robert Parker has stressed that Greeks generally recognized the obligation to bury a potential source of pollution and that prolonged public exposure of a corpse is shocking and not the practice of Greek states. Hence Creon's first speech would disturbingly combine the citation of democratic topoi concerning the interests of the state with a policy that not only failed to correspond to the usual treatment of traitors, but would threaten the state with pollution.[35]

Read in context, details of Sourvinou-Inwood's argument become difficult to accept. She argues that Antigone herself confesses that she is acting against the *polis*. In fact, Antigone originally makes the claim to Creon that the chorus supports her act (504–505, 509); it is only in her final speech at 904ff. that she says that she is acting *biai politon* (907). Either she here contradicts herself, or she has changed her mind about the views of the *polis* after hearing the chorus' negative reaction to her deed. If we treat the play as an evolving narrative rather than as a text from which details may be picked to support an argument without their context, the latter explanation (if, as is by no means certain, we can view Antigone as a consistent character) seems more likely if by no means verifiable. Sourvinou-Inwood adopts the position that tragic characters are not static or necessarily endowed with psychological coherence, but are created interactively by the text, the author, and the audience;[36] yet although she insists on an evolving perspective on Creon's character (in her view, he evinces tyrannical behavior, and thus incurs audience disapproval, for the first time in the scene with Haemon), she does not do the same for Antigone. Furthermore, on what basis are we entitled to assume that the death Antigone receives is a just or divine punishment? The text, in contrast to Creon's case, does not say so. Indeed, as was remarked earlier, the chorus tries to console Antigone by mentioning the praise that she will win with this death (if not with her rebellious act).[37]

If Creon's behavior is consistently evaluated in terms of *polis* ideology (and I would argue that it is not), why does the play repeatedly show him making a mistake in exercising these familiar assumptions about men and women, youth and age, city and family? I have space here only to offer one example of Creon's repeated failures (familiar in the criticism of the play) to make these assumptions work in the actual situation with which he is faced. The audience, who has heard Antigone in the first scene, knows that the guard is telling the truth and is not part of a political conspiracy, as Creon assumes. Hence tragic irony undercuts Creon's assessment of the situation before him.[38] His error may be reasonable, but by the time he has misjudged every character who appears before him on stage, the errors begin to appear to be more than simply ironic. Most of Creon's democratic topoi appear early in the play and are gradually eroded by his later tyrannical behavior.[39] Indeed it has been argued that as the play evolves Creon symbolically rejects the central effort of the democracy to advocate listening to good advice and building consensus rather than unilateral action and exposes the tendency of the *polis* itself to become a tyrant.[40] If we adopt Sourvinou-Inwood's own approach of reconstructing democratic ideology in order to interpret the play, Thucydides' Diodotus expresses this ideal concerning receptivity to advice to an assembly shortly to be almost equally divided on the issue in the Mytilenean debate (Thuc. 3.42), even as he then despairs of the democracy following its own precepts: "The good citizen ought to triumph not by frightening his opponents but by beating them fairly in argument; and a wise city, without overdistinguishing its best advisers, will nevertheless not deprive them of their due, and far from punishing an unlucky counsellor will not even regard him as disgraced. In this way successful orators would be least tempted to sacrifice their convictions to popularity, in hope of still higher honours, and unsuccessful speakers to resort to the same popular arts in order to win over the multitude."[41]

Such details are important in demonstrating the need for accounting both for the entire drama and for the full range of perspectives offered in nondramatic representations of democratic ideology. Yet there are larger issues at stake. The Athenian audience was used to being nurtured by poetry with an ethos that did not correspond fully to its own. At recitations of Homer during the Panathenaia or in quoting him at home, the Athenian audience did not expect literature to mirror in any obvious way its own reality and ideology. How can Sourvinou-Inwood be sure that the reverse was true (even intermittently) of drama, especially when comedy often explicitly claims to be urging the members of the audience to change their views? Even if comedy makes many of these claims tongue-in-cheek, a democracy that did not suppress contradictory discourses in its assembly and law courts would be unlikely to do the exact reverse in its drama. Within the *Antigone* itself, the chorus remains far more dubious as to the correct course of action and far more persuaded by alternative points of view than Creon. In other words, a contemporary audience would be accustomed to negotiating among points of view that had equally valid claims to representing the interests of the *polis*. It seems sensible then to assume as a critical principle that Athens was in reality populated with citizens with different and changing views and that democratic ideology, which itself contains contradictions, was hard to apply with any consistency.

Central to the *Antigone* in the view of most critics is the tension—central to Attic democracy as well—between the interests of family *(oikos)* and *polis*. Attic democracy put the institution of the family under attack in certain respects by favoring the interests of the *polis*, yet it also defended the interests of the family. For example, the institution of the *epikleros*, or "heiress," functioned to preserve the continuity of the male lineage in individual households. And if funeral orations aimed to mute the losses presented by the war dead, the state was certainly concerned with reproducing its male citizens; the *polis*, for example, took care to raise war orphans at its own expense. We cannot dismiss Creon's cavalier rejection of family concerns—Antigone's role as *epikleros* in the house of Oedipus and fiancée to his son, his refusal to bury a nephew—by blaming everything on Antigone's inappropriate intervention and her purported neglect of her duty to marry.[42] Are the concerns of the family so simply sacrificed to those of the state? Is Antigone, as Sourvinou-Inwood claims, simply neglecting her obligation to marry or is she regretting that her obligations to her brother have forced her to make a tragic choice between two familial obligations?

It is important to emphasize here that Antigone is a virgin,[43] not a married woman as in Herodotus' story of the wife of Intaphernes (3.119), from which Sophocles may have borrowed Antigone's argument, and that by the time she gives this explanation of her choice, Creon has ruled out marriage as an option. Hence Antigone represents herself as choosing between a concrete obligation to a brother and a hypothetical set of relations to which she now has no access. Furthermore, in Creon's own case his punishment is—one might imagine, significantly—the extinction of his family. The play seems rather to show that when one eliminates the family, nothing is left, and that if *polis* ideology does not dwell on the family, this is because it is urging a new attitude to a set of priorities that are taken for granted as fundamental. As Aristotle says in the *Poetics* (13.1453a), the best tragedies concern the troubles of certain families, and one can hardly imagine that the genre and its frequently outrageous defenders of the family would have continued to attract an audience if issues where family and state interests come into conflict were so obviously and easily resolved in the minds of the audience. The Athenians, unlike the Romans, did not seem to favor black-and-white Horatia stories, in which a brother justifiably kills a sister for mourning the fiancé whom two of her brothers had just slain in battle, dying themselves in the process.

Attic law and ideology seem to insist that adequate leadership rests on having familial ties. Pericles asserts in the Thucydidean funeral oration (2.44.3–4) that those who do not have children to hazard cannot offer fair and impartial counsel to the *polis*; Dinarchus (*Against Demosthenes* 71) says that a rhetor or a *strategos*, in order to get the people's confidence, must observe the laws in begetting children. Both apparently refer to a law (cited in Arist. *Ath. Pol.* 4.2) that required an archon or a hipparch to have a child over ten. In *Against Ctesiphon* 77–78, Aeschines argues that Demosthenes is not fit to be a political leader, because he put on white clothes, sacrificed, and took part in public affairs only seven days after the death of his only daughter. Such a bad father, he argues, could never be a proper political leader. Those who do not feel proper affection for the ones most closely related to them will never value nonkin as they should. When Creon says that those depraved in private life can never properly direct public affairs (661–662), he inadvertently condemns himself.[44] I would argue that, despite democratic ideology that privileges the interests of the state, Creon's blanket denial of the importance of kin ties may well have signaled an inadequacy in his attitude to leadership from the first speech on.

In addition, we cannot be certain what range of historical attitudes there were on certain issues raised by Sourvinou-Inwood, and we sometimes have to rely on tragedy itself for historical evidence rather than on sources external to it. For example, I agree with Sourvinou-Inwood that a knowledge of Athenian attitudes toward funerary behavior helps in reading the play and that Athens did attempt to control women's behavior in funerals. Yet how do we know what the popular view would be in a case where there were no male relatives taking responsibility for a burial? In Sophocles' *Oedipus at Colonus*, Polynices, in urging Antigone to promise to bury him, cites the praise that she will win for doing so (1411–1413)—a praise that sounds entirely similar to that cited by Haemon for Antigone's action. Even Ismene hopes to be forgiven for not burying Polynices, although she will not act in defiance of Creon's edict. Either Sophocles repeatedly creates a fictive responsibility for his female characters that did not exist in Attic reality, or, as is the case in some modern Mediterranean villages, female relatives were felt in popular Attic ideology to have the responsibility to act in defense of relatives if there were no men to do so.[45] Sourvinou-Inwood herself admits that some grave stelae may have been put up by women (perhaps again in the absence of male relatives to do so).[46]

This is not to deny that characters in the play criticize Antigone for an *au-*

tonomia and a disobedience to the ruler inappropriate in any citizen, but especially in a woman—or to imply that Sourvinou-Inwood is wrong to stress the disastrous implications of Antigone's almost incestuous rejection of marriage. At the same time, the later popularity in Euripidean drama of the virgin who sacrifices marriage for family or state makes clear that marriage is not consistently to be celebrated as the highest female priority in tragedy (reality is an altogether different case here); Antigone in her final speech offers a justification (however controversial) for why she had to reject marriage to protect the interests of a brother. Thus it seems important to entertain the possibility here that popular (or fictional) ideology, which might expect a virgin to act in her family's interest when there is no male to do so, did not always conform perfectly to a changing *polis* ideology, which generally aimed to control and curtail funerary rites and women's participation in them.

Bennett and Tyrrell's discussion of the importance of funerary topoi to an interpretation of the play makes clear Sourvinou-Inwood's unwillingness to see democratic ideology operating in the language of characters other than Creon in the *Antigone*. Athens' heroic championing of the unwritten laws concerning burial in the case of the Theban invaders after the war of the Seven against Thebes was a popular topos in funerary oration. Sourvinou-Inwood assumes that this topos is not yet in place at the time of the *Antigone*. Indeed, she argues that it became a topos after Sophocles' play, a point which incidentally undermines her argument, for if Sophocles created this topos, his play is not defending *polis* ideology, but attempting to change it.[47] Yet her assumption is in itself problematic. Nicole Loraux dates the beginning of the funeral oration to the 460's.[48] The questionable ending to Aeschylus' *Seven against Thebes* raises the same issue about Polynices' burial as Sophocles' play does, and his lost *Eleusinioi*, to which Euripides' later *Suppliants* is responding, almost certainly told the story of Athens' championing of the Theban dead. In Herodotus (9.27.3) the Athenians cite this deed to justify their place on one of the fighting wings against the Persians at Plataea. Tiresias raises the issue of the burial of all dead Theban invaders in the *Antigone* (1080–1083).[49] Even the *Iliad* will not permit Achilles to continue his abuse of Hector's corpse, and Sophocles' Ajax wins burial despite his treachery to his fellow Greeks. Despite the impossibility of securely dating a topos of this kind, I think Bennett and Tyrrell assume on reasonable grounds that it could well have been in place before the *Antigone* was composed.[50] In any case, at a later date this very topos not only failed to contradict the ideology of the Attic funerary oration, but was central to it.

As Bennett and Tyrrell point out, when the story of the Theban dead is told in tragedy and funerary oration (e.g., Lys. 2.7–10), the Athenians, alone among the Greeks, deliberately choose to risk their lives to champion justice and the customary rites due to the dead. The Thebans generally reject peaceful intercession, while the Athenians abjure personal gain by fighting only to the point where they have reappropriated the corpses; the bodies are buried, despite their dubious behavior in life, at Eleusis. Even if the Seven acted wrongly, they have paid their penalty in death and the gods below deserve their due. In these funerary myths the city nobly scorns life and gain for the higher and eternally meaningful traditional customs of the Greeks. In Bennett and Tyrrell's view the isolated Antigone's actions exactly parallel those in the funerary topos, whereas Creon rejects the rites due the dead and the intercession of Haemon, and only surrenders to the inevitable. From this perspective, Antigone nobly sacrifices marriage for her brother—just as warriors sacrifice their lives for the city and its causes—whereas Creon is simply impious for exposing the corpse. Bennett and Tyrrell acknowledge that Athens attempted to control women's role in civic funerals, but in their view Sophocles pits the state's right to bury the dead against the family's and women's traditional prerogatives over the corpse and "reveals through Antigone's 'intrusion' the sexual intrusion at the base of the public funeral."[51]

There are difficulties as well as advantages in this argument. In this play we are not dealing directly, as in the Attic funerary topoi, with a conflict between Thebes and Athens, but with a conflict within Thebes; this interpretation does not come to terms sufficiently with the fact that, at least in the view of Ismene, Creon, and the chorus, Antigone is acting against the city and disobeying its ruler. Although Bennett and Tyrrell do not argue for a crudely literal reading, the fact that Antigone is a young woman—not, as in the topos, a warrior sacrificing his life for a civic cause—is more critical than they allow.[52] Furthermore, as Sourvinou-Inwood rightly points out, democratic topoi also appear in the speeches of Creon. Yet it does seem to me that if the funerary topos about the Athenian burial of the Theban invaders was familiar to the audience (or congruent with the ideology that was soon to invent it), then the audience's knowledge of this topos counters Creon's position on Polynices and makes irrelevant the bickering on Attic attitudes to burying traitors so familiar in the historical criticism of the play. On the whole, Athenians apparently did view unwritten laws as natural, unchanging, and superior to particular laws such as those concerning traitors, which were subject to controversy and change (see Arist. Rh. 1.13 [1373b] and 1.14–15 [1375a–b], which quotes favorably Antigone's lines on the unwritten laws, despite Aristotle's generally conventional views on women in both life and drama). Furthermore, even if Antigone would in reality be a significantly anomalous choice to champion civic ideology on this issue, Bennett and Tyrrell make a convincing case that we can hardly view her simply as the utterly anticultural figure that she appears to be in the argument of

Sourvinou-Inwood. Nevertheless, Bennett and Tyrrell still cannot offer a satisfactory explanation for the profoundly interesting question of why Sophocles chose a rebellious woman to make the same case as the gods and Tiresias.[53]

As a whole neither of these arguments based on democratic ideology succeeds in supporting the view that the play is unambiguously taking the side of either Antigone or Creon. Each position requires us to suppress or to give insufficient weight to parts of the text in order to make the case for either. Taken collectively, these articles suggest that the language and arguments used by both Antigone and Creon could evoke democratic ideology in the minds of the audience, whereas the overall dramatic context raises questions about the actions of both characters in pursuing the ideology they favor. It should be stressed here that democratic ideology also appears in the language of Ismene and Haemon.[54] Inadvertently, these arguments bring us back to a more complex and interesting battle—also familiar in the criticism of the play—among at least four characters (and the chorus) whose claim to authority is ambiguous, even if Creon clearly turns out to have been in error. And they show us that much depends on our using our knowledge of democratic ideology and practice to ask the right question, or at least an answerable question, about a play. A close reading of the text has shown that Attic practice concerning burial of traitors may not be relevant to interpreting this particular play, for what we know of the practice is apparently contradicted by the topoi of the funerary oration; prolonged exposure of dead bodies is not a Greek practice under any circumstances. The concluding predictions of Tiresias, which culminate in the burial of Polynices in Thebes, apparently close the question.

A knowledge of democratic ideology certainly helps us to understand what cultural background the original audience of the *Antigone* brought to the play and to judge more accurately the implications of the issues raised therein. Yet it should be stressed that most of the points raised on both sides by these analyses based on democratic ideology are explicitly present in the text. The text itself certainly makes the case against Antigone's rebellious and unfeminine behavior in the words of Creon and Ismene, and it makes the case for her act in the words of Antigone and Haemon. It appears that it is possible to be both subversive and at least partially right on the tragic stage—that the notorious and dangerous "female intruders"[55] who often stalk the tragic stage have a point and, despite the possible eroding effects of *eros* on his attitudes,[56] Haemon and the populace whose views he reports are there in the play to represent this point of view.

Tragedy may at best marginally defend the interests of the family in relation to those of the *polis*, yet it also holds up to view contradictions in *polis* ideology. Those points at which conflicting obligations to *oikos* and *polis* come into conflict are of central interest in tragedy. And the fact that our play's internal audience of citizens, the chorus (who are older and confirmed supporters of the royal household and its rulers) and those citizens mentioned by Haemon, does not have the same views on Antigone's act seems to suggest that the audience of the play itself might be expected to divide along similar lines. I do not mean to argue that a knowledge of the historical and cultural context is irrelevant to our understanding of the texts. But historical readings must account for the full text that we have, and we cannot assume that tragedy will conform either to reality or to ideology in a direct fashion or that it will easily distinguish where and to what degree it is doing so. Instead it tends repeatedly to go beyond the cultural map on which it is drawn.

Those who defend what they characterize as a nonanachronistic reading of the *Antigone* repeatedly and in my view unnecessarily seem to come up with a unilateral and antidialogic reading of the play.[57] Whereas Sourvinou-Inwood and Bennett and Tyrrell agree in principle that tragedy stages a plurality of voices and does not give full authority to any single voice, their historical readings tend to privilege one voice over another. We must make a point of giving full weight to the other players in the drama's dialogue whose voices have a claim on the attention of an audience that also contains a plurality of perspectives, and we should judge each character by the standards applied to the others. Synnøve des Bouvrie, who, like Bennett and Tyrrell, favors Antigone's position on the grounds of contemporary ideology, demonstrates the extreme to which such interpretations can go. She argues that tragedy does not present "a problem or discussion of values" or dramatize "alternatives to be reflected upon."[58] In her view, "tragic drama does not discuss ideas, it presents unarguable truths through a 'symbolic' medium."[59] Furthermore, "these truths lie at a less abstract level than is often assumed, and are directed at the collective audience rather than the individual spectator."[60] What is at stake in this play, she argues, is *philia,* kinship, and rites due to a deceased *philos.* "The *message* of the drama is that human rational thought may err, while divinely inspired or mantic knowledge guides human actions unerringly" (my italics).[61] The audience is not invited to reason about which point of view is preferable. "Knowledge about divine truth . . . is independent of empirical experience and rational, i.e. human, knowledge" and is enforced "by divine anger, plague, and pollution."[62] This knowledge must be represented as "unwritten, eternal, 'natural'" and "transmitted by way of emotional conditioning rather than by intellectual reasoning."[63] Creon's disaster in des Bouvrie's view simply reinforces this conditioning.

On the other hand, the recent book of Oudemans and Lardinois argues for reading the *Antigone* as a case study in tragic ambiguity, in which the play, by presenting the strengths and weaknesses of both Creon's and Antigone's actions and views, leaves its central issues without a clear resolution.[64] Our historically based readings seem in any case to have driven us on entirely different grounds to agree on the difficulty of judging the positions taken by all the major characters. Nevertheless, to what degree is even the ambiguity of these texts controllable through interpretation?[65] Many critics, for example, have pointed to the instability of the very language in this play, where Antigone and Creon use words like *philos* (friend or relative) and *echthros* (enemy) to make diametrically opposed arguments.[66] The text blurs the distinction between its principal characters through the use of imagery as well. Both Creon and Antigone are described with the dehumanizing imagery of the natural world; both, as virgin and the ruler/scapegoat, are marginal figures. Oudemans and Lardinois stress the irony of Creon's total identification with the city, ending in his total isolation from its citizens, and argue that one-sided adherence to any category in this play leads ironically to the destruction of that adherence.[67]

Oudemans and Lardinois' arguments introduce other problems—to give one example, their case for the authority of Creon's position relies heavily on Sourvinou-Inwood.[68] I treat some aspects of the other side of the case in a forthcoming essay.[69] Yet despite the ambiguity and instability of tragic texts, the slipperiness of their dialogic form, and the questions that they raise about cultural commonplaces, I believe that we should continue to investigate, as I certainly have myself, the role that the democratic debate plays in tragedy (and vice versa). I hope this examination has shown something that is banal as a generalization but more complex in practice. Overall, attempts to make a putatively more objective and culturally unbiased reading of the *Antigone* have confirmed the need to reconsider whether a play, or even one character within it, can be said to argue from a clearly defined, logically consistent, and easily assimilable viewpoint. The Creon who mouths democratic ideology in his first speech is not the tyrannical father who rejects popular opinion and a reasoned attempt by Haemon to represent an alternative that might well avoid stasis. Nor does this democratic ideology sound the same in the final scenes as it did in Creon's first speech. To categorize Antigone either as a "bad woman," which, from the perspective of some characters in the play, she certainly is, or as a heroic representative of civic ideology, which the topoi she adopts also suggest is at least partially the case, is only the first step in exercising a critical judgment of the *Antigone* as a whole. Instead, dramatic narrative requires its audience (each different member of it) not to uncover a message, nor to leave the theater in a state of helpless *aporia* (inability to make a judgment), but to negotiate among points of view just as it would in a court of law or an assembly.

Although I cannot argue this case here, I wish to insist that tragedy does not aim to make judgment impossible. In the *Antigone*, at least, the principles espoused by the major protagonists still stand, however difficult it may be to exercise them in practice; the unwritten laws, the interests of the gods of the dead, and the interests of the family prove in this case to coincide with the interests of the city. Understanding the cultural grid on which tragedy is built and to which it reacts does facilitate the process of exercising judgment. Equally important is the awareness that tragedy is a complex dialogue that evolves in space and time. Hence those who advocate (and I should stress that both Sourvinou-Inwood and Bennett and Tyrrell are among them) a partnership between history, anthropology, and literary critical readings of tragic texts are, despite the many pitfalls, blindly tapping, like Tiresias, in the right direction.

NOTES

I would like to thank Carolyn Dewald, Simon Goldhill, Richard Seaford, and Oliver Taplin, as well as the participants in the Austin symposium, for comments on an earlier draft of this paper.

1. See especially Loraux 1981 and aspects of Loraux 1986.

2. Sourvinou-Inwood 1989*a*, 1989*b*, 1990, 1991; and Bennett and Tyrrell 1990. I shall cite Sourvinou-Inwood's arguments primarily from Sourvinou-Inwood 1989*a* and from the other articles only where they expand on this comprehensive version. I shall not discuss the version of this argument offered in Tyrrell and Brown 1991:203–215. I wish to stress my general admiration for the work of these authors; we share a common interest in using history, anthropology, and literary criticism to interpret Greek literature. I selected these papers because their articulate arguments raise critical and as yet unresolved questions about the interrelations among history, tragedy, and theory central to this book.

3. 1989*a*:134; see also 1990:12–13. Here Sourvinou-Inwood attempts to adapt the insights of reader-oriented criticism to the reading of Greek literature (see 1989*a*:134, n. 1). Sourvinou-Inwood makes a valuable attempt to use contemporary literary theory in a constructive fashion, even though, as I shall argue below, I do not think she ultimately stands by the principles of interpretation that she initially sets out.

4. 1989*a*:135.

5. Calder 1986:404.

6. 1986:117. See Bennett and Tyrrell 1990:441–442 and n. 4.

7. See Bennett and Tyrrell 1990:456. In their view, Creon is wrong to expose Polynices' corpse, but he follows Attic ideology in attempting to control women's behavior in the context of death ritual. They adopt the views of Zeitlin 1986 on dramatic Thebes as an anti-Athens.

8. Bennett and Tyrrell 1990:442.

9. 1989*a*:138. All women are outside the house in drama, hence the setting of first scene is not necessarily significant. See Easterling 1987.

10. For the discussion on women and burial see 1989a:138–140 and 1990:30–31.

11. The covering of the corpse with earth seems to have been a male task in both public and private funerals in both archaic and classical periods. In fact, however, without Ismene's help Antigone only laments, pours libations, and scatters dust on the body, rather than attempting to inhume it. Ismene herself, who takes a traditional position on the limits women should observe in a man's world, acknowledges that, if it were not for Creon's decree, the sisters ought to bury their brother (65–68). This implies that as women they would have under other circumstances obligations in this matter on which they should act. Finally, by the standards of archaic poetry and society at least, women were given a considerably more prominent role in burials; hence, the audience must read the scene anachronistically (not by the standards of heroic Thebes) for Sourvinou-Inwood's argument to work.

12. On Antigone's claims in this speech, see Sourvinou-Inwood 1989a:146, 1989b, and 1990:18–21.

13. Arist. *Rh.* 3.16. Despite the fact that the later author Plutarch approved the choice of Herodotus' Persian woman to save the life of her brother (*Mor.* 481e), Sourvinou-Inwood (1990:20) argues that Antigone is borrowing in this speech the inverted views of a Persian, representative in Attic culture of the Other. Here she assumes that the audience recognizes the borrowing from Herodotus 3.119, and that Herodotus designed this story as exemplary of Persian rather than Greek mores.

14. 1989a:140.

15. 1989a:143 and 148.

16. 1989a:148.

17. 1989a:140.

18. 1989a:140. See also 141.

19. 1989a:144. Oudemans and Lardinois (1987:164) take Sourvinou-Inwood one step further and argue that Creon is tragically forced on multiple political grounds to act against the family and deny burial to Haemon.

20. 1989a:138.

21. Yet in this corroborating example the generals were condemned for failing to pick up the dead.

22. 1989a:142.

23. 1989a:145.

24. 1989a:146–147 on the burial of Polynices. See further below on the obvious objection to this point, that when Creon begins to act the part of a Theban stage tyrant, the audience is dramatically prepared for his downfall.

25. 1989a:147.

26. 1989a:148. Note the equation of Creon and the *polis* here, even though Haemon has argued that many in the *polis* do not agree with Creon.

27. 1989a:136. For examples, see 142, 144.

28. 1989a:136.

29. 1989a:137 and 145.

30. For example, Creon is not only failing to act as her guardian by denying her marriage to Haemon, but also preventing the birth of a Labdacid who would legitimately inherit his throne.

31. In effect, they become the mourners that Antigone denies that she has. Bennett

and Tyrrell (446–447) argue that the audience will give more weight to the topoi about the unwritten laws than the one about civil disobedience, whereas Sourvinou-Inwood takes the opposite stance.

32. 1990:24. Yet Zeitlin shows that Creon's behavior from the first scene is evocative of the Theban stage tyrant, and Blundell 1989 has a very balanced discussion of the pros and cons of Creon's behavior in the light of contemporary political attitudes. See further below.

33. 1989a:144–145.

34. Sourvinou-Inwood (see esp. 1990:26–28) argues that Tiresias simply says that Creon kept the corpse in the upper world and deprived the nether gods of their due (1064ff.); Creon's response, which is to bury Polynices honorably in Thebes, rather than to pick a more effective way of disposing of a traitor, is an excessive reaction to a previous excess. I do not find this convincing. Tiresias is here predicting what will happen and explaining why Creon is in error, not giving instructions. The chorus certainly interprets Tiresias' words as Creon does (1101). Furthermore, would casting the body in a pit or the ocean give the nether gods their due? Finally, since the ending conforms with the topoi of the funeral oration and earlier tragedy on burial, the audience had no absolutely compelling reason to privilege Creon's initial position (at any time in the play) over the final resolution.

35. 1983:44 and 47. Even in changing Antigone's mode of punishment from stoning to confinement in a cave, Creon seems less concerned with pollution than a fear of dissent (stoning requires the consent of the population). See Knox 1956:72.

36. 1989a:136. The controversy over consistency of characterization in Greek tragedy has been hotly debated, above all since Tycho von Wilamowitz in 1917.

37. Sourvinou-Inwood (1989a:143) also asks us to agree that divine approval of the burial does not indicate divine support for Antigone's action—something that I think is impossible to determine either way. There are many divine secrets to which tragedy gives us no access. In addition, although Antigone is punished for her act of disobedience, she receives after death from Haemon both lamentation and a symbolic marriage.

38. It is certainly true, as Sourvinou-Inwood argues (1989a:137), both that Greek religion was under the control of the *polis* and included chthonic as well as Olympian cults and that Creon champions *polis* religion; but this argument can be turned against him, in that his *polis* religion does not in Antigone's and Haemon's view sufficiently respect the rights of Hades. It is not enough to say in defense of Creon's violation of the rites due to the gods below that he was "simply exercising the polis' taken-for-granted right to deny burial to a traitor" (137). This gives priority to political legislation over the unwritten laws, whereas the discourse of the democratic funerary oration, for example, insists on respect for both.

39. Another irony is that Creon's actions are in fact more destructive to the city than Antigone's, since the pollution of the unburied body endangers its well-being, and his rejection of Haemon and the marriage with Antigone endangers the royal succession.

40. Blundell 1989:123–126.

41. Trans. Crawley (Modern Library 1951).

42. In Foley 1993:111–113 I argued that the audience has no way to interpret Antigone's insistence (despite Ismene) that she is the last of her family line (895–896; 940–943) except through the institution of the *epikleros*. Hence Creon is preventing An-

tigone from producing a male heir for her natal family and violating his role as her guardian.

43. On Antigone's virginity, see also Goldhill 1990:103–104.

44. On related issues, see Leinieks 1962:78 and 85.

45. See Deliyanni 1985 and Holst-Warhaft 1992:77–84, 91–93. I treat this issue in more detail in Foley, forthcoming.

46. 1990:30. This material is hard to interpret, since we do not know exactly what role female initiative actually played in such cases.

47. 1989a:143.

48. Loraux 1986:56–69 and 198.

49. These lines are thought to be spurious by some, however.

50. Bennett and Tyrrell (1990) do not in fact address the problem of dating the funerary oration and its topic in relation to the play.

51. 1990:454. In their view, Creon improperly excludes women and the family from the burial that he finally gives Polynices (p. 456).

52. See their discussion at 1990:453–456. They justify their position by taking for granted women's responsibilities in the area of burial, a responsibility that Sourvinou-Inwood questions.

53. Ibid.

54. The quotation of phrases from Haemon's speeches in Antiphanes fr. 231K and Eupolis' *Propaltioi* (fr. 260, Kassel-Austin) makes it likely that Haemon is using democratic topoi as well. Ismene's initial stance on the place of women in a *polis* and on obedience to the city anticipates that of Creon and echoes popular Attic views.

55. See Shaw 1975 and Foley 1982.

56. The problematic but critical role that *eros* plays in this drama is beyond the scope of this paper.

57. Goldhill (1986:89) suggests that critics' attempts to define an audience's (univocal) point of view mirror the attempts of the characters to lay claim to the views of the city.

58. 1990:170.

59. 1990:170.

60. 1990:170.

61. 1990:191.

62. 1990:192.

63. 1990:192. Here des Bouvrie denies any relevance to the claims of the state or Attic laws concerning traitors.

64. 1987. I am here accepting Oudemans and Lardinois' thoughtful case against a Hegelian reading (although their own reading develops out of Hegel's). Goldhill (1986:105) similarly argues that the text resists the stability of the opposition Creon:city and Antigone:family.

65. This is a question raised by a variety of poststructuralist critics.

66. See Knox 1956; Kitzinger 1976; and Goldhill 1986.

67. 1987:182–183.

68. On Creon, see 1987:164–165, 174. For their acceptance of her views on Antigone, see 167. They refer to an unpublished version of Sourvinou-Inwood in manuscript form.

69. Foley, forthcoming.

REFERENCES

Bennett, Larry J., and Wm. Blake Tyrrell. 1990. "Sophocles' *Antigone* and Funeral Oratory," *AJP* 111:441–456.

Blundell, Mary Whitlock. 1989. *Helping Friends and Harming Enemies: A Study in Sophocles and Greek Ethics.* Cambridge.

Calder, William. 1968. "Sophocles' Political Tragedy, *Antigone*," *GRBS* 9:389–407.

Deliyanni, H. 1985. "Blood Vengeance Attitudes in Mani and Corsica." Unpublished ms. University of Exeter.

des Bouvrie, Synnøve. 1990. *Women in Greek Tragedy: An Anthropological Approach.* Oslo.

Easterling, P. E. 1987. "Women in Tragic Space," *BICS* 34:15–26.

Foley, Helene. 1982. "The 'Female Intruder' Reconsidered: Women in Aristophanes' *Lysistrata* and *Ecclesiazusae*," *CP* 77:1–20.

———. 1993. "The Politics of Tragic Lamentation." In *Tragedy, Comedy and the Polis,* A. H. Sommerstein, S. Halliwell, J. Henderson, and B. Zimmermann, eds., 101–143. Bari.

———. forthcoming. "Antigone as a Moral Agent." In *Tragedy and the "Tragic,"* M. Silk, ed. Oxford.

Goldhill, Simon. 1986. *Reading Greek Tragedy.* Cambridge.

———. 1990. "Character and Action, Representation and Reading: Greek Tragedy and Its Critics." In *Characterization and Individuality in Greek Literature,* C. Pelling, ed., 100–127. Oxford.

Hester, D. A. 1971. "Sophocles the Unphilosophical," *Mnemosyne* 24:11–59.

Holst-Warhaft, G. 1992. *Dangerous Voices: Women's Laments and Greek Literature.* Ithaca, N.Y.

Kitzinger, Rachel. 1976. "Stylistic Methods of Characterization in Sophocles' Antigone." Diss. Stanford University.

Knox, Bernard M. W. 1956. *The Heroic Temper.* Berkeley and Los Angeles.

Leinieks, V. 1962. *The Plays of Sophocles.* Amsterdam.

Loraux, Nicole. 1981. *Les enfants d'Athèna.* Paris.

———. 1986. *The Invention of Athens: The Funeral Oration in the Classical City.* Trans. Alan Sheridan. Cambridge, Mass. (Originally published in French, Paris 1981.)

Oudemans, C. W., and A. P. M. H. Lardinois. 1987. *Tragic Ambiguity: Anthropology, Philosophy, and Sophocles' Antigone.* Leiden.

Parker, Robert. 1983. *Miasma.* Oxford.

Rabinowitz, P. J. 1986. "Shifting Stands, Shifting Standards: Reading, Interpretation, and Literary Judgment," *Arethusa* 19:115–134.

Shaw, Michael. 1975. "The Female Intruder: Women in Fifth-Century Drama," *CP* 70:255–266.

Sourvinou-Inwood, Christiane. 1989a. "Assumptions and the Creation of Meaning: Reading Sophocles' *Antigone*," *JHS* 109:134–148.

———. 1989b. "The Fourth Stasimon of Sophocles' *Antigone*," *BICS* 36:141–165.

———. 1990. "Sophocles' Antigone as a 'Bad Woman.'" In *Writing Women into History,* Fia Dieteren and Els Kloek, eds., 11–38. Historisch Seminarium van de Universiteit van Amsterdam: Amsterdam.

————. 1991. "Sophocles *Antigone* 904–20: A Reading." *A.I.O.N.* (Annali dell'Istituto Universitario Orientale di Napoli) IX-X (1987–1988): 19–35.

Tyrrell, Wm. Blake and Frieda S. Brown. 1991. *Athenian Myths and Institutions: Words in Action.* New York and Oxford.

Wilamowitz, T. von. 1977 (1917). *Die dramatische Technik des Sophokles.* Berlin. (Originally published 1917 as vol. 22 of *Philologische Untersuchungen.*)

Zeitlin, Froma I. 1986. "Thebes: Theater of Self and Society." In *Greek Tragedy and Political Theory,* J. Peter Euben, ed., 101–141. Berkeley and Los Angeles.

SIX

WOMEN ON THE TRAGIC STAGE

Bernd Seidensticker

The extraordinary significance of women and their cause on the Attic stage[1] constitutes a striking contrast to their muted role and marginalization in Athenian society. The paradox is made more acute by the fact that the conception of women as presented in the theater seems in many ways to contradict the picture that may be reconstructed from other sources.

In the following discussion I want to challenge the widespread assumption of a fundamental difference between life and dramatic poetry, between image and reality. I begin with a survey of what is known about the political, social, and economic structures and the ideological discourse that appear to have formed the conditions and defined the parameters of women's life in classical Athens. Despite the manifold problems presented by the grave limitations of our material and by the nature of the available sources,[2] the combined efforts of historians, philologists, philosophers, anthropologists, archaeologists, historians of medicine, and others have established a general picture that is basically clear and widely accepted, even if many details are still controversial. Since a number of excellent summaries of the present state of our knowledge are available,[3] the following outline can be brief.

For the whole of her life the Athenian woman was a person of limited rights. With the exception of a number of functions and responsibilities in cult, she was excluded from all political rights and duties. Women had no right to vote, to speak, or even to be present in the *ekklesia*. Formally speaking, they were not a part of the *polis*, for women were not entered in the register of the deme, nor were they, in all probability, registered as members of the phratry.[4] "Their citizenship was latent; it consisted in the capacity to bear children, who would be citizens."[5]

Legally, a woman was a perpetual minor. For the whole of her life she stood under the guardianship of a male (her *kyrios*).[6] The testimony of a woman could be accepted in court, but she could not plead her own cause.[7] Furthermore, her right to inherit, to own, and to control property was severely restricted.[8] As these drastic limitations show, the Athenian woman in political, legal, and economic contexts was not a *persona sui iuris*. As part of the *polis* she existed only through men and for men: as daughter, wife, and mother, as producer of male citizens and heirs, as an instrument for the reproduction of family and *polis*.[9]

While the Athenian man spent most of his time outside his home, women, being excluded from large provinces of the male world, stayed inside;[10] and the spatial separation of men *(polis)* and women *(oikos)* continued even inside the house. The women's quarters were located either on the second floor or in the remoter part of the house—in any case as far removed as possible from the main entrance and the *andronitis*.[11] Respectable women did not participate in the social life of men, not even in their own home.[12] The Athenian woman was a housewife in the true sense of the word. She was educated only in her duties as a housewife;[13] these duties occupied her completely and tied her to the house, which many women probably did not even leave to fetch water or to go to market.[14]

The ultimate reason for the careful separation of the living quarters and the restriction of women to the private sphere lies in the fact that the unquestionable origin of the male offspring was decisive both for the legitimacy of his rights as a citizen and for the guarantee of his claims to his inheritance. The future position of the man, both in *polis* and *oikos,* depended on the strict supervision of women.[15] The ideal of chastity and the strict spatial separation protected adolescent girls and young wives[16] in particular from dangerous contacts with the male world.

Both the political and legal restrictions and the rigorous spatial separation were based on the ideological assumption of the natural inequality of the sexes. As indicated by all our mythological, literary, historical, and philosophical sources—from Hesiod's myth of Pandora to Aristotle, whom Gomme aptly characterizes as a "consistent believer in the inferiority of the female sex"[17]—women were regarded as "deuxième sexe," as comparable to slaves and barbarians,[18] and as perpetual children. They were a *kalon kakon,* characterized by fickle irrationality in contrast to the temperate rationality of man—emotional, self-indulgent, and weak-willed. They were thus morally, intellectually, and financially unreliable, both endangered and dangerous. This entails, as formulated with disarming candor in many traditional metaphors, that women had to be subdued and tamed, broken in and put to the yoke of matrimony; in short, they had to be domesticated.[19] Then, like a plowed field, they could receive the male seed and bear fruit; then, under rational male guidance, they could act for the benefit of their husband and his *oikos;* then, in the orderly paths of family life, their dangerous irrationality could be transformed into loving care and compassion.

It is obvious that this set of ideas and images about the nature of woman (analyzed in great detail by the French anthropological school)[20] is closely linked to the body of legislation and custom in "a mutually sustaining and mutually revealing combination."[21] Yet it is possible to raise objections against this dismal picture, and a number of such objections demand some clarification and modification.

(1) Important elements of our portrait are representative only of a particular section of the female population in Athens, namely of the wives, daughters, and mothers of the free and prosperous Athenians. This qualification is, however, less significant than it may appear at first sight. For, as Gould and Just have pointed out, it is highly probable that the described class of women was the socially dominant class, the lifestyle and ideals of which determined to a considerable extent the actions and attitudes of the other classes.[22]

(2) The assertion of a fundamental, practical, and conceptual orientation of women toward the private realm is not refuted by the correct observation that the Athenian woman was allowed to leave the house—probably veiled—not only in order to visit the wife of a neighbor, but also on the occasion of family celebrations and state festivals, sacrifices, and funerals. On these occasions she did not have to fear the reproachful glances of the men of her family.[23] These occasions, however, are evidently exceptions to the rule of everyday life, occasions when women remained for the most part among themselves or at least among relatives. Thus even these comparatively short moments of "public" life were of a quasiprivate character.

(3) On closer inspection, even the significant and active role of women in cult,[24] which is adduced frequently in this context, fits quite well into the picture of the Athenian woman that I have sketched. This is not primarily because cults and rituals, even when women played an important part, were often ultimately supervised and controlled by men. The main reasons are that some of these occasions appear to have been safety valves, short moments of release, which served to reinforce the restraints[25] and that the rituals themselves symbolized and stabilized, sometimes blatantly, the traditional female role as housewife and mother. This is the case both for the rituals of initiation by which young girls, acting as representatives of their age-group, were prepared for their future role as wives,[26] and for the manifold fertility festivals and rituals by which the reproductive function of women and their importance for the continuity of *polis* and *oikos* were celebrated and sanctioned.[27]

Although this picture of the position of Athenian women and their life, presented to us by our fragmentary sources, possesses a number of regrettable lacunae and is certainly not equally detailed and informative in all aspects, it is, as a whole, consistent and instructive. It is characterized by the almost complete exclusion of women from public rights and duties (cult being the sole exception) and by their spatial and conceptual restriction to the private domain and to the function of housewife and mother. Apart from the practical skills and qualities required of the woman for the fulfillment of her domestic duties, her most important virtue is female *sōphrosynē*, i.e., chastity and general restraint in all contacts with the male-dominated public realm. As Pericles said: "The greatest glory is hers who is least talked about by men, whether in praise or in blame." [28]

At first glance no genre seems to present more of a contrast to this picture than does drama. One only has to think of the pervasive presence of women on the Attic stage in general or specifically of powerful heroines such as Clytemnestra or Medea, Antigone or Lysistrata, to understand why so many critics have spoken of a fundamental discrepancy between social reality and poetic fiction. In my opinion, however, the paradoxical first impression can be considerably modified by a more detailed analysis.

On the one hand we have to keep in mind that the archaeological and literary sources provide us with a set of rules but do not show us how the game was played in reality. Deviations from the norms and wide variations in the ways that they were complemented are not improbable.[29] On the other hand our testimonies, especially those that most decidedly advocate or represent the separation of domains, such as Xenophon's *Oikonomikos*, leave us in no doubt that in the private sphere women were accepted as equal partners and that the successful woman and mother was as respected and honored as the successful man.[30] A number of interesting cases document that in family matters women had their say, even if they did not formally possess the right to take part in the decision. Women might be heard, for example, in the case of a daughter's marriage, in financial matters, or in questions of adoption or inheritance. In addition to this we may assume that women commented on political, legal, and economic questions as well, and in this way indirectly influenced public affairs to some extent.[31]

Once we add these aspects of private influence and the actual exercise of informal power to our earlier picture of the Athenian woman, the apparent difference between reality and poetic representation in fifth-century drama is already somewhat diminished. It may be further reduced if one properly accounts for the nature of the medium in which their representation appears.[32] The aristocratic world of tragedy with its extraordinary freedom of action and speech for women stood in clear contrast to the social reality of the audience. But the spectators were used to other conventions of the genre, such as the masks and costumes, the highly rhetorical quality of much of the text, or the absurd reversal of reality in comedy. In my view, they regarded the special position of women too as no more than an easily bridgeable distance of aesthetic alienation.

Similar considerations apply to another convention of the ancient theater that has often been held partially responsible for our paradox. In contrast to the modern stage, the ancient open-air theater knew no interior scenes (if one disregards the few *ekkyklema* scenes). This condition of production has the inevitable consequence that both men and women always act outside the *oikos* proper, which per se generates a certain tension between the real and the fictional world. In the case of tragedy, however, this tension is reduced considerably by the way in which theatrical space is handled. As a rule, the action takes place in the immediate vicinity of the private domain, in front of the palace. Where this is not the case, as for instance in the Trojan plays of Euripides, the tents of the captured Trojan women have the same effect. Thus the outdoor scenes can, and many scenes do, possess the intimate atmosphere of interior scenes.[33] More important, however, are the flexibility and elusiveness of the settings of tragedy, of which Easterling has recently reminded us.[34] Part of the public space with which Greek theater presents us can pretend to be private.[35] It is therefore quite wrong to assume the public quality of an action or a situation simply on the basis of its being performed or happening outside the stage-building.

Equally misleading, or at least overstated, is Gould's magisterial statement: "Greek tragic drama is a theatre of public events. . . . The chorus, exerting the pressure of being heard and witnessed upon the stage figures, is the constant visible symbol of this public world."[36] For quite often the presence of the chorus does not diminish the atmosphere of private intimacy. In many tragedies, in which women play the central part, the choruses consist of close confidantes of the heroine (friends, slaves, or fellow-sufferers). This establishes a rather private public that comes close to social reality, where the main interlocutors of women are also relatives, friends, and neighbors; one may add that the appearance of women and female choruses in public is often explicitly or implicitly motivated by occasions that are justified by the conventions of social reality. At this point suffice it to say that the distance between the role of women in day-to-day life and the poetic conception of women on the stage, on the one hand, is smaller than may appear at first sight and, on the other hand, loses some of its significance because the spectator understands it and accounts for it as a result of theatrical convention.

In this way the paradoxical discrepancy between poetry and reality from which we started out is reduced to a further degree. But a crucial question remains. The question is whether the image of women in fifth-century drama, despite the superficial differences that depend on the nature of the dramatic medium, is at its core identical with the historical picture that the other available material and literary sources provide of the nature and social role of women, their rights and duties, arguments and achievements, weaknesses and virtues. In my opinion one can answer this question positively. I will try to justify this thesis in three stages.

First, it can be shown that the essential elements of the historical role of women—general inferiority and physical and conceptual confinement to the private domain—are indeed stated and shown everywhere in tragedies (and in comedies).[37] Everywhere in classical drama, especially in Aeschylus and Euripides, we find maxims in which the fundamental subordination of women and their traditional social role are expressed in a catchy formula. They are used by men like Creon and Pentheus when they fear that the public order or their own status could be jeopardized by women.[38] More often, however, they are used by women themselves, and above all by female choruses who frequently express the emotions and values of the "normal" woman.

To be sure, the dramatic context must not be ignored if one wants to understand what the author intends to achieve by the evocation of the conventional norms and attitudes. But even in the frequent cases where a remark or dramatic situation that refers to the traditional conception of women is modified, ironized, criticized, or repudiated by the speaker or the context, it remains part of the dramatic discourse and attests to the omnipresence of this conception on the tragic stage as in the everyday life of the audience. In view of the enormous mass of relevant material, the following documentation has to be confined to the most important aspects (and a few examples in the footnotes):

(1) The power and authority of men, in *polis* and *oikos*, remain essentially unquestioned in drama. Throughout the world of tragedy, including the plays dominated by women, it is the man who rules; he decides and gives orders, without consulting women.[39] The latter react, are objects and victims of male politics, or sacrifice themselves for it.[40]

(2) Where men rule, women must be silent, or at least restrain themselves.[41] As dramatic characters women must of course speak and speak out, but again and again the violation of the traditional code of behavior is expressly emphasized. Women are constantly told to keep silent

or to stop talking; time and again women ask whether they may speak, apologize for their boldness, assert that for once they have something reasonable to say or that they have learnt what they know from men.[42]

(3) In drama, as in the world of the audience, women are told that they should not interfere in the affairs of men, but rather stay at home and cause no trouble.[43] Quite often the fundamental separation and difference of male and female space is not only shown, but explicitly emphasized.[44]

(4) In drama as in life, women live, above all, for the family, as wife or mother, as daughter or sister. The girls wait impatiently for their wedding day or lament the loss of their dreams. The women are concerned for their marriage, for their husbands and children; they fight and sacrifice themselves for them and grieve their fates. Outside their family roles women often appear in their traditional religious contexts: they carry offerings and lament the dead, they dance and pray to the gods of the house or the city, or act as priestesses.

(5) Since I have discussed the way tragedy presents the life of women, let me add a brief reference to the "tragic ways of killing a woman." Nicole Loraux's analysis[45] has made us aware of the clear distinction between male and female forms of death. Women, in tragedy, die by men, for men, with men; they die, after a silent exit, in the innermost part of the house, in the orbit of their marriage. Their death often appears as symbolical marriage, as it does for Iphigenia, Polyxena, and Deianira. Antigone "found in her death a femininity that in her lifetime she had denied with all her being, and also found something like a marriage."[46]

(6) Finally, the dramatists also seem to regard vulnerable and dangerous irrationality as the crucial characteristic of the female psyche.[47] Tragedy presents us, above all, with both the positive and negative extremes of female emotionality: the ability to love passionately or to hate passionately; altruistic willingness to make sacrifices, but also self-destructive vindictiveness; the capacity to endure suffering and hardship and the ability to pity and to mourn, but also the tendency to excessive lamentation.[48] Chastity and general restraint are the most widely praised virtues of women.

While this brief survey was intended to show that the essential elements of the conception of Athenian women, as established on the evidence of our non-poetical sources, are also omnipresent on stage,[49] the second phase of my argument is to recall the often neglected fact that, apart from the exceptional heroines who are mainly responsible for our paradox, fifth-century drama presents us also with images of women who are in total conformity with the social norms and ideals. In fact, these women, to whom one has to add the numerous female choruses, are not at all "rare instances of an adherence to the ideal," [50] but clearly form the majority. Nor do they play only insignificant, subordinate roles. As Loraux points out,[51] good wives (and mothers) may not be material for tragedy, but they are an important part of the tragic world, from Aeschylus' Atossa and Hypermestra to Sophocles' Tecmessa, Iocaste, and Euridice, and to Euripides' Alcestis, Andromache, Euadne, and Iocaste.

Positive images of women as guardians of the values of kinship and religion clearly prevail. Such are, for instance, the altruistic daughter Antigone (Soph. *OC*), who accompanies her blind father in his wanderings; the self-denying sister Electra (Eur. *Or.*) attending Orestes, who is haunted by wild fits of insanity; the devoted wife Euadne (Eur. *Supp.*), who follows her husband to death; the loving mother Iocaste (Eur. *Phoen.*), who all alone attempts to prevent the imminent fratricide; and, finally, to name an example from Aeschylus, Atossa, the Persian queen who in her worries over her son, driven by nightmares, leaves the palace only in order to seek comfort and advice from the chorus of the elders. Atossa is a typical woman, who (as her conversation with the chorus shows) has not given much thought to the Persian army's operations; a typical wife, who goes to Darius' grave in order to implore help from her dead husband; a typical mother, who at the end of the play, following the advice of the elders, welcomes her beaten and tattered son with new clothes and comfort. It is Euripides especially who has enriched this impressive array of positive images of women with his memorable representations of female strength and self-sacrificing devotion in danger and grief: young girls who sacrifice themselves for the benefit of the community (Iphigenia) or the deliverance of the family (Macaria); the spouse who follows her slain husband to death (Euadne); and, of course, the wife and mother Alcestis as the radiant model of the perfect woman, the dream of every male spectator.

The female choruses, finally, also appear in typically female roles and situations: as victims of war (Eur. *Hec., Tro., Hel., Phoen.*), as the objects of sexual aggression (Aesch. *Supp.*), as virgins fearing the enemy's soldiers (Aesch. *Septem*), as mothers fighting for the funerals of their sons (Eur. *Supp.*), and frequently as servants (Eur. *Ion, IT*), acquaintances and friends of the heroine (Soph. *El., Trach.*; Eur. *Hipp., Andr., El.*).

The ubiquity of this conformity to the female role becomes even more evident if one remembers that it appears even in those plays in which the heroine violates it drastically. Thus Aeschylus' Clytemnestra pretends to be the loving wife and faithful guardian of house and bed, first to the herald (587ff.) and then to her husband, in order to lure him into her trap (855ff.). Medea outwits the two men she wishes to destroy by putting on the mask of a woman who, conscious of her weakness and in the interest of her children, is prepared to bow to the decision of king and husband (271ff., 866ff.). Even the masculine Antigone, condemned to death, returns in the end to a female role, first in her lament over the loss of marriage and the joys of motherhood and then, as we saw, in the manner in which she dies.[52]

Considering the two preceding arguments it would still be possible to say that the omnipresence of the traditional image of women has the function of forming the background or foil against which the spectacular deviations from the rule stand out even more clearly.[53] In the following pages I therefore intend to show, as the third step in my argument, that even the extraordinary women of classical drama, as women, are not all that extraordinary. Rather, in many respects, even they strongly confirm the traditional image. This is not only true of Aristophanes' housewives, Lysistrata and Praxagora, but also of Clytemnestra, Antigone, and Deianira, of Medea and Phaedra, Electra and Hecuba.

(1) It can be shown that women in tragedy usually react to a threat to or violation of their domain, namely the world of the family and its values or, as in the case of Antigone, the family and the religious laws that protect a central right of the family.

(2) As a rule, they react inside their world, that is in the private sphere of their home or in the realm of cult.

(3) The traditional image of women is confirmed both by the manner in which the heroines react and by the actual means they employ. Ever since Penelope, cunning is the quintessential female weapon, and ever since Penelope, the means of female cunning are the loom or its products. Given the fact that no other activity defines the traditional role of the Greek woman in myth, cult, and reality as much as spinning and weaving, the exceptional dramatic significance of these activities and their products as instruments of female cunning is hardly surprising. The other instrument they use, poison, is of course the negative side of the other important female activities, cooking and nursing.[54]

(4) In cases where women, in their reaction to male injustice (and often in the interest of a close male relative),[55] have left the female realm, they return to it in one way or another; in tragedy they pay for this intrusion into the male world either with death or with the loss of their femininity—or with both.[56]

I will illustrate these claims by a brief interpretation of one female character of each of the three tragedians. These interpretations do not claim to do justice to the complex figures of the selected heroines, but rather exemplify the four aspects of their characterization that I have just outlined.[57]

AESCHYLUS' CLYTEMNESTRA[58]

In her proud apology over Agamemnon's corpse Clytemnestra finally discloses her personal motives for the deed. The first and last argument she puts forward in her dispute with the chorus is the sacrifice of Iphigenia. Agamemnon slaughtered her daughter, whom she "bore with dearest travail" (1415ff.), like an animal on the altar. And when at the end the chorus in their desperation asks her who could raise the funeral lament for Agamemnon (1541ff.) Clytemnestra retorts sarcastically that Iphigenia will be waiting for her father at the Acheron in order to greet him with embrace and kiss (1555ff.). Apart from this central motive of the violation of her sacred right as a mother there appear, however marginally, also her husband's escapades at Troy (1439) and his return with Cassandra (1440ff.). The sexual offenses of her husband complete Clytemnestra's portrait of a man who has offended against child and bed. Her bitter characterization of Agamemnon as *lymanterios* (1438)—a word signifying physical and psychical defilement and abuse—combines the two aspects of his guilt.

It is therefore not quite correct to say that Clytemnestra resists marriage and confinement to the house;[59] and Winnington-Ingram's thesis[60] that Clytemnestra's main motive is not the sacrifice of Iphigenia but her desire to maintain the freedom and power she has enjoyed while Agamemnon was away, although highly suggestive, is based on fairly little textual evidence. The treacherous ruin "he brought on his house" (1523f.)—as she calls the murder of Iphigenia—is avenged by the mother inside the house. Whereas Agamemnon sacrifices Iphigenia in public space, Clytemnestra "sacrifices" him in the most private part of the house, in the bath, and alone (1107ff., 1127–1128). To the perversion of his duties as father and husband Clytemnestra responds with a perversion of her duties. Instead of washing the home-coming husband, she kills him. Instead of making love to him, she rejoices with the clearly sexual allusion:

> Spouting out a sharp jet of blood
> He struck me with a dark shower of gory dew,
> While I rejoiced no less than the crop rejoices
> In the Zeus-given moisture of rain.
> (1389–1392)

Woven fabrics are the female instruments of her female revenge. In the carpet scene she persuades him to enter the house by stepping on the fabrics she spread out in front of the palace (905ff.)—fabrics that, by reminding the audience of her duties as mistress of the house, symbolize the perversion of her duties. In the bath she casts a large garment like a net over him and slays him (1115–1116, 1126ff., 1382–1383, 1492–1493, 1516–1517).

It is worth noticing that the masculine Clytemnestra—"the woman with the heart of a man" (11)—does not act the female part of a good housewife simply to lull Agamemnon into security (855ff.); at the end of the play, after the murder, she appears to move back closer to the traditional female role. When Aegisthus enters (1557ff.) she stays in the background; she intervenes only when the quarrel between him and the chorus is coming to a dangerous head, and asks him to return into the palace with her (1654ff.). Aeschylus' Aegisthus, "the woman" (1625), as he is called by the chorus, "the wolf in the bed of a lioness" (1258–1259), is certainly not the master of the palace, as he is in Sophocles and Euripides, but even Aeschylus' Clytemnestra, when the chorus threatens her, refers to Aegisthus as to her protector, her *kyrios:*

> The hope that walks my chambers is not traced with fear
> While yet Aegisthus makes the fire shine on my hearth,
> My good friend, now as always, who shall be for us
> The strong shield of our defiance.[61]

Clytemnestra's abandonment of the female role eventually destroys her and threatens to destroy the next generation as well. In the trilogy's final scene the disturbed order is once again restored. The female is assigned its proper place: inconspicuous, yet honored; inferior, but nevertheless important for the protection of the traditional male order and the continuance of the *polis.*

SOPHOCLES' DEIANIRA[62]

Deianira also kills her husband, but, unlike Clytemnestra, not out of hatred but out of love. In general, Clytemnestra and Deianira, the most "masculine" and the most "feminine" of all great female characters of the Greek stage, represent extreme opposites, yet seen under the aspect in which I am interested they reveal surprising parallels.

In the first scenes of the *Trachiniae* Sophocles carefully exposes the heroine's total dedication to home and marriage (103ff.). When her beloved husband finally seems to be returning home for good, she has to realize that he is bringing a beautiful young woman back as his mistress and concubine (536–

542). Threatened in the most elementary aspect of her life she decides to act (or better, to react). Like Euripides' Creusa she reacts out of passionate jealousy that stems ultimately from the threat to her position in the *oikos*, and, just like Clytemnestra, she reacts within the boundaries of her domain and with her own female means. In the innermost corner of the house (686) she has kept a supposed love charm, given to her by the centaur Nessus. She applies it to a festive gown and sends it to her husband. Herakles puts it on and burns to death. Once again a ruse, once again a garment. What is added this time is poison, the other typically female device. When her son rushes home with the terrible news and curses her, she retreats silently into the palace, bids farewell to her world, her household, and the altar, and kills herself with Herakles' sword on Herakles' bed, the center of her life.[63]

Loraux has pointed out that although she uses a male instrument, her way of killing herself is female. Answering the question that has bewildered many critics, why Deianira strikes on her left side, she states: "It is a textual ruse, a contradiction deliberately presented to emphasize that a woman's death, even if contrived in the most manly way, does not escape the laws of her sex."[64]

EURIPIDES' MEDEA[65]

Although Medea is certainly more the sister of the masculine Clytemnestra than of the feminine Deianira, one can nevertheless find a number of parallels to the latter as well. For Medea (as for Deianira) her husband is the center of her life. For her love of Jason she has sacrificed everything; for Jason she has betrayed her father, left her native land, and during her flight, in order to save her lover, killed her own brother. Expelled from Iolcus, she now lives in Corinth, a stranger, isolated, except for her husband and children. At the very moment when she finally hopes to find peace, her husband, whose life she saved more than once, decides to leave her and to marry the daughter of Creon, the king of Corinth. Her life is destroyed (225–229). The situation is further aggravated by the fact that the king fears her revenge and wishes to expel her from the city and that she does not know where to find a new shelter for herself and the children (502–505). Totally isolated and deeply hurt in her sense of loyalty and justice as a wife, in her pride as a woman, and in her love of Jason, she decides to take revenge.

> For in other ways a woman
> Is full of fear, defenseless, dreads the sight of cold steel;

But, when once she is wronged in the matter of love,
No other soul can hold so many thoughts of blood.
(263–266)[66]

Here too it is not the case that Medea resists marriage and confinement to the *oikos* or "that she has subordinated her feminine skills to a purely masculine desire to dominate," as Shaw puts it.[67] Rather, as in the cases of Clytemnestra and Deianira, we have a violation of the female sphere by the husband, and here too the reaction takes place in the woman's own domain and with the typically female weapons: cunning, fabric, poison. She invokes Hecate—the goddess of magic and witchcraft who resides in the hearth, the very center of the house (395ff.)—to help her and kills Creusa, her rival, and her father, the king, who, as *kyrios*, is responsible for the marriage, by means of a poisoned gown that she sends to the bride as a wedding gift. Yet this is not enough; in order to completely destroy her treacherous lover and unfaithful husband, she uses, after poison and fabric, the most horrible of possible female weapons, the murder of her own children.

For one who, in a terrible perversion of her sacred duties as daughter, sister, wife, and mother, has destroyed her family, first in Colchis and now in Corinth, no return to any form of a family context is possible. In the end Medea disappears out of the spectator's sight in a serpent-chariot.[68] The destruction of her happiness as a wife and mother forces her, like Clytemnestra, into a masculine role. And the price she has to pay for her revenge is high. Not death, like Clytemnestra, but the loss of herself as a woman and mother.

Other Euripidean women appear to be cast in a similar mold. Creusa, raped by a god and forced to expose her newborn child, finally reacts with cunning and poison when her last hope of finding her son has been disappointed and her husband, with the help of her divine lover, appears to introduce an extra-marital son into the family and onto the throne. Electra hates Clytemnestra and Aegisthus not—like her Aeschylean and Sophoclean sisters—because these two have killed her father, but because, by marrying her off to a poor farmer who has not touched her, they have deprived her of a suitable marriage and of children. She helps Orestes kill their mother with a sword, but her main contribution to the matricide is cunning, and she uses a particularly female trick when she lures Clytemnestra into the deadly trap by sending her the message that she has borne her first grandchild. Hecuba endures sheer endless suffering; in the end, however, when she must face the fact that a supposed friend of the royal house has killed her last son, she takes a revolting revenge on the murderer, and she takes it inside, with female cunning and female weapons. She entices Polymestor into her tent, where she and her servants first kill his sons with daggers they have hidden in their robes, and then blind him by piercing his eyes with brooches. But Hecuba also has to pay the price for the brutal revenge with the loss of humanity; as her victim predicts, she will be changed into a bitch.[69]

The main, tripartite section of my paper aimed to demonstrate the following points:

1. The picture of the social position of women in the fifth century reconstructed from our nondramatic sources is also expressed and evoked everywhere in classical drama in the form of maxims and dramatic situations.

2. The majority of female characters and choruses do indeed conform to the social norms and ideals of fifth-century Athens.

3. Even the extraordinary female characters of the Attic stage correspond to and thus confirm essential elements of the traditional image of women in so far as they react to threats to and violations of the female realm and its values. They do so in the female world and with female weapons, often driven by emotional forces that are considered typical of women, namely jealousy and vindictive passion on the one hand and self-sacrificing altruism on the other.[70]

On the basis of the material presented under these three headings it seems justified to maintain that the apparently enormous discrepancy between the binding social norms and conceptions and the poetic images of women in the fifth century largely disappears, and that the frequently stated paradox loses much of its paradoxical quality.

But here I do not want to be misunderstood. To argue that Clytemnestra, Antigone, and Medea conform in many ways to the traditional image of women is not to say that they are unexceptional women or that much of what they say and do does not violate the traditional norms and values of the society, in which and for which they were created. This aspect, as well as the extraordinary significance of women in Attic drama, remains surprising and calls for an explanation.[71]

Tragedy, as we have learned to understand better and better over the last two decades, is part of the discourse of the *polis*. Whereas the French anthropological school has emphasized that and how the tragic poets—consciously and subconsciously—worked with the conscious and subconscious conceptions of their society about the nature of women and their place in the *polis*, other critics have tried to analyze the dramatic images not in terms of the deep structures of the Greek mind, but rather in terms of historical reality, and to understand them as responses to and reflections of the rapid political, social, and intellectual developments that characterize the fifth century and to the strains and tensions produced by them. Above all there were the vast and profound consequences of the Greek victory over the Persians, which catapulted Athens overnight into the position of a world power; the progressive democratization of the *polis*, which accelerated around the middle of the century; and, finally, over the last three decades, the Peloponnesian War, which profoundly affected the traditional value systems, as we know from Thucydides' vivid description. Christian Meier[72] has recently stressed again the momentous impact these political events and developments must have had on what he, using a favorite concept of Max Weber, calls the "nomological basis" of Athens. The theater in the fifth century is the institution that serves as the central medium for the necessary discussion and analysis, evaluation and readjustment of the various mutually interconnected elements of the nomological basis, which is essential for the success of the polity, if not for its survival.

As far as women are concerned, it has often been pointed out that the rapid development toward radical democracy had momentous consequences for the relation between *oikos* and *polis*, between family and polity, and between the sexes. "The radical separation of the domestic sphere from the political sphere, and the relatively greater subordination of household to state and of female to male undoubtedly posed more problems in reality than it did in the ideal. Too radical a privatization and cultural isolation of the female accompanied by extensive public demands on the male created a potential imbalance between the values, needs and interests of the two spheres."[73]

Tragedy (and comedy) dealt with the ambivalence and unease, tensions and conflicts in the nomological basis that resulted from the marginalization of women, and it is here that we find the ultimate reason for the enormous importance of women in Attic tragedy.

It would therefore be most interesting and most important for our understanding of both this momentous phase in the European "histoire de la mentalité" and the political function of drama if we could determine the intentions of the authors and the effect on the audience that the dramatic discourse may have had. Does the drama of the fifth century—or any particular drama— describe and analyze or evaluate and judge the tensions between *polis* and *oikos* and the various aspects of the conflict between the sexes? And if the latter is the case, does it affirm or challenge the traditional image of women? Does it thus destabilize and even destroy or rather consolidate and reconstruct?

As the history of interpretation shows, it is exceedingly difficult (if not impossible) to reach widely accepted answers to these questions, and the more general the answers are, the less consensus they will muster. The differences between the three tragedians and between single plays of the same author are too manifest. The fact that tragedy is an "epistemological genre par excellence" (Zeitlin) is undisputed. "It brings into view ambiguities, tensions and fears, deep-seated fears, which the norms of law and custom are intended to control or even suppress."[74] Gould's statement relates to myth. But it can help to define the function of tragedy, if we remember that the tragedians used myth only as raw material for their intellectual constructs, and that we therefore have to try to determine what their positions and intentions may have been.

Since Vernant defined tragedy as the "genre of ambiguity,"[75] it has become fashionable to assume that classical tragic drama presents questions rather than answers, problems rather than solutions, diagnosis rather than therapy. I would argue that the Athenian tragedians, who were seen and saw themselves as teachers of their *polis*, offered or at least tried to offer answers for the questions they dealt with. Of course, they did not have answers for all of the questions of their time and, of course, they could not offer simple, pat solutions. As one would expect, their answers were not always the same nor free from contradictions. But answers they gave, and despite the major differences among the three as to which aspect of the complex syndrome of problems they address and despite the fact that their images of women differ considerably, their answers seem to agree in one fundamental point. From the *Oresteia* to the *Bacchae* Greek tragedy appears to tell its predominantly male audience that what is essential for a healthy and stable society is a fair balance between the basically different interests of *polis* and *oikos*, public and private, male and female. Whereas Aeschylus uses the dialectic form of the trilogy to present and justify the necessary balance in the third play, Sophocles and Euripides rather concentrate on the destructive effects of various forms of imbalance between the two mutually dependent worlds and their qualities. The catastrophes are usually caused not by female but by male intruders who ignore or violate the rights, needs, and qualities of women. Formulated ex negativo the basic imperative of their texts is the same and, as the insistent portrayal of the disastrous results of any disturbance of the delicate balance indicates, the message is basically affirmative. It is not, however, a simple reassertion of the cultural norms and practices. The emphasis on the female perspective is a clear reminder of how important a well-balanced compromise between the sexes is and how difficult this is to achieve and preserve.

As the continuous challenge to a one-sided male worldview shows, all three tragedians champion the women's cause.[76] Aeschylus, whose solutions seem to be the most conservative, nevertheless shows in the *Oresteia* clear signs of understanding, if not sympathy, for Clytemnestra, and at the end of the trilogy he stresses the indispensable nature of the female and its powers for the survival and renewal of the *polis*. Sophocles not only presents a number of positive female role models, such as Tecmessa or the sisters Antigone and Ismene in *Oedipus at Colonus*, but, in a more powerful indirect comment, creates heroines like Antigone and Electra who impressively hold their own against his great tragic heroes Ajax, Philoctetes, and Oedipus. Finally, Euripides, who from Aristophanes to our own days has often been totally misunderstood as a misogynist,[77] is in fact the most eloquent and insistent advocate of women's cause. It is not so much the heroines' rather sporadic criticisms of the position of women [78] that prove this point as it is the constant presentation of women as victims of men, the sensitive analysis of the female psyche that allows him to produce understanding and sympathy even for his "bad" women (like Phaedra or Medea), and, above all, the creation of numerous female characters whose intellectual and moral strength proves itself triumphantly in personal and public crises and catastrophes, for which men have to accept all or most of the blame.

Living in a society that had marginalized women further than any other Greek *polis*, all three tragedians in different ways and to a different degree appear to plead the female cause, but they do so without challenging the traditional casting of social roles and the underlying conceptual assumptions.

NOTES

An earlier version of this paper appeared in *Humanistische Bildung* (Zeitschrift des Württembergischen Vereins der Freunde des humanistischen Gymnasiums) 11 (1987) 7–42. Permission to reprint has kindly been granted. I am grateful for the opportunity to present the revised paper to a wider public.

1. Eight of the seventeen preserved plays of Euripides are named after women and five more after female choruses; in only four do male heroes have the title role, and even in two of these the main tragic characters are women. Three of the seven extant Sophoclean tragedies are plays with female protagonists (only the *Philoctetes* has a purely male cast), and, as Aeschylus' *Oresteia, Suppliants,* and *Seven* show, the first of the three great tragedians took the lead in creating monumental female characters and addressed time and again the fundamental tension between the sexes.

2. Cf. Gomme 1925/1967; Pomeroy 1975:59–60; Just 1989:1ff. Gould 1980:38–42; Sealey 1991:1ff.

3. Cf. esp. Pomeroy 1975; Foley 1981*b*; Just 1989; Clark 1989; Sealey 1990.

4. Gould 1980:40–42; but cf. Golden 1985. For the position of women in politics in general Just 1989:13–25.

5. Sealey 1990:14.

6. Harrison 1968:I.108–115; Just 1989:26–39.

7. Harrison 1968:II.136ff.

8. Harrison 1968: I.108–109, 132–148; Schaps 1979; Just 1989: 76–104.

9. It is therefore not surprising that we know comparatively few women by name—and, significantly, these few from dedications or tombstones. In historical and legal texts, however, they mostly appear, in accordance with their functional importance for the *polis*, as mother of . . . , sister of . . . , daughter of . . . , wife of . . . . Cf. Schaps 1977: 323–330.

10. Pomeroy 1975: 79–84; Gould 1980: 46–48; Vernant 1969.

11. Cf. Walker 1983: 89–91; differently, Isager 1978; Schuller 1985: 44–45.

12. Lacey 1968: 159; Starr 1978.

13. Clark 1989: 12: "The general rule was domesticity and lack of training for anything else." For literacy cf. Cole 1981; Harris 1989: 106–108.

14. Dover 1973; Pomeroy 1975: 72; Clark 1989: 17ff.

15. Pomeroy 1975: 86.

16. Cf., e.g., Lys. 1.6; Lacey 1968: 169–170, 175.

17. Gomme 1925/1967: 17; but cf. Fortenbaugh 1977: II.135–139; Said 1983.

18. Hall (1989: 202–203) notes that "when women in tragedy 'get out of hand' reference is frequently made, whether explicitly or implicitly, to barbarian mores."

19. Gould 1980: 53; Just 1989: 153–193. For the merits and limits of the anthropological nature-culture dichotomy cf. Foley 1981*b*: 140–148.

20. Gernet, Detienne, Vernant, Vidal-Nacquet; see the relevant literature in Zeitlin 1982: 154–157.

21. Just 1989: 192.

22. Gould 1980: 48–49; Sealey 1990: 10.

23. Lacey 1968: 168; Pomeroy 1975: 80.

24. Farnell 1971; Deubner 1932; Burkert 1977; Garland 1984: 75–123; Pomeroy 1975: 75–78; Just 1989: 23–24; Clark (1989: 33–37), who points out "that religious duties were not likely to conflict with family commitment." For the sexualization of public and cultic space cf. Vernant 1969.

25. Zeitlin, cf. n. 21.

26. Cf. Burkert 1966.

27. Cf. the Thesmophoria; Burkert 1977: 365–370; Zeitlin 1982.

28. Thuc. 2.45.2.

29. Sealey 1990: 4; Just 1989: 1–2.

30. Cf. Lefkowitz 1983: 31–47.

31. Cf. Lacey 1968: 151–153, 159–171, 172–174; Gould 1980: 49–50; Just 1989: 126–152.

32. One argument that has been used repeatedly in the past to explain—or rather, explain away—our paradox does not bear closer scrutiny. It is not the nature of the inherited mythical or literary material used by the tragedians that is ultimately responsible for the distance between the great female characters of classical tragedy and their Athenian sisters, but the authors themselves who, as a closer look at the mythological tradition shows, either created or at least expanded and accentuated the special roles of women in many cases and particularly in the most spectacular ones (e.g., Clytemnestra, Antigone, Medea).

33. Cf. e.g. Antigone and Ismene, Ajax and Tecmessa, Phaedra and her nurse.

34. Easterling 1987.

35. This is the case, as Easterling convincingly shows, e.g., in the first half of the *Trachiniai*, where Sophocles leaves the dramatic space quite vague and invites the audience to imagine Deianira "at home" (at least in private rather than in public space).

36. Gould 1978:49.

37. E.g., Eur. *IA* 1392–1394; *IT* 1005–1006.

38. Creon: Soph. *Ant.* 484–485, 525, 678, 740, 756; Pentheus: Eur. *Bacc.*, esp. 785–786, 803. Cf. B. Seidensticker 1972:46–47.

39. E.g., Aesch. *Septem* 200–201; Soph. *Ant.* 484–485; Eur. *Andr.* 214ff., *El.* 930–933, 1051–1053, *IA* 568–572. Aristophanes' utopias, as perversion of the natural order, confirm this picture as a whole and in detail. Mary Lefkowitz' statement (1983:54) about the *Thesmophoriazusae* applies to *Lysistrata* and *Ecclesiazusae* also: "Aristophanes realizes that his audience would find the very notion of women, meeting together, making speeches and voting hilariously funny."

40. Cf. p. 159.

41. E.g., Soph. *Aj.* 292–293; Eur. *IA* 829–830; Ar. *Lys.* 507ff.

42. E.g., Eur. *Andr.* 364–365; *Herakl.* 474ff.; *Supp.* 293ff.; *Herakles* 534–535; *El.* 945ff.; *Hel.* 1049; Ar. *Lys.* 1124ff.

43. E.g., Aesch. *Septem* 201, 232; Soph. *El.* 328–329, 516ff.; Eur. *Herakl.* 476–477; *Andr.* 876–878; *Tro.* 647ff.; *El.* 343–344; *Phoen.* 88ff., 193ff.; *Or.* 108; *IA* 731ff.(!), 992ff., 1338ff.; Ar. *Thesm.* 785ff.; Gould 1980:40.

44. See, for example, the Electra of Euripides, who does not listen to the advice of her poor husband not to work too hard and answers: "You have enough to do outside. / The things inside are my duty. / It's sweet for the man coming home from work / to find everything in good shape."

Aeschylus' *Seven* and Sophocles' *Trachiniae* present the clearest examples of the rigid separation of the two worlds, and even at the tragic climax of the *Oresteia* there is a reference to the social hierarchy that has been violated by Clytemnestra. Orestes rebukes his mother, who tries to defend herself by pointing to her long years of loneliness: "The man's hard work supports the woman who sits at home" (*Cho.* 920–921).

45. N. Loraux 1987.

46. Loraux 1987:32.

47. For general criticism of women as "kakai" see Eur. *Hipp.* 616ff.; *Andr.* 269–273, 352–354; *Hec.* 1177–1182; *Ion* 398–400; *Phoen.* 198–201. Women are considered as vain (e.g., Eur. *Tro.* 990ff., 1020ff.; *El.* 1069–1070; *Or.* 1110), loquacious (e.g., Eur. *Hipp.* 383ff.; *Andr.* 930ff.) and cunning (e.g., Eur. *Andr.* 911; *Hel.* 1621; *IT* 1032).

48. Cf. Eur. *Andr.* 91ff., 241–242; *Herakles* 533ff.; *Hel.* 991; *Or.* 1022.

49. To the sheer endless list of brief or detailed explicit statements by the dramatic characters there could be added a large number of scenes that implicitly visualize central elements of the traditional image of women, e.g., at the beginning of the *Phoenissae* where Antigone is cautiously led out of her seclusion in the palace by the old pedagogue to look down at the battlefield from the wall (88ff.).

50. Foley 1981b:156–157.

51. Loraux 1987:28.

52. On the comic stage the revolutionary women of Aristophanes, though usurping male dominance, remain good housewives who simply intend to use their domestic abilities and virtues for the administration of the *polis* and in this way confirm the

traditional distribution of roles exactly where they reverse them; for women in Aristophanes see esp. Vaio 1973; Vidal-Naquet 1979; Foley 1982; Zeitlin 1981.

53. Two well-known examples are Ismene and Chrysothemis, the ordinary, untragic sisters of Antigone and Electra, who each serve as a foil for the greatness and tragic stature of Antigone and Electra; they are representations of women who, conscious of their female weakness, succumb to male predominance and adapt themselves to a situation that is unbearable for the heroines despite the fact that they share similar feelings.

54. Clark 1989:12; for women as poisoners see Just 1989:264–276.

55. Lefkowitz 1983:49.

56. Pomeroy 1975:98–101; Shaw 1975:262; Foley 1981b:135, 153, 155.

57. Critical discussion of the vast secondary literature is impossible; references are kept to the minimum.

58. For women and sexual conflict in Aeschylus cf. esp. R. Winnington-Ingram 1983a; Gagarin 1976, esp. 87–118 and 151–162; Zeitlin 1984; Podlecki 1983.

59. Foley 1981b:142, 151.

60. Winnington-Ingram 1983a:105–106.

61. 1434–1437. See Pomeroy 1975:98: "The double entendre is especially shocking because the woman traditionally lit the fire on her father's or husband's hearth."

62. For women in Sophoclean tragedy see Winnington-Ingram 1983b; Wiersma 1984.

63. See Seidensticker 1983:113–115, 122.

64. Loraux 1987:55.

65. For women in Euripidean tragedy cf. esp. Nancy 1983; Powell 1990; Harder 1993.

66. Cf. also 569ff.; 1367–1368.

67. Shaw 1975:263.

68. For the deus ex machina ending of the play Knox 1977:206–211.

69. Many other examples from tragedy could be added to further prove the claim that even the extraordinary heroines of classical drama in many respects correspond to the traditional image of women, and Foley 1982 has convincingly shown that what I have tried to argue for Aeschylus' Clytemnestra, Sophocles' Deianira, and Euripides' Medea (and a number of other Euripidean heroines) in a quite similar way also holds true for Aristophanes' women.

70. Usually they act on behalf of a male relative and in most cases under some kind of male protection; cf. Zeitlin 1985:67: "Functionally women are never an end in themselves, and nothing changes for them once they have lived out their drama on stage. Rather they play the roles of catalysts, agents, instruments, blockers, spoilers, destroyers, and sometimes helpers or saviours for the male characters." Rarely do they move outside their world to assume political responsibilities, and when they do, they do so in the interest of the family (Antigone, Macaria) or can only play the traditional role of sacrificial victim (Macaria, Iphigenia).

71. The common explanation that since Greek tragedy is to a large extent family tragedy—that is to say, the portrayal of intrafamilial conflicts—women, of course, play a central role as wives and mothers, daughters and sisters, is not sufficient. Philip Slater's psychopathological theory, on the other hand, has been rightly criticized and rejected by a number of scholars (cf. especially Foley 1975), but he deserves the credit for having

reminded us that literary female characters of male poets are always not least the expression of "male fantasies." It is not improbable that the extensive social repression of women turned them into especially fascinating objects of male curiosity and fantasy, male dreams and fears.

72. Meier 1988.

73. Foley 1981b:151.

74. Gould 1990:55.

75. Vernant 1988:29–48.

76. For a totally different view see Zoepffel (1989:443–500), who speaks of the conspicuous misogyny of many classical tragedies (pp. 495, 498).

77. The numerous testimonia about the alleged misogyny of Euripides appear to go back to Aristophanes (esp. *Thesm.*); cf. Lefkowitz 1981:88–104. Pomeroy (1975:106) reminds us how small the number of misogynistic statements in extant Euripidean tragedy actually is; cf. also March 1990.

78. Eur. *Med.* 230ff.; *Ion* 1090ff.; *Melanippe Desmotes* fr. 491–494 N, 499 N; also Sophocles fr. 583R; cf. Knox 1977.

REFERENCES

Burkert, Walter. 1966. "Kekropidensage und Arrhephoria," *Hermes* 94:1–25.

———. 1977. *Griechische Religion der archaischen und klassischen Epoch.* Stuttgart and Berlin.

Cameron, Averil, and Amélie Kuhrt, eds. 1983. *Images of Women in Antiquity.* London and Sydney.

Clark, Gillian. 1989. *Women in the Ancient World.* (*Greece and Rome New Surveys in the Classics* no. 21.) Oxford.

Cole, S. G. 1982. "Could Greek Women Read and Write?" In Foley 1981a:219–245.

Deubner, Ludwig. 1932. *Attische Feste.* Berlin.

Dover, K. J. 1973. "Classical Greek Attitudes to Sexual Behaviour," *Arethusa* 6:143–157.

Easterling, Patricia E. 1987. "Women in Tragic Space," *BICS* 34:15–26.

Farnell, Lewis Richard. 1971. *The Cults of the Greek City States.* Chicago. (Originally published Oxford 1895–1909.)

Foley, Helene. 1975. "Sex and State in Ancient Greece," *Diacritics* 5:31–36.

———, ed. 1981a. *Reflections on Women in Antiquity.* London.

———. 1981b. "The Conception of Women in Athenian Drama." In Foley 1981a:127–168.

———. 1981c. "The 'Female Intruder' Reconsidered: Women in Aristophanes' *Lysistrata* and *Ecclesiazusae*," *CP* 77:1–21.

Fortenbaugh, William. 1977. "Aristotle on Slaves and Women." In *Articles on Aristotle* Jonathan Barnes, Malcolm Schofield and Richard Sorabji, eds., II.135–139. London.

Gagarin, Michael. 1976. *Aeschylean Drama.* Berkeley, Los Angeles, London.

Garland, Robert S. J. 1984. "Religious Authority in Archaic and Classical Athens," *BSA* 79:75–123.

Golden, Mark. 1985. "'Donatus' and Athenian Phratries," *CQ* 35:9–13.

Gomme, A. W. 1925/1967. "The Position of Women in Athens in the Fifth and Fourth Centuries," *CP* 20:1–25. (Reprinted in A. W. Gomme, *Essays in Greek History and Literature* [New York 1967] 89–115.)

Gould, J. 1978. "Dramatic Character and 'Human Intellegibility' in Greek Tragedy," *PCPS* 24:43–67.

———. 1980. "Law, Custom, and Myth: Aspects of the Social Position of Women in Classical Athens," *JHS* 100:38–59.

Hall, Edith. 1989. *Inventing the Barbarian: Greek Self-Definition through Tragedy.* Oxford.

Harder, Ruth. 1993. *Die Frauenrollen bei Euripides.* München.

Harris, William Vernon. 1989. *Ancient Literacy.* Cambridge, Mass.

Harrison, Alick Robin Walsham. 1968. *The Law of Athens.* 2 vols. Oxford.

Isager, Signe. 1978. "The Women's Quarter," *Mus. Tusc.* 32/33:39–42.

Just, Roger. 1989. *Women in Athenian Law and Life.* London and New York.

Knox, Bernard M. W. 1977. "The Medea of Euripides," *YCS* 25:193–225.

Lacey, Walter K. 1968. *The Family of Classical Greece.* London.

Lefkowitz, Mary. 1981*a. The Lives of the Greek Poets.* London.

———. 1981*b. Heroines and Hysterics.* London.

———. 1983*a.* "Influential Women." In Cameron and Kuhrt 1983:49–64.

———. 1983*b.* "Wives and Husbands," *G&R* 30:31–47.

Loraux, Nicole. 1987. *Tragic Ways of Killing a Woman.* Trans. Anthony Forster. Cambridge, Mass.

March, Jennifer. 1990. "Euripides the Misogynist?" In Powell 1990:32–75.

Meier, Christian. 1988. *Die politische Kunst der griechischen Tragödie.* Munich.

Nancy, Claire. 1983. "Euripide et le parti des femmes." In *La Femme dans les sociétés antiques,* E. Levy, ed. Strasbourg.

Podlecki, Anthony J. 1983. "Aeschylean Women," *Helios* 10:23–47.

Pomeroy, Sarah B. 1975. *Goddesses, Whores, Wives, and Slaves: Women in Classical Antiquity.* New York.

Powell, Anton, ed. 1990. *Euripides, Women, and Sexuality.* London and New York.

Said, Suzanne. 1983. "Féminin, femme et femelle dans les grands traités biologiques d'Aristote." In *La Femme dans les sociétés antiques,* E. Levy, ed., 93–123. Strasbourg.

Schaps, David M. 1977. "The Woman Least Mentioned: Etiquette and Women's Names," *CQ* 27:323–330.

———. 1979. *Economic Rights of Women in Ancient Greece.* Edinburgh.

Schuller, Wolfgang. 1985. *Frauen in der griechischen Geschichte.* Konstanz.

Sealey, Raphael. 1990. *Women and Law in Classical Greece.* Chapel Hill.

Seidensticker, Bernd. 1972. "Pentheus," *Poetica* 5:35–63.

———. 1982. "Die Wahl des Todes bei Sophokles." In *Sophocle: Entretiens sur l'antiquité classique* 29:105–153.

Shaw, Michael. 1975. "The Female Intruder: Women in Fifth-Century Drama," *CP* 70:255–266.

Starr, Chester G. 1978. "An Evening with the Flute-girls," *PP* 33:401–410.

Vaio, John. 1973. "The Manipulation of Theme and Action in Aristophanes' *Lysistrata*," *GRBS* 14:369–380.

Vernant, Jean-Pierre. 1969. "Hestia-Hermès: Sur l'expression religieuse de l'espace et du mouvement chez les Grecs." In *Mythe et pensée chez les Grecs*, 97–158. Paris.

———. 1988. *Myth and Tragedy in Ancient Greece*. New York. (Originally published *Mythe et tragédie en Grèce ancienne*. Paris 1972.)

Vidal-Naquet, Pierre, ed. 1979. *Aristophane: Les Femmes et la cité*. Paris.

Walker, Susan. 1983. "Women and Housing in Classical Greece." In Cameron and Kuhrt 1983:81–91.

Wiersma, S. 1984. "Women in Sophocles," *Mnemosyne* 37:25–55.

Winnington-Ingram, R. P. 1983*a*. *Aeschylus*. Cambridge.

———. 1983*b*. "Sophocles and Women." In *Sophocle: Entretiens sur l'antiquité classique* 29:233–49. Geneva. First published in *JHS* 88 (1949) 130–47.

Zeitlin, Froma I. 1981. "Travesties of Gender and Genre in Aristophanes' *Thesmophoriazusae*." In Foley 1981:169–217.

———. 1982. "Cultic Models of the Female: Rites of Dionysus and Demeter," *Arethusa* 15:129–157.

———. 1984. "The Dynamics of Misogyny: Mythmaking in the Oresteia." In John Peradotto and John P. Sullivan, eds., *Women in the Ancient World: The Arethusa Papers*, 159–194. Albany.

———. 1985. "Playing the Other: Theater, Theatricality, and the Feminine in Greek Drama," *Representations* 11:63–94.

Zoepffel, Renate. 1989. *Aufgaben, Rollen und Räume von Mann und Frau im archaischen und klassischen Griechenland*, in Jochen Martin und Renate Zoepffel, eds., *Aufgaben, Rollen und Räume von Mann und Frau*, II:443–500. Munich.

SEVEN

ART, MEMORY, AND *KLEOS* IN
EURIPIDES' *IPHIGENIA IN AULIS*

Froma I. Zeitlin

Ⓘt is a seldom noted fact that the evolution of dramaturgical techniques and concerns in the fifth century closely coincides with the development of the figurative arts (sculpture, reliefs, painting). Theater in fact contributes to this development through the advances made in perspective, coloration, perceptions of distance and proximity, and general interest in pictorial space, starting with scene painting, called *skēnographia* (a term that later comes to cover the general category of perspective).[1] The painter Agatharchos, whose work spans the period in question, is credited with being both the first to introduce scene painting for the Aeschylean stage and also, in the latter part of the century, the first to decorate a private dwelling with paintings (the house of Alcibiades).[2] This same artist is reputed to have written a treatise on perspective, as are the two philosophers Anaxagoras and Democritus, following their interest in optical phenomena.[3]

Additionally, in the opinion of some scholars, the technique of *skiagraphia* (interpreted variously as chiaroscuro effects of modeling through light and shade, outline drawing, impressionistic use of color, or *trompe l'oeil* effects) can also be ascribed to the influence of the theater, originating toward the end of the fifth century.[4] And if we can detect a growing influence, for example, of theatrical scenes and stage effects in vase painting of the period[5]—such as experiments in hinting at an imagined interior space[6]—the reverse may also be true in that initially the theatrical medium may itself have borrowed from the plastic arts such stylized conventions as gestures, poses, motifs, compositional schemes, and tableaux.[7] As we also know from at least one famous instance, the theater must invent an iconography for mythic figures that have never before been depicted and hence cannot be named. The Erinyes whom the Pythia sees for the first time at the opening of Aeschylus' *Eumenides* are unknown to her. They are creatures "terrible to speak of, terrible to gaze at with one's eyes"

(*Eum.* 34). They are female, it is true, but they may be Gorgons, she thinks, yet they do not exactly resemble Gorgonic types (Γοργέοισιν εἰκάσω τύποις). They might be Harpies whose painted image she once had seen, but they do not have wings as Harpies do, and besides they are black, and their eyes drip with a disgusting ooze (*Eum.* 48–54). If the Pythia is unable to identify the intruders at Apollo's shrine, she can at least, through her experience with art, place them in a general field of iconographical signs by which they may be defined both visually and thematically in the company of other monstrous females.

The evidence of our ancient sources for these reciprocal influences between the visual and dramatic arts is far from satisfactory. Yet it seems beyond dispute that the experience of the *theatron* and the growing interest in various techniques of representation, including the rise of monumental painting, placed a new emphasis on the role of the spectator and enlarged the uses of visual perception in the cultural life of the city. The sheer profusion of public artistic monuments and architectural programmes (along with painted pottery and votive offerings) attests to this broader trend, as do the marked theoretical interest in dramatic and artisanal techniques, the mathematics of optics, and the issue of mimesis itself. Clearly, "art" and "theater" cannot stand as alone as monolithic and unitary terms nor can they be treated as commensurate with one another simply on the grounds that both are visual phenomena. Nevertheless, both share the requirement of an attentive gaze as well as a stylized and informed mode of viewing, which, beyond its emotive qualities, engages the cognitive skills of spectators in learning how to recognize, evaluate, and interpret the visual codes of what they see.

The complexities of this topic are far too vast for an adequate discussion here. For the theater, at least, it would have to involve a more detailed review of the development of different aspects of the stage and a comparative survey of the major dramatists in their uses of visual language and gesture, along with analysis of themes and vocabulary drawn from the figurative arts.[8] Certainly, as my examples drawn from Aeschylus suggest, the tendency I am indicating begins already with the first tragic poet, who, according to tradition, was known for his bold experiments with spectacular effects in the theater. But in this brief essay I want to focus on Euripides, whom ancient biographers claim began his career as a painter before turning to tragedy. The veracity of this information is less significant than the implied observation that Euripidean drama displays some marked affinity for the visual arts as reflected, for example, in the new pictorial quality of his imagery, the emphasis on the keen and practiced eye of the spectator on stage, and, more directly, in the use of embedded ecphrases, or descriptions of works of art, and framed aesthetic scenes as actual elements in his text.

From the start, the tragic stage was organized in both its spatial and mental horizons around the dialectical relationship between what can be seen and what cannot, and it extended the practical problems of vision and visibility that belong to the conventions of its *mise en scène* into an epistemological concern with insight, knowledge, revelation, and truth. Sight is a privileged source of knowledge; it is also the delusive basis of appearance. Both aspects are played out in the course of dramatic enactment and through the wide-ranging use of visual language. This combination often creates a "double perspective" for the audience which "looks at the action . . . through its own eyes and through the eyes of those on stage," thus producing the characteristic trope of tragic irony.[9] Or, in another vein, we are shown figures who are keenly aware of themselves as the cynosure of others' eyes, demanding sometimes that we "witness the spectacle of their suffering so we may pity them, or calling for a covering to hide their shame, sometimes wishing to be hidden inside the house, or again sometimes yearning for some supernatural way to disappear from public view."[10]

Euripides himself goes further than his predecessors in thematizing the implications both of vision and of the interplay between illusion and reality, whether in exploring and enforcing the proprieties of reciprocal viewing in a social world of human relationships (*Hipp.*),[11] or in testing the trustworthiness of visual perception and the world of appearances in the extreme case of Helen and her *eidōlon* (*Hel.*).[12] This look-alike phantasmatic double will vanish into thin air at the opportune moment, but Helen initially holds her own enticing appearance to blame for her misfortunes, as though she were a work of art. "If only," she says, "I could have been erased, like a painted image *(agalma)*, and have gotten an uglier form *(eidos)* instead of the beauty I have now" (*Hel.* 261–263; cf. Aesch. *Ag.* 1329). Painting serves as the ground of comparison between the permanence of a human form and the evanescence of an art that its creator can remake at will, but it serves too as the touchstone of an enduring aesthetic value for this self-regarding spectator. In another play, the *Hecuba,* which is also centered in its own way on the primacy of sight and vision,[13] the aged queen likewise views herself in the painter's idiom, this time as an object to be gazed at from afar so she may be apprehended in the totality of her physical bearing. "Pity me, behold me *(idou),*" she says in her appeal to Agamemnon, "and like a painter, standing at a distance, gaze at me *(athrēson)* in my sufferings" (*Hec.* 807–809). The emotive power of the image, the formal perspective of distance, and the reference to the painter's technique as he works to perfect his art are projected on to the other as spectator. But the comparison depends on the prior objectivization of a self who must first imagine herself in the picture in order to elicit the empathetic response to her psychological distress that she so intensely desires.

These two examples of self-reflexive viewing on the part of major characters are only special cases of this pervasive tendency in Euripidean theater to emphasize the conditions and details of visual experience, whether to expand the imaginative field of vision far beyond the confines of the theater (chorus) or to register private emotional states that are vividly realized (lyric monody), or to give the impression of objective eyewitness reports.[14] A recent study of messenger speeches demonstrates the degree to which the first-person narrator sees himself as a *theatēs* in his own right—an observer and eyewitness of the events he reports, which he more than once calls a *theama*.[15] "I stood at the Electran gate as a spectator *(theatēs)*, occupying the tower that gives a good view *(euagēs)*, and I beheld *(horō)* . . ." (*Supp.* 651–653). The acuteness of his vision is guaranteed by the quality of light, for it was the time when "the shining ray of the sun, the standard of clarity (κανὼν σαφής) was just striking the ground" (*Supp.* 650–651). The messenger, as always in Greek tragedy, stands in for the spectators, those both on and off the stage. But in Euripides, his function as a spectator at another drama, another *drōmena*, is specified, not only in these explicit gestures to theatrical viewing, but in the narrative style that never "loses sight of the action" and, among other devices, uses "the combined qualities of setting, grouping, and perspective-change" to "make the narrative clearly visible" to the audience.[16]

All these effects contribute to a sense of an authentic happening that can persuade the audience of the veracity of the report, but it is also worth noting that a large number of vase paintings identified as scenes from Euripidean drama represent messenger speeches, as if confirming their strikingly visual appeal.[17] But rather than accounting for this evidence, as some have claimed, as a sign just of the popular interest in these speeches[18] or as indicating a one-way influence of drama on art, we might consider, as I will later, how the organization of visual experience in the verbal medium sometimes reflects the aesthetic conventions of pictorial display. And to add yet another dimension to these relations between the arts, the language of visual description may also resonate with echoes of other previous ecphrastic texts to produce an effect of montage or a species of double vision that evokes a sense of *déjà vu* in present theatrical time.

This effect is one I will show in more detail for a single play, the *Iphigenia in Aulis*, with the general aim of exploring some of the implications of the increasing importance of visualization and spectatorship as a technique of Euripides' theater in the later fifth century, when both dramatic and iconographical repertories are firmly established and when the uses of the observing eye are put at the service of both aesthetic and instructional use. Aesthetically speaking, the eye of the beholder is subject to two contradictory (but related) impulses: on the one hand, the so-called reality effect deriving from a more fully described world of color, texture, light, and shade, and on the other a self-reflexive awareness of the mimetic qualities of the artistic medium in both theatrical and figurative domains. Neither, I maintain, would be possible without the shaping and organization of perceptual reality through the images of the plastic arts that press for verisimilitude but also stimulate the powers of the visual imagination, of seeing with the mind's eye through the pictorial description of objects and places that are not directly present to the viewer. Beyond aesthetic considerations, however, art is shown as a source of information, a mode of learning, whether of ordinary matters or of weightier cultural traditions. Hecuba in the *Troades* has never set foot on a ship, but she knows about ships and the sea from paintings she has seen (*Tro.* 686). Likewise, the virtuous Hippolytus claims ignorance about sex, except for what he has gleaned from viewing pictures or has heard from others (*Hipp.* 1004–1006), while the young Ion, brought up at Delphi, derives his knowledge of the mythic history of Athens in a similar way (*Ion* 271). This last instance reminds us that the cognitive effects I propose cannot be separated from the environment of the *polis* that promoted such aesthetic productivity and which, in its monumental art and building programmes for the adornment of the city, also educated its citizens through recodings of mythic traditions into visual narrative and form.

What interests me most in this context is the shaping and cultivation of cultural memory (and also inevitably of political ideology), not just as a way of "divulging and perpetuating myths and with them, the legendary history of men and the communities in which they lived," [19] but as an active engagement, conditioned by a sense of historical process, that refashions the past in the present and the present in the past through the differing modalities of visual and verbal idioms.[20] Tragedy itself consists, of course, in a dialogical representation of ancient myths in the present that operates as a complex set of "interferences" between the two. But in Euripides, as is often remarked, these "interferences" are most pronounced, and a more troubling distance opens up between the two worlds of then and now, usually with disconcerting effects. These dissonances are often lamented as painful indications of cultural crisis, but they should also be taken as signs of a changing mentality that reflects a more formal historical consciousness, which is manifested, for example, in an awareness of multiple and competing traditions and in an antiquarian interest in cultural lore. This outlook, which in the next era will result in more systematic efforts at codification,[21] also takes a more extended view over events in time than tragic convention usually allows and, in keeping with its literary status, it engages with the past in a denser network of intertextual readings, which include replays of visual scenes, now translated at a second level into the visual space that is the *theatron* and its stage.

Such effects are most evident in what I would call examples of "hyperviewing": that is, those moments in Euripidean drama of ecphrastic discourse, which, in their absorptive gaze that is focused on a visual scene or tableau, join word and image in pictorial language. This genre of discourse begins, of course, in Homer with Achilles' shield,[22] but in the visual setting of the theater, it is framed as a second and heightened order of observation, whose mimetic effects are to be communicated to the spectators as part of the stage action itself. Most often dismissed as decorative ornaments or virtuoso displays, or treated only as symptoms of the disjunction between a romantic past and a more sordid present, between sacred authority and secular aesthetics, these moments are precisely those that exemplify the issues I have raised about the interrelations between art and theater, between specularity and interpretation.

It is noteworthy, first of all, that in the three plays I chose for discussion in my full exposition[23] (the *Ion*, the *Iphigenia in Aulis*, and the *Phoenissae*), the scenes in question all belong to the opening segments of prologue or *parodos* (choral entrance song). They take place as a counterpoint to an initial speaker or speakers, and their immediate function is to shift the perspective to expand in detail and scope the sense of the actual visual decor as well as to set the scene in the mind's eye. These ecphrastic moments are dramatized from the point of view of the spectators on stage, and it should be noted that all are first-time viewers, who, in fixing their gaze on a new and arresting sight, derive both pleasure and instruction from what they purport to see.

Second, and not surprisingly, these naive spectators turn out to be women who have been sheltered from the outside world, consisting as they do of the Athenian attendants of Creusa *(Ion)*, the thrill-seeking girls of Aulis *(IA)*, and the young Antigone with her elderly tutor *(Phoen.)*.[24] A third and essential point is that all three plays are preoccupied with a longer diachronic view of a narrative history shaping that tragic "interference" between ancient myths and contemporary concerns, and all introduce expansive epic elements of theme and structure into their dramatic composition. Spatial viewing anticipates and symbolizes temporal extension under the idea of a continuously evolving mythic history in the light of civic and national identity.

The *Ion*, which reveals the true identity of the foundling at Delphi, the unknown son of the god Apollo and the Athenian princess Creusa, treats the last moment in the prehistory of Athens in the consolidation of its founding dynasty that sustains contemporary claims to hegemony over Greece. By contrast, the *Iphigenia in Aulis*, which relates the circumstances leading to the sacrifice of Agamemnon's daughter, stands midway in the saga of the Trojan War, between the events that led up to the mustering of the Greek expedition and the actual war in Troy and its aftermath in the fortunes of the House of Atreus. By this route it arrives not only at a *déjà vu* of epic and tragedy in current dramatic time but at a more up-to-date vision of collective action in the idea of Panhellenic unity, now codified in public discourse and art since the Persian Wars. Lastly, the *Phoenissae*, characterized as depicting the "tragedy of civilization,"[25] is epic in its proportions (and in its language), as it surveys the entire history of Thebes from its very foundation, just at the critical moment when the city is besieged by its Argive attackers and Oedipus' two sons are to confront one another in fratricidal battle. At the same time, the ecphrastic scenes in all these plays have an historical dimension in their own right: that is, they are complex reworkings of both poetic and pictorial traditions and, taken on these terms, their representational value is inseparable from the larger cultural project they are designed to represent.

The *Ion*, in its direct confrontation with different works of art (the sculptures of the temple façade, the tapestries of Ion's tent) thematizes the uses of pictured images across a whole spectrum of values, both old and new. Its vivid iconography, set in the hallowed oracular seat of Delphi, exemplifies the traditional function of reading symbolic images as divinatory signs, but its emphasis in the text also suggests an increased awareness of the visual medium as a distinctive mode of instruction about the legacy of the past. The shift during the course of the play from stone to textile, from the straightforward representation of time-honored myths to a creative and composite design, may chart the correlative development of Ion's identity and a politically imagined history of Athens.[26] But the sequence may also signify in its own right as a gesture toward the sense of a history of artistic styles.[27] On the other hand, the *parodos* of the *Iphigenia in Aulis*, in which the local women come to see the army massed at Aulis, is an example of an ecphrastic description that, in its visual details, suggests a transference from epic poetry to painted images as a mode of knowing, and a reconfiguration of the *kleos*, or renown, guaranteed by the bard to hint at the *topoi* (places) and *eikones* (images) of a nascent memory system. Finally, for the *Phoenissae*, there are several moments that best represent the problems of specularity and of interpretation, both of which are central to the thematics of this panoramic play that ranges over the whole conflictual history of Thebes. The first is the view over the massed Argive army at the gates of Thebes, the second is the messenger's description of the Argive shields. These are echo texts that refer to earlier textual versions in epic and tragedy. Both are exemplary specimens of telescopic and panoptic viewing from the vantage point of a city's walls, within which, in this case, the aged Oedipus still dwells in hidden seclusion; his belated entrance on stage in the figure of an archaic *eidōlon* image marks him truly as an image of the past.

Let us look more closely, however, at a single play, the *Iphigenia in Aulis*, the centerpiece in the triad of dramas I have identified as important examples of heightened relations between art and theater. This piece, the last in Euripides' repertory (along with the *Bacchae*), dramatizes the sacrifice of Agamemnon's daughter as the precondition for the launching of the Greek expedition to Troy. In this fast-paced drama of surprising twists and turns, Iphigenia is lured to Aulis on the pretext of a marriage to Achilles, but the intrigue quickly unravels and the deception is exposed to all concerned, including the would-be bridegroom and the bride's mother, Clytemnestra, who has unexpectedly appeared in company with her daughter. Played out against the background of a restive, even seditious, army at odds with its leaders, whose vacillating resolve and opportunistic motives suggest an uncomfortable degree of contemporary realism, the issue of Iphigenia's sacrifice questions the heroic values of the Homeric tradition but also ambiguously reinstates them in the maiden's sudden decision to offer herself for the sake of all of Greece. Turning from the pitiful victim, whom now all the characters would save, even at the cost of not going to Troy, Iphigenia takes on the starring role to embrace a destiny decreed by her myth, preferring to offer herself as the bride of Hellas rather than risk the overwhelming coercion of the Greek host. Long regarded as a problem play, particularly with respect to textual anomalies of form and structure at the beginning and the end,[28] the *Iphigenia in Aulis* is nevertheless a brilliant theatrical piece of artful design. Structured around the oppositions between love and war, between marriage and sacrifice, public and private, family and country, and, of course, between the two worlds of men and of women, the play is psychologically astute, politically aware, and provocative in its uneasy confrontations between a demystified present and those hallowed epic ideals that are framed from the start in the choral *parodos*.

In the *Iphigenia in Aulis*, by contrast to the *Ion*, with its temple sculptures and woven tapestries, the visual description in the choral *parodos* is not an ecphrasis in its familiar, restricted meaning of a description of a work of art. Technically, the panoramic view over the encampment of the Greeks at Aulis, together with the scene of ships in the harbor, conforms to the general category of ecphrasis, or vivid description, as codified in the rhetorical handbooks of the later Greco-Roman period *(Progymnasmata)*, which classify such descriptions into four main categories: persons *(prosōpa)*, places *(topoi)*, periods of time *(chronoi)* and *pragmata* (activities or circumstances), among which group scenes of armies and fleets are specifically mentioned.[29] As in so many of Euripides' other innovations in theme and technique that anticipate later literary developments of the Hellenistic period, this lengthy choral description already exemplifies the conditions expressly associated with the topos of ecphrasis, whose aim is to produce a visual clarity *(saphēneia)* and vividness *(enargeia)* in words designed "to make hearers into spectators."[30] Yet, as we shall see, what is recounted by the chorus of Euboean women as they gaze over the entire field is already conditioned by experience with works of art, both of single scenes and of larger and more complex paintings.

The sense of an artistic pictorial display is reinforced by the identity of the chorus itself. Unlike Creusa's attendants in the *Ion*, who have accompanied their mistress from Athens to Delphi, these women have no reason for being there other than the simple fact that they live in the vicinity and are driven by curiosity to take in the impressive sight. Although they too, like their counterparts in the *Ion*, repeatedly refer to the act of looking, here the emphasis falls on the emotive and aesthetic aspects of the experience: their desire to see (190–191), the joy they take in sating their eyes with the spectacle (232–234), and the beauty that arouses their astonished gaze (203, 205).[31] Their eagerness to look upon this world of men and arms is so strong that, despite their scruples of feminine modesty (185–188), it impels them to leave their town of Chalcis and to come at a run "through the sacred grove of Artemis." What draws their attention is not a well-established locus of visual treasures like Delphi, but rather a transient scene of real life and a fortuitous point in time that allows the women to glimpse the visual splendor of the expedition assembled on the shores of Aulis. Whereas in the *Ion* the question of realism revolved around what might have been depicted on the façade of the actual stage building that represented the temple at Delphi, here the impression is one of a full *skēnographia*, a painted backdrop to frame the drama of Iphigenia as it unfolds on stage before the eyes of the spectators in the audience. But aside from the impossibility of mounting such an ambitious representation in the theater, this extensive description goes far beyond the usual function of an initial choral song to identify the locale of an individual play in its spatial and temporal coordinates, and it does so, like a monumental wall painting, in a series of aesthetically constituted scenes.

The *parodos* falls into two distinct parts: the first, consisting of strophe, antistrophe, and epode (164–230), is followed by a second, composed of three pairs of strophes and antistrophes (231–302). What the women claim they have come to see are "the army of the Achaeans and the seafaring ships of the proud demigods" (171–173), further specified as the "bulwark of shields, the tents of the Danaans filled with arms," and the "masses of horses" nearby (189–191). But in the first part they actually describe various heroes at leisure, engaged in pleasurable sports, in states of both repose and activity. Eight heroes are named in the antistrophe, divided into two groups. The two Ajaxes are sitting side by side. Near them is Protesilaos playing at draughts, "delighting in the intricate shapes of the game"; his partner is Palamedes (191–198). The women's gaze then shifts to Diomedes, "taking joy from the pleasures of the discus," followed by Meriones, "a marvel to mortals" (199–202), Odysseus, "that man from the mountainous isle, son of Laertes," and finally Nireus, "the fairest of the Achaeans" (204–206).

Others have pointed to the artistic layout of the scene—its spatial relations organized on different planes with a careful positioning of figures, viewed from a distance[32]—and they have suggested a tableau reminiscent of the techniques of monumental painting pioneered by Polygnotus.[33] Mention has also been made of vase paintings with scenes of Homeric heroes intent upon their game of draughts, and the pose of the discus thrower finds analogies, for example, on Panathenaic vases and in bronze or marble statuary.[34] Homeric epithets that describe the outstanding valor of heroes merge with the aesthetics of viewing (*thauma, kalliston*), and the visual pleasure of the women matches the pleasure of those delighting in their games. Palamedes, the man of intricate thought, enjoys the "intricate shapes" (*poluplokois morphais*, 196–197) of the dice: complexity of mind is refracted both through visual patterns and through the nature of the activity in which they figure.

In the epode, too, there is a similar convergence of figure, image, and action in the description of Achilles' race against the four-horse team of the chariot driven by Eumelos. The unusual contest between a single man and a team of horses acts out in graphic and compelling detail the hero's most characteristic epithet.[35] In this fully imagined scene of movement and color that brings the entire description of the Homeric heroes to a climax, the terms "swift-footed" (*laipsēdromos*) and "fleet as the wind" (*isanēmon*) are animated into reality before the chorus' eyes (206–230). What they see is how Achilles in his armor was rounding the goalpost and how the shouting charioteer was plying his whip against the most handsome horses (*kallistous . . . pōlous*) the women had ever seen. With their magnificent panoply of gilded bit and bridle (*chrusodaidaltous*) and their different shades of dappled gray and fiery red, manes flecked with white, feet of piebald color, the horses are truly a splendid sight. It is a fitting close to the entire scene that moves from repose (the game of draughts) and a single activity (the discus throw) to the more complex action that culminates in an explosion of visual energy that trains the spotlight on the most preeminent hero and gives immediate proof of his traditional prowess. Dramatically speaking, the emphasis is justified. Achilles is the only one named who is to play a part in the stage action to come, and because he is first introduced to the spectators through women's eyes, aesthetic appreciation is already tinged with an erotic coloring that foreshadows Iphigenia's own first bedazzled view of her pretend bridegroom.[36]

In the second part of the *parodos*, the women turn to the ships. There are compositional links between the two sections: one is internal (Achilles is last among the heroes and first in the enumeration of his ships) and the other describes a wide arc of ring composition whereby Ajax, "crown of Salamis," leads the ranks of heroes (along with the other Ajax), and the same "nursling of Salamis" brings the series of ships to a close. The elaborate description of his intricate naval maneuvers emphasizes his position in the structural design and gives an Athenian audience pride of place in commemorating their recent historical past in the naval battle that won them the victory against the Persians.

The chorus begins this section (the authenticity of which many suspect) by first stating its wish to count the ships. They emphasize their intense desire to see this "indescribable sight" *(thean athesphaton)*, a spectacle "to fill their feminine eyes, a greedy pleasure" (234). In the list that follows, spatial indications of proximity, direction, and serial position give the impression of an actual scene. The most remarkable feature, however, is the addition of the painted (or possibly sculpted) golden emblems *(chruseois eikosi*, 239) that adorn some of the prows of the ships and are identifying signs of the different contingents. These emblems vary in their synecdochic value. The Myrmidons are represented by the pedigree of their leader ("twenty golden Nereids, the sign of Achilles' host," 239–241), the Attic forces by their patron goddess ("Pallas in her winged chariot of single-hoofed horses, a sight of fair sign for sailors" *[eusēmon . . . phasma]*, 250–252). Thebes prefers an image of its founder ("Cadmus holding a golden serpent," 256–257), Pylos a geographical marker in the bull-footed figure of its neighboring river, the Alpheus (275–276). These figured insignia,[37] or *sēmata* (252, 255, 275), may be likened to shield devices or, even better, to emblems on coins that identify the cities of their issue. Beautiful to see, they enliven the details of a lengthy catalogue and, as coded signs, they impress the spectator's memory with visual cues that may prompt an easier recall.

In closing, the chorus twice refers to ears and eyes as the twin sources of what they know. "Such is the naval host I have heard about, such the one that I have seen," they declare after describing Ajax and his ships (294–296). But vision takes precedence in the coda that rounds off the entire *parodos:*

> Such is the navy's setting forth/that I've seen here,
> So when at home I hear it spoken of *(kluousa),*
> I will guard the memory *(mnēmēn sōizomai)*
> Of the gathering of the host.
> (299–302)[38]

These may be innocent words, designed to enhance the realism of the scene and to give credence to what they have described. Certainly, this ending creates an interesting tension between the visual immediacy of the scene and the traditions of epic poetry, whose diction and content pervade their song. Yet there may be something more in the elaborate ecphrases of this unusual choral entrance song that addresses the question of cultural memory in this period— how it is shaped and how transmitted. On the one hand, the chorus performs as a good historian might, appealing to hearsay but deriving authority from an eyewitness report and signaling, as Herodotus does in his proem, the magnitude of the event it takes credit for perceiving at the outset. On the other hand, given the gestures to the artistic conventions of the day and the casting of the scene into recognizably aesthetic form, this instance of theatrical "hyperviewing" may indicate some greater role for pictorial information in relaying the legacy of epic narrative sources. Unlike the images of the Delphic temple in the *Ion* (Herakles and the Hydra, Bellerophon and the Chimera, the Gigantomachy) which are among the most popular iconographical themes in Greek art, the *parodos* draws on a general recognition of familiar artistic scenes (e.g., games and sport) and of painterly techniques in organizing complex scenes into a spatial whole. Still further, it might be suggested that the *parodos* even validates the use of pictorial images located in well-defined spaces as an aide-mémoire to assist in the historical recording of people, places, and events. Euripides writes at a time when certain mnemonic techniques were already available. Although the evidence is far from secure, there are reasons to suspect that the rudiments of what in the next era was to develop into a fully articulated memory system were already in place. The explicit mention of *mnēmē* at the close of the choral song may thus intimate to the spectators that what they have witnessed through the women's eyes is a process of memorization for future recollection that itself is indebted to experience with newer artistic conventions and graphic images.

Simonides, we may recall, was credited with the invention of the first memory system, based on the recollection of seeing persons in the order of seating in a given place,[39] and attributed also to him was the famous dictum that "painting is silent poetry and poetry is painting that speaks."[40] Themistocles, possibly his acquaintance, was reputed to have refused to acquire the new art of memory, claiming he would prefer to learn an art of forgetting rather than a technique of remembering (Cic. *De Orat.* 2.74.299–300). Despite the disagreement of scholars on the status and nature of memory systems during the fifth century, they generally concur that the question of memory training, particularly in the use of visual cues, was of current interest among the sophists, who have left some suggestive traces of their activities.[41] Hippias, for example, was proverbial for his remarkable memory. According to many sources, including Plato, he seems to have been acquainted with a mnemotechnics, and perhaps even taught it. He was especially famous for his feat of repeating fifty names in a series after only one hearing (although we do not know what means he used) and he was said to have possessed a vast storehouse of encyclopedic knowledge, which probably was fortified by a mnemonic system.[42] There is no doubt that a true architectural art of memory, which relies on *loci* and *imagines*—that is, the mental construction of a defined space with images distributed at specified intervals—was developed afterward in the Hellenistic period, although elements of its system may well have been in use even before.

The visual arts have their role to play in this development. Given the widespread notion of memory, attested from Aeschylus on, as a wax tablet that receives all sorts of graphic impressions that can be read or seen,[43] it follows that the process of recollection can eventually be theorized from the experience of viewing paintings. Aristotle, for example, in his treatise on memory (*De Mem.* 450b11–20) likens "the image within us" to a painted panel that may be treated both as a figure (*zōon*) and as a copy/likeness (*eikon*). If a figure is regarded in itself, it is "an object of contemplation" (*theorēma*) or a visual "image" (*phantasma*). But if it refers to something else, then it is a sort of copy (*hoion eikon*) and a reminder (*mnēmoneuma*). The influence of the theater on such an art of memory should also be considered, as it is, in fact, in later Roman sources (Cic. *De Orat.* 2.88.359), since the system works best with constructing memorable scenes and framed tableaux, along with figures that can be turned into active, lively, and notable images.

For the end of the fifth century, our claims must be more modest. In the context of the *Iphigenia in Aulis,* the emphasis on vision, the deployment of figures in space, and the catalogue itself—starting with the desire to count (*arithmos*) and ending with the specific mention of *mnēmē*—may indicate the uses of mental scene-making, particularly with respect to the management of lists of names and numbers that are enhanced by the iconic shorthand of the naval emblems. In general, given the spatial and somatic nature of memory images, the entire *parodos* answers to some more general principles advised for secure recollective procedures: a strong affective engagement of the viewer (visual intensity, pleasure in seeing) "sensorily derived and emotionally charged," associations both verbal and visual, marked positions in a series constituted as "scenes," and an experience that can be "reenacted" later in the mind.[44]

Yet even granting some validity to this suggestion of a visual mnemonics at work, the mention of *mnēmē* (memory) in context must refer to the traditional values of Homeric epic itself as the guarantor of memory in the making of *kleos* (glory) for its heroes, an oral memory that will "forever live on the lips of men" (e.g., *Theog.* 237–254). As many have noted, the *parodos* is saturated throughout by Homeric language, with direct allusion to the epic tradition— the *Iliad* as well as the lost *Cypria,* the cyclic poem that contained the actual story of Iphigenia. The viewing of the chorus bears a resemblance in a sense to the famous *teichoskopia* on the walls of Troy in *Iliad* 3, when Helen identified the Greek heroes on the plain before her to Priam and the other Trojan elders, while the catalogue of ships recalls more directly its counterpart in *Iliad* 2 (and possibly also a similar catalogue in the *Cypria*).[45] The past is therefore invoked in a deliberate intertextual relation with the epic idiom and, by association, with those same epic values of *aretē* (valor) and *kleos* that attract heroic images and mythic scenes into their orbit. Panoramic viewing in space corresponds to the narrative sweep of epic, and the text itself enters into relations with other texts, as well as with the already constituted dramatic repertory of previous plays that concerned the war at Troy and its aftermath in the fortunes of the House of Atreus.[46]

In Book 2 of the *Iliad*, the poet invoked the Muses in a special proem as he prepared to deliver his tour de force in the catalogue of ships. The Muses know everything, the poet only the report (the *kleos*) of what he has heard. He needs their help because otherwise he "could not narrate or name the multitudes," not even if he had "ten tongues, ten mouths, an unbreakable voice, and an iron heart within him" (2.484–493). Here too, in the *Iphigenia in Aulis*, the chorus introduces its catalogue with a new beginning, but Homeric speech gives way to visual spectacle ("the desire to fill their eyes with the sight") and the emphasis passes to the experience, not of words, but of theatrical viewing. This revision of Homeric method may also refer, as I have claimed, to the techniques of a nascent memory system, but it also advertises in the present tense of the play that what follows will be a momentous epic event.

The chorus cannot know, of course, that the drama to ensue will jeopardize the expedition we know has already taken place, an expedition they, in fact, will imagine in the third *stasimon* (choral song) as having crossed the seas to Troy (751–800). They cannot know as yet that the reason will be Agamemnon's daughter, Iphigenia, whose sacrifice is essential if the ships are to sail. Hence if the specular aspect of the *parodos* suggests a possible contest between verbal and visual means, between epic narrative and theatrical vista, between the past and the present, two further questions arise. The first is the issue of epic ideals and how these are confronted and shaped in the rest of the play. Do *kleos* and *mnēmē* recur as operative terms in the course of the action and with what effects? The second is whether, in its foregrounding of spectacle, the *parodos* already suggests to the audience a cue to the import of future visual experience in the economy of the play. How is vision organized and to what does it lead?

This *parodos* of unusual length follows after a distinctly unusual prologue (in which Agamemnon attempts unsuccessfully to prevent his daughter from coming to Aulis), and both sections have been subjected to harsh scrutiny by critics, who have often claimed, for a variety of reasons, that neither is entirely the authentic work of Euripides. Recent defenses, however, have pointed to, among other factors, the elaborate symmetry that organizes the two, individually and together, to comprise a formal ensemble of technical virtuosity.[47] Although Agamemnon's brief mention of how the Greeks came, marshaling their ships, shields, horses, and chariots (84), finds an immediate echo in the chorus' first panoramic viewing, the prologue and *parodos* are marked by striking contrasts and different perspectives. In particular, there is the basic opposition between insiders and outsiders, proximity and distance, between the conspiratorial secrecy of the prologue in the conversation between Agamemnon and his messenger servant and the unrestricted public gaze of the chorus. The women do not know, of course, the reasons why the expedition has lingered at Aulis for the pleasure of their viewing, and against the true unhappy details revealed in Agamemnon's anguish over sacrificing his daughter, the chorus sees a broad, diversified scene, colored by a romantic aesthetic haze.

On the other hand, there is an interesting tension between the stated theme of the play and the potential of the prologue, if the servant's mission succeeds, to short-circuit the entire heroic *geste* previewed before the chorus' eyes. If Iphigenia does not come, the Trojan War will not take place, and in this suspended moment of the theatrical present, the realization of the myth is threatened, as typically in Euripides, with the possibility of its nonperformance.[48]

The chorus of women will become progressively more involved in the brute reality of the action, while still retaining their lyric role as custodians of past poetic traditions.[49] Remarkably, as they come to identify more and more with Iphigenia and her female predicament, she in turn eventually absorbs their epic perspective in the service of a political ideal of Panhellenic solidarity to justify the Greek expedition, going so far as to adopt their lyric voice in the form of her own monodic song that precedes her decision (1280–1335).[50] The female voice, whether chorus or character, upholds the higher virtues of both epic past and political present against the male world of deception, expediency, instability, strife, and violence, and in so doing promotes an uneasy, if ironic, equilibrium that defies any simple resolution.

Iphigenia's change of mind in deciding to accept her role as sacrificial victim as a patriotic gesture to safeguard Greek communal values has disturbed critics, from Aristotle onward (*Poet.* 15.1454a26), for its apparent abruptness and lack of explicit psychological motivation. The scene has also had defenders on several grounds, based, in particular, on the intricate relations, noted above, between the chorus of women and their feminine counterpart in the person of Agamemnon's daughter. But if we focus on the semantics of *mnēmē* and heroic *kleos* as well as on the explicit language and action of viewing, some interesting highlights emerge from within the text that affect the quality of Iphigenia's decision, as she shifts from the private to the public sphere and reimagines herself as the sacrificial bride and heroine of all of Greece.

Iphigenia's long supplication of Agamemnon (1211–1252) appeals to the intimate relations between father and daughter. In pleading with him for her life ("Sweet it is to look upon the light; do not compel me to behold the world beneath the earth," 1218–1219), she recalls their mutual affection and promises to one another for the future. Quoting the direct words of their earlier conversation, (1221–1230), she reproaches him for the fact that while she has kept the *memory* of his words (λόγων μνήμην ἔχω), he has forgotten them. She implores him now to *gaze* at her (βλέψον), to give her both his *eye* and his *kiss* (ὄμμα δὸς φίλημά τε) so that if her words fail to persuade him, she will, in her dying, at least have this *souvenir* of him (μνημεῖον, 1238–1240). And she concludes with a general plea for the value of life: "The light is sweetest for mortals to *look upon* (βλέπειν); beneath the earth is nothing. . . . Better a wretched life than a glorious death" (1250–1252).[51]

Agamemnon, in his reply, picks up her reference to the power of the gaze but bids her rather to direct it to the present scene spread out before her eyes, the vista of army and ships, the multitude of leaders and their panoply of arms (1259–1260) that the spectators already know in detail from the choral description in the *parodos*. The Greeks cannot sail without the sacrifice of his daughter, Agamemnon argues, and they are determined to do so, he argues, in the name of the freedom of all of Greece against the barbarians and of the protection of their wives against unlawful seizure (1264–1275).

Whatever the logic or sincerity of Agamemnon's defense in its appeal to the watchwords of Greek *eleutheria* that come into common usage after the Persian Wars, Iphigenia's subsequent change of mind (after her lyric monody and Achilles' promise of protection) changes the visual focus of attention as well: "All of Greece in its majesty looks at me (*apoblepei*)," she declares, and this in both literal and figurative ways. Upon her depends the sailing of the expedition, the destruction of Troy, as well as the future fate of all Greek womanhood, put into jeopardy by the theft of Helen (1378–1382). Clytemnestra bore her not for her mother alone, but to be shared in common for the sake of Hellas (1386). What Iphigenia will gain by her glorious deed in thus liberating Greece from the barbarian threat is an enduring *kleos* (1376; 1383–1384) as fitting recompense for her savior role. Her sacrifice and the sack of Troy will be "her memorials for the length of time (μνημεῖα μοῦ διὰ μάκρου); these will be her children, her marriage, and her good name" (1398–1400).

This *kleos*, of course, is one familiar from epic ideology. But in keeping with its Panhellenic tone, the terms recall more closely the ideal of a patriotic heroism that had long translated archaic *kleos* into the praise of civic virtue for those citizen soldiers who had died in battle. Thus in giving instructions for her mother to follow after her death, Iphigenia underlines the triumphal theme by forbidding all mourning. In words that closely echo Simonides' famous epigram over those who died at Thermopylae (fr. 26.3; 531 P), she wants no tomb: the altar of Artemis will be her memorial (*mnēma*), and as she dictates the ceremonial protocols of prayer and procession for her sacrifice—her marriage with death—the women confirm the idea that *kleos* will be hers forever (1504). This *kleos* even spreads by contagion to her mother ("I am saved and through me you will get fair renown" *[eukleēs esēi]*, 1440) and for the chorus in their closing words, it applies to her father as well: "Let Agamemnon wreathe Greek spears with garlands of renown *(kleinotaton stephanon)* and place on his own head a glory that will always be remembered *(kleos aeimnēston)*" (1528–1531).

The invocation of a collective memory is finally the essential link that binds the beginning of the play to its end. The chorus had earlier vowed to remember what they had seen and heard that day in Aulis (299–302). Now their commemorative urge is one conditioned by the completed action of the play and the unusual context of Iphigenia's *kleos*, whose import is heightened by the ring composition that rounds off the theme in the same epic idiom (cf. 185–186).[52] Iphigenia's reversal of her previous position and the reversal in gender, whereby a woman, not a man, claims the traditional epic and civic values and passes them on to the greatest of all Greek heroes, have not gone unnoticed by critics of the play. The inversions, especially with regard to the heroic self-sacrifice of young girls, are a favorite theme of Euripides, carried to its furthest degree, however, in this drama that focuses entirely on the circumstances that lead to that action.[53]

What I wish to stress, however, is that, for all its ironies and uncertainties about Iphigenia's role and behavior, the play acts out on stage a dramatic process of *kleos* in the making that was already implied in the beginning choral scene. This now is a *kleos* that in the present tense of the action is reviewed against the historical backdrop of Panhellenic slogans about the unity of Greece confronting barbarian enemies in the East which came into currency after the Persian Wars. But it acquires a further and novel dramatic twist at the end in the miracle that transports Iphigenia to the realm of the gods and earns her instant acclaim from those who saw her achieve a divinely bestowed *kleos* before their eyes. While the Trojan War is always available for use as a paradigm of relations between East and West—in art as in the theater—this play constructs its own particular (and challenging) version of a deed to be remembered that, through the chorus' eyes, spans the temporal distance between epic convention and its theatrical reenactments, between the bardic voice of the past and the specular properties of the fifth-century stage. The *Iphigenia in Aulis* addresses the dissonances between these two extremes of past and present without ever wholly discrediting either the epic glamor surrounding the Trojan expedition or the stirring Panhellenic rhetoric, both of which seem to be compromised by the figures of those who claim to support them, whether through shallow opportunism or youthful naiveté.[54] The political realism of a military undertaking, subverted by internal *eris* and unmastered *eros*, may clash still more harshly with the divinely engineered fantasy of the maiden's rescue, but it does so in the frame of a vividly reported ceremony that engages its spectators from within the play to witness a memorable visual scene.

In the messenger's speech that narrates the scene of the sacrifice at which the savior of Greece will herself be saved,[55] these specular properties indeed come to the fore. The vivid details of a ritual staged as a public performance, followed by the dramatic intervention of a sudden apparition, strengthen my contention that an extraordinary visual emphasis in the first part of a play has some predictive value for the later dramaturgy. At the very least, it prepares the audience to expect some other unusual spectacle before the play is done. Ironically perhaps, critics have turned to depictions in art for assistance with the text, since this scene of Iphigenia's sacrifice became a popular theme in iconography, no doubt due in part to Euripides' play. A famous painting by Timanthus, dated to around 400, may have been directly inspired by the performance of the play, but the reverse may also be true, and, as one noted scholar suggests, Euripides might actually have borrowed his description from the painting itself.[56]

In the lively pictorial style of the narrative, the uses of the gaze are prominent, particularly in Agamemnon's memorable gesture of turning aside and veiling his eyes with his peplos to hide his tears at the sight of his daughter's arrival (1547–1550). At the fateful moment when the scene at the altar is set and all is prepared, the army too cannot bear to look, but fixes its gaze on the ground (εἰς γῆν βλέπων, 1577), and the messenger confesses he did likewise (1581). What interrupts this averted gaze is a remarkable prodigy, "a sudden marvel to see" (θαῦμα αἴφνης ὁρᾶν, 1581). "Everyone clearly heard the sound of the blow but did not see where the girl had gone" (1582–1583), and amidst the shouts of the priest and the echoing cries of the army, they all beheld "an unexpected apparition sent by some god (ἄελπτον εἰσιδόντες . . . φάσμα), whose viewing could scarcely be believed" (1585–1586). What met their eyes was a large and beautiful deer, a remarkable sight (ἰδεῖν, θέαν, 1587; cf. 1591). Sent by Agamemnon to report to Clytemnestra, the messenger declares that their daughter had won "imperishable glory" (δόξαν ἄφθιτον) throughout Greece, adding that he can vouch for the veracity of the account because he was there and saw what happened (τὸ πρᾶγμα ὁρᾶν) with his own eyes: Iphigenia indeed was saved by the gods on a day that saw her "both die and look again upon the light" (θανοῦσαν καὶ βλέπουσαν, 1604–1612).

A fragment ascribed to Euripides as quoted in Aelian (*Hist. Anim.* 7.39 = fr. 857 N2) suggests that in the true *exodos*, Artemis appeared ex machina before Clytemnestra to announce that she would substitute a deer for Iphigenia and transport the girl among the Taurians. If this were the case (although it seems highly unlikely),[57] then the *Iphigenia in Aulis*, like many other Euripidean plays, would have resorted to a divine epiphany as a concluding visual experience. Far more interesting (and convincing) from a spectator's perspective is the present sequence in our extant text. The miraculous event that guarantees Iphigenia's special *kleos* is witnessed, not predicted for the future, and its mystery as a sign of Artemis' favor is enhanced by the need for others to interpret it. Moreover, the scene itself is predicated on an uncanny visual sleight of hand, by which the deer's replacement for the girl relies on the simultaneous appearance of one and the disappearance of the other from the astonished gaze of the onlookers. The import of eyewitness testimony recurs at the end in Clytemnestra's telling skepticism as to what she has only heard. "How can I be sure," she says, "that these are not empty tales that have been told to assuage my grief?" (1617), a parting shot that Agamemnon's immediate entry on stage to confirm the supernatural event can do nothing to gainsay. Like the chorus' concern in the second *stasimon* that the marvelous story of Helen's birth was a *muthos* recorded "on the tablets of the Muses" to lead mortals astray (794–800), Clytemnestra hesitates between credulity and disbelief in the face of a story she has merely heard but did not see with her own eyes. Despite all these assurances that the play, in effect, was not just a theatrical *tour de force*, a *muthos* in its own right, and its ending not merely a comforting fiction that just replaces the earlier deception of Agamemnon's lying letter to Clytemnestra, the eye still remains the touchstone of reality. "Not seeing," in the case of the *Iphigenia in Aulis,* amounts to "not wholly believing."

To sum up, the *Iphigenia in Aulis* engages in a series of intricate relations with both epic and dramatic traditions, invoking both myth and history in its rewriting of the maiden's sacrifice. In typical Euripidean fashion, it subjects all its terms to a penetrating irony through the naiveté of its young and inexperienced heroine, who, in a deft reversal of roles, gets to exemplify and even appropriate twice over the heroic glory reserved for men in war, first in her noble gesture and then in her unexpected apotheosis. But in so doing, the play offers invaluable testimony to the theater's engagement with the visual arts, in these closing years of the fifth century, as a self-conscious mode of representing the creation and transmission of cultural memory for both the ear and the eye of those who will come hereafter. The drama maintains but reconfigures the traditional sense of recording memorable deeds in the immediate bestowal of a divine *kleos* and, at the same time, transforms the process of recollection into a visual experience that incorporates into its *mise en scène* the techniques required to remember them in a newer and more complex age.

This moment of cultural transition may be embedded in the curious phrase the "Pierian tablets," or books of the Muses, mentioned above. The Muses are primarily associated, of course, with oral transmission and not with writing in books. To be sure, the idea is not entirely new to Euripidean theater. Aeschylus, in crediting Prometheus with the invention of writing (the "arrangement of letters"), calls it "the memory of all things" ($\mu\nu\acute{\eta}\mu\eta\nu$ $\dot{\alpha}\pi\acute{\alpha}\nu\tau\omega\nu$) and in boldly adding the phrase "artisan, mother of the Muses" ($\mu o\nu\sigma o\mu\acute{\eta}\tau o\rho'$ $\dot{\epsilon}\rho\gamma\acute{\alpha}\nu\eta\nu$,

PV 460–461), he bestows upon the *grammata* of a written text the epithets that more properly apply to the traditional figure of Mnemosyne, Zeus' consort. Yet, apart from Euripides' reputed bookishness, including the tradition of a personal library,[58] the reference to myths as inscribed in writing reminds us that an important and recurrent metaphor for memory is a wax tablet on which impressions, like letters and images, are recorded.[59] Given the importance of the written letter in the prologue of the play, by which Agamemnon had hoped to forestall his daughter's arrival, this allusion to the tablets of the Muses may simply recall the epistolary theme that is now echoed in another key. But the implicit relation between an actual library of myths and a mental "book of memory," whose images can be visually "read" by its owner, may also suggest that the role of the Muses, daughters of Mnemosyne, is also subject to revision in the evolving cognitive techniques of the day, whereby they too must now be schooled in written texts and visual aids. Even more compelling, however, the image of Pierian tablets is one already familiar in the iconographical repertory, since a number of fifth-century vases depict Muses with book rolls in their hands, along with other tools of writing.[60] Memory of distant mythic events is encoded in a phrase that evokes a recognizable visual icon, even if the chorus has reason to doubt the veracity of the tales these tablets record. But the vista of army and fleet, framed as a series of pictorial scenes, has shown us how the theatrical art transmutes visual spectacle into a memorable new event in present time to impress the eyes and minds of actors and audience alike.

NOTES

This essay is an excerpt from a longer piece, Zeitlin 1993, under the title "The Artful Eye: Vision, Ecphrasis, and Spectacle in Euripidean Theatre." It has undergone some revisions for this volume and the notes are expanded. Permission to reprint has kindly been granted by Cambridge University Press.

1. For the most extensive recent discussion with bibliography, see Rouveret 1989a: 65–127. For another view of the evidence, see Padel 1990:347–349. Throughout this discussion and what follows, I am indebted to Rouveret's meticulously documented study.

2. Vitruv. *De Arch.*, 7. pref. 11. Cf. Dem. *Against Meid.* 147; schol ad loc; Ps. Andocides *Against Alcib.* 17; Plut. *Alcib.* 16. More generally, see Rouveret 1989a:106–115.

3. Vitruv. *De Arch.* 7. pref. 11; Diog. Laer. *Vit. Democr.* 9.46, 9.48; and cf. Diels-Kranz, A.33. See also the discussion of Rouveret 1989a:100–106. On ancient optical theories in general, see Simon 1988.

4. See the extensive discussion with bibliography of Rouveret 1989a:16–63.

5. In addition to the usual iconographical reference works, see Trendall and Webster 1971 and Séchan 1926. On the "mythological image" and its relation to texts,

see the cautionary remarks of Bazänt 1981; Moret 1984:153–162; and Lissarrague 1990: 231–235.

    6. See, most recently, the discussion of Padel 1990:356–358.

    7. Golder (1993), noting the preference in Greek art for "monoscenic ... representation" focused on a concentrated, dramatic moment, argues for the priority of the visual arts in determining the dramaturgy of the Attic stage. "The scenic forms of Greek drama," he suggests, "must have arisen out of the prior visual culture, whose icons and images had shaped the audience's visual imagination. Images formed of compositional schemes, gestures, postures, and motifs had become through long visual habit and association, conventional" (325). Golder raises an intriguing point, but his argument would require closer attention to the chronological developments in Greek art as well as to those in the theater. An even more serious problem is the underlying notion that both art and theater are closed worlds, mimetically dependent on one another, with no reference to larger cultural and social attitudes, behaviors, and gestures.

    8. For a convenient listing and discussion of relevant passages, see Philipp 1968: 26–41.

    9. Seale 1982:20–21.

    10. Zeitlin 1985b:72.

    11. I have treated this topic at length in Zeitlin 1985a.

    12. Many critics have discussed these problems. See most recently Zeitlin 1981 and 1985b, with bibliography.

    13. I have treated the multiple implications of vision in this play in Zeitlin 1991.

    14. No one who approaches this topic of visual effects in Euripides can fail to acknowledge the remarkable work of Shirley Barlow (1971), whose organization of the subject and acute analyses of the relevant texts remain a landmark in Euripidean criticism. See also, among others, Jouan 1966:418–419, 436–439; di Benedetto 1971a:245–269 and 1971b; and, more extensively, Sousa e Silva 1985–1986.

    15. *Theama* in *Med.* 1167, 1202; *Hipp.* 1216–1217; *Phoen.* 1139; *Bacch.* 1063. Sometimes, *thauma* (the indication of a powerful reaction to what is seen) is used instead: e.g., *IT.* 1142; *Bacch.* 693. See de Jong 1991:9–10 and appendix B ("The Messenger as Eyewitness"), 183–184.

    16. Barlow 1971:67, 65.

    17. De Jong (1991:118, n. 5), estimates the number at more than half of the representations in Trendall and Webster 1971.

    18. De Jong 1991:118.

    19. Sousa e Silva 1985–1986:81.

    20. The case of the Stoa Poikile in the Athenian Agora, built before the middle of the fifth century, is informative for approaching the complex relationships between past and present as well as between art and politics. Of the four paintings known (attributed to different artists), two are mythic in content (Amazonomachy, aftermath of the fall of Troy), two historical (Battle of Oenoe, Battle of Marathon), but all feature Athenian interests and personages, and the historical paintings in particular reflect changing political agendas as well as concern about the dangers of self-promotion of individuals through new advances in realistic portraiture. The fact that the painter Mikon was forced to pay a fine for having represented the Persians as larger than the Greeks in the Marathon painting leads Rouveret (1989b:104) to suppose "a conflict between a 'popu-

lar' representation founded on the hierarchy of personages by reason of their social or political importance and the first forms of a naturalistic representation aimed at creating illusions of visual appearance." On the other hand, this same painting seems to have directly influenced Herodotus' account of the battle, a significant testimony to the mutual influences between art and text. On all these issues, see Rouveret 1989*b*:101–104, with relevant bibliography. See too Castriota 1992 on the uses of public art in this period as a means of enforcing Greek ethical standards.

21. On the growth of historiographical awareness, see, for example, Steinmetz 1969; Rösler 1980:305–306; and Rösler 1990:236.

22. The bibliography on the shield is too vast to cite here. Homeric scholia also praise similes for their pictorial vividness, and Lonsdale (1990) views them as miniature ecphrases. On ancient ecphrasis in general, see Friedländer 1912; Palm 1965; and the convenient summary in Hagstrum 1958:3–36. Space does not permit a discussion of theoretical positions on the nature and function of ecphrastic descriptions. Despite important critiques of older views and more sophisticated frames of analysis, I find the current, almost exclusive, focus on an implied contest (or even reconciliation) between word and image to be both reductive and even, at times, grossly inaccurate.

23. See Zeitlin 1993.

24. I expect to take up elsewhere the marked prominence of the "female gaze" in tragedy.

25. I owe this phrase to Arthur [Katz] 1977.

26. The myths represented on the temple façade (Herakles and the Hydra, the Gigantomachy) are among the most familiar in Greek art on public monuments as well as in painted pottery. (The third myth depicted, Bellerophon and the Chimera, is less popular in the iconographical repertory; it also, perhaps not coincidentally, gets the briefest attention in the text.) The tapestries of Ion's tent display three different kinds of images, all of different provenances and theme: one of a night sky, another of Cecrops and his daughters, and a third, of barbarian fabrication, showing naval battles and combats with monstrous beasts.

27. There is evidence to demonstrate that artists in the sixth century were already aware of their debts to a pictorial tradition. See De Angeli 1988:34. On the archaizing tendencies in Attic pottery, starting in the period 480–450 B.C., see the discussion in Pollitt 1972.

28. These problems, along with other technical difficulties, have often tempted critics into practicing extreme forms of philological surgery on the text. For recent extensive discussion of these problems, see the editions of Jouan 1983 and Stockert 1992, and see further below in respect to particular passages.

29. On the classifications of the Greek rhetoricians, see, for example, the recent discussion of Bartsch (1989:8–10) in connection with the Greek novel.

30. *Enargeia* is a much earlier concept than ecphrasis. For a history of these terms, see Zanker 1981; further discussed in Zanker 1987:39–52.

31. Other references to seeing: 171, 191, 192, 210, 218, 232ff., 254, 275, 295, 298. The text of the *Iphigenia in Aulis* will be cited from Jouan's Budé edition, 1983.

32. Barlow (1971:183, n. 21), for example, points out that "the 'actual' positioning is echoed in the positioning of the words. *Protesilaon-Palamēdea* are placed at either end of the sentence and enclosed between them is the description of counters and boards."

33. Jouan 1966:438; Sousa e Silva 1985:52–53.

34. Barlow 1971:20 and 138, n. 22; Sousa e Silva 1985:53.

35. See Jouan 1983:67, n. 3. Di Benedetto 1971a:258–259, connects this joy to what he calls "a Homeric poetics of pleasure" as well as to contemporary taste in art for beauty in "decorative" and "ornately" detailed style, also designed, as he claims, to give immediate gratification.

36. On this point, see Foley 1985:80. Burkert (1993:88–89) argues that the unusual race between a runner and four-horse team would remind an Athenian audience of a special contest *(apobates)* in the Panathenaia (Dem. *Erot.* 61.21), thus identifying Achilles as a Panathenaic victor. Even more to my point, the ecphrastic description of Achilles' race finds its counterpart in actual vase paintings of such contests as well as on a dedication relief found on the Acropolis. For bibliography, see Burkert 1993:89, n. 13.

37. On ships' figureheads, see Stockert 1992:259, and bibliography. The evidence for the images used for actual figureheads is too scanty to permit any correlation with these emblems.

38. The syntax is somewhat ambiguous here, and no two translators render it alike. Jouan 1985: "I had already heard talk of it at home, but I keep in myself the memory of this warrior expedition." Walker 1958: "So when at home I hear men speak of it, my vision of the marshaled ships will live in memory." Merwin and Dimock 1978: "I have seen the whole fleet, and when it is famous and they tell of it where I live, I will remember" (compressing 293–295 with 300–302). On the textual problem, see Stockert 1992 *ad loc.*

39. The sources are many and late: e.g., Cic. *De Orat.* 2.86.351–354; Quint. *Inst. Orat.* 11.2.11–12; Callim. frag. 64 (Pfeiffer); Marmor Parium; Pliny *HN* 7.89; Ael. *De Nat. Anim.* 6.106; Longinus 1.316 (Spengel). For discussion of the evidence, see Yates 1966: 27–32; Blum 1969:41–46; Simondon 1982:181–183; and Rouveret 1989a:303–305.

40. Plut. *De Glor. Athen.* 3 (*Mor.* 346f; cf.17f58b). He expands the analogy: "For the actions which painters depict as they are being performed, words described after they are done." This famous statement, often misunderstood (as is the Horatian *ut pictura poesis*), needs further discussion, which cannot be undertaken here. The essential point in these stories about Simonides, whatever their factuality, is the linking of "poetry, painting, and mnemonics in terms of intense visualization" (Yates 1966:28). On the revolutionary aspects of Simonides' career, see Detienne 1967:106–119.

41. On the evidence and the relevant texts, see Blum 1969:46–55; Yates 1966:29–30; and Simondon 1985:185–186. The entire topic of memory and recollection deserves fuller discussion than can be given here.

42. Plat. *Hipp. Min.* 368d and *Hipp. Maj.* 285e; Xen. *Symp.* 4.62. On Hippias' reputation and accomplishments, see Blum 1969:48–51; and Simondon (1985:184–185), who also considers relevant the "great 'lectures' given by Hippias at Sparta," which contained disquisitions "on the power of letters, genealogies of heroes and men, stories of foundations of cities, and an entire archaeology" (Plat. *Hipp. Maj.* 285d).

43. To be discussed further below.

44. See Carruthers 1990:59–60. *Thauma* (marvel) and *ekplēxis* (astonishment) are, of course, typical Greek reactions to aesthetic experience, from Homer on.

45. There are echoes too of the funeral games in *Iliad* 23 among other borrowings. See the detailed discussion in Jouan 1966:293–298.

46. Euripides had also written a *Palamedes* and a *Protesilaos*.

47. See Irigoin's meticulous analysis (1988). For other arguments on the prologue and/or the *parodos*, see Knox 1972; Mellert-Hoffmann 1969; Jouan 1966:293–298 and 1983:29 and *ad loc;* and Stockert 1982 and 1992 *ad loc.*

48. These are almost the exact words of Agamemnon to Iphigenia; to persuade her, he bids her, in a quasi-echo of the *parodos*, to gaze at the vast array of the army, fleet, and bronze weapons of the Hellenic heroes (1259–1264). On the possible nonfulfillment of the preordained myth (plot) as a technique of Euripidean drama, see Zeitlin 1980; for this play, in particular, see Foley 1985, who follows this dramaturgical principle.

49. Mythically speaking, the play stands at a midpoint in the saga of Troy. Its causes, which are celebrated in other choral odes, include the judgment of Paris, the birth of Helen, Paris' arrival in Sparta, the abduction of Helen, and even the wedding of Peleus and Thetis. This is the event that was the occasion for the irruption of Eris that led to the judgment of the goddesses and also was the necessary prelude to the birth of Achilles. This comprehensive scope of the tradition is another instance of Euripides' longer view over the events he dramatizes, which brings epic into a historical perspective of causally linked episodes.

50. Iphigenia's lyric monody refers to the birth of Paris and his exposure as an infant on pastoral Mount Ida, and the judgment of the three goddesses there: a contest of beauty which ends with glory *(onoma)* for the Danaans but with many echoes of choral diction. On the correlation between the odes and the action, see, e.g., Bonnard 1945; Walsh 1971; Parry 1978:186–192; and Foley 1985:78–84. As Foley observes (84), "the further the action in the corrupt political world of the play veers from the predicted sequence of myth [the sacrifice of Iphigenia, the expedition to Troy], the less relevant the ideals of the odes seem to become. Yet because the distance of the chorus from the action actually makes the odes more and not less relevant to an interpretation of the play," she argues, we must consider both perspectives (disjunctive and integrative), which remain in uneasy counterpoint with one another.

51. In Iphigenia's first meeting with Agamemnon, she also emphasizes vision. She has come at a run, because she "desires his *eye*" (ποθῶ γὰρ ὄμμα δὴ σόν, 637), i.e., a reciprocal gaze. She rejoices, *seeing* him after all this time (640). Observing his downcast look (οὐ βλέπεις εὔκηλον, 644), she urges him to extend her a loving *eye* (ὄμμα τ' ἐκτείνον φίλον, 648). He complies, but, as she notes, tears fall from his *eyes* (ἄπ' ὀμμάτων, 649–650).

52. The first *stasimon* prepares for this gender reversal. The chorus, commenting on the different natures of mortals and their modes of life, praises virtue, especially the *charis* of taking a decision in view of necessity. Thus "reputation *(doxa)* confers an unaging glory *(agēraton kleos)* upon life," they claim, defining the term in accordance with traditional feminine and masculine roles. The woman's part is *aretē* through the intimacy of love *(kata Kuprin kruptan)*, but for a man, his task is to enhance the city, counting on an inner sense of order *(kosmos)* that takes a multitude of forms (558–573).

53. Cf. *Herakleidae*, *Erechtheus*, and *Hecuba* (especially pertinent to Iphigenia's decision).

54. Much has been written on the subject of Panhellenism in the play, its dramatic import, and its possible connections to current political debates. For a recent discussion

and bibliography, see Saïd (1989–1990), who rejects both the accuracy of such claims as well as their validity in the play. Yet, in basing her definition of Panhellenic unity against the barbarians on fourth-century authors (particularly, Isocrates), she does not address the present political realities that might lie behind them. I have come to the conclusion, however, that the idea of Panhellenic unity, as coded through the expedition to Troy, is probably not a contemporary issue. Rather, we should understand it as having been an integral part of the city's ideology since the period following the Trojan War, long depicted on public monuments and more recently given expression in Herodotus' views on the mythic aspects of the struggle between Greeks and Persians. This traumatic struggle, so decisive for Greek self-definition, has already passed into paradigmatic status and is enshrined as such in collective memory. Hence, for example, Ajax is featured prominently in the *parodos*, both in the list of the heroes and the catalogue of ships, precisely because of his associations with Salamis. Rather than speaking of past (epic) and present (Panhellenism), we would do better to articulate the "interferences" between them as two stages of the past, whose value lies in the dually anachronistic relation to a demystified present, as represented in the atmosphere of the play.

55. The text, in whole and in part, has been subject to much critical suspicion. Some would even excise it entirely. In general, I concur with the opinion that the ending is genuine, even if marred by some serious infelicities. We should note in particular that the double twist of the savior who herself is saved takes Euripides' characteristic emphasis on the theme of salvation to new heights of ingenuity. For the best general summary, see Jouan 1983:26–28, and see too his sensible discussion 1966:281–283.

56. On this second theory, see Séchan 1931:392–430. For discussion of the iconography, see Jouan 1984. See also Jouan 1983:50–51 and *ad loc*; Jouan 1966:282, n. 6.

57. I agree with Jouan's assessment 1966:283.

58. His association with books is satirized in Aristophanes' *Frogs* (48–54; 868–869; 1407–1409), and for his library, see Ath. *Deipnosoph.* 1.3.

59. See, for example, Aesch. *Supp.* 179; *PV* 789; *Eum.* 275; and cf. frag. 281a.20 Radt; Soph. *Trach.* 683; frag. 597 (Radt); and Euripides, frag. 506.2 (Nauck²); Plato, *Theaet.* 191c–d, etc. On the metaphor, see, most recently, Nieddu 1984 and Steiner 1994: 100–105.

60. On Muses with books on vases, see Immerwahr 1964 and Nieddu 1982:255–258, with further bibliography. Immerwahr counts sixteen examples, dating from 440 to 400. Other, nonmythic representations begin much earlier, c. 500–490.

REFERENCES

Arnott, Peter. 1962. *Greek Scenic Conventions in the Fifth Century* B.C. Oxford.
———. 1989. *Public and Performance in the Greek Theater.* London.
Arthur [Katz], M. 1977. "The Curse of Civilization: The Choral Odes of the *Phoenissae*," HSCP 81:163–185.
Barlow, S. 1971. *The Imagery of Euripides.* London.
Bartsch, S. 1989. *Decoding the Ancient Novel: The Reader and the Role of Description in Heliodorus and Achilles Tatius.* Princeton.
Bažant, Jan. 1981. "Art and History," *ListFil* 104:13–33.
Blum, Hedwig. 1969. *Die antike Mnemotechnik. Spudasmata* 15. Hildesheim.

Bonnard, André. 1945. "*Iphigénie à Aulis:* Tragédie et poésie," *MH* 2:87–107.

Burkert, Walter. 1993. "Attische Feste in der 'Aulischen Iphigenie' des Euripides," *Grazer Beiträge*, Supplementband 5, *Religio Graeco-Romana: Festschrift für Walter Pötscher*, Joachim Dalfen, Gerhard Petersmann, and Franz Ferdinand Schwarz, eds., 87–92. Graz-Horn.

Carruthers, Mary. 1990. *The Book of Memory: A Study of Memory in Medieval Culture.* Cambridge.

Castriota, David. 1992. *Myth, Ethos, and Actuality: Official Art in V B.C. Athens.* Madison.

De Angeli, Stefano. 1988. "Mimesis e Techne," *QUCC* 57:27–45.

de Jong, Irene. 1991. *Narrative in Drama: The Art of the Euripidean Messenger Speech.* Leiden.

Detienne, Marcel. 1967. *Les Maîtres de vérité dans la Grèce archaïque.* Paris.

di Benedetto, V. 1971a. *Euripide: Teatro e società.* Turin.

———. 1971b. "Il rinnovamento stilistico della lirica dell'ultimo euripide e la contemporanea arte figurativa," *Dionisio* 45:326–333.

Donohue, Alice A. 1988. *XOANA and the Origins of Greek Sculpture.* Atlanta.

Faraone, Christopher A. 1992. *Talismans and Trojan Horses: Guardian Statues in Ancient Greek Myth and Ritual.* Oxford.

Foley, Helene. 1985. *Ritual Irony: Poetry and Sacrifice in Euripides.* Ithaca, N.Y.

Friedländer, Paul. 1912. *Johannes von Gaza und Paulus Silentiarius.* Leipzig-Berlin.

Golder, Herbert. 1993. "Visual Meaning in Greek Drama: Sophocles' Ajax and the Art of Dying." In *Non-verbal Communication*, F. Pyatos, ed., 323–360. Amsterdam.

Hagstrum, Jean H. 1958. *The Sister Arts.* Chicago.

Hammond, N. G. L. 1972. "The Conditions of Dramatic Production to the Death of Aeschylus," *GRBS* 13:387–450.

Hourmouziades, N. 1965. *Production and Imagination in Euripides: Form and Function of the Scenic Space.* Athens.

Immerwahr, Henry R. 1964. "Book Rolls on Attic Vases." In C. Henderson, Jr., ed., *Classical, Medieval and Renaissance Studies in Honour of B. L. Ullman*, 1:17–48. Rome.

Irigoin, Jean. 1988. "Le Prologue et la parodos d'Iphigénie à Aulis," *Revue des Etudes Grecques* 101:240–52.

Jouan, François. 1966. *Euripide et les chants cypriens.* Paris.

———. 1983. *Euripide. Iphigénie à Aulis,* vol. 7 (Budé). Paris.

———. 1984. "Autour du sacrifice d'Iphigénie." In *Texte et Image*: Actes du Colloque international de Chantilly (13 au 15 octobre 1982), 61–74. Paris.

Knox, Bernard M. W. 1972. "Euripides' *Iphigenia in Aulide* 1–163 (in that order)," *YCS* 22:239–261.

Lissarrague, François. 1990. "Why Are Satyrs Good to Represent?" In Zeitlin and Winkler 1990:228–236.

Lonsdale, Steven. 1990. "Simile and Ecphrasis in Homer and Virgil: The Poet as Craftsman and Choreographer," *Vergilius* 36:7–30.

Mellert-Hoffmann, Gudrun. 1969. *Untersuchungen zur 'Iphigenie in Aulis' des Euripides.* Heidelberg.

Merwin, W. S., and Dimock, George E., trans. 1978. *Euripides' Iphigeneia at Aulis.* Oxford.

Moret, Jean-Mare. 1984. *Oedipe: La Sphinx et les Thèbains.* 2 vols. Geneva.

Nieddu, G. F. 1982. "Alfabetismo e diffusione sociale della scrittura nella Grecia arcaica e classica: Pregiudizi recenti e realtà documentaria," *Scrittura e Civiltà* 6:233–261.

———. 1984. "La metafora della memoria come scrittura e l'immagine dell'animo come *deltos*," *Quaderni di Storia* 19:213–215.

Onians, John. 1979. *Art and Thought in the Hellenistic Age.* London.

Padel, Ruth. 1990. "Making Space Speak." In Winkler and Zeitlin 1990:336–365.

Palm, Jonas. 1965. "Bemerkungen zur Ekphrase in der griechischen Literatur," *Kungliga Humanistiska Vetenskapssamfundet* 1:108–211.

Parry, Hugh. 1978. *The Lyric Poems of Greek Tragedy.* Toronto.

Philipp, Hanna. 1968. *Tektonon Daidala.* Berlin.

Polacco, Luigi. 1989. "Il teatro greco come arte della visione: Scenografia e prospettiva," *Dioniso* 59:137–171.

Pollitt, Jerome J. 1972. *Art and Experience in Classical Greece.* New Haven.

———. 1986. *Art in the Hellenistic Age.* Cambridge.

Rösler, Wolfgang. 1980. *Dichter und Gruppe: Eine Untersuchung zu den Gedingungen und zur historischen Funktion früher griechischer Lyrik am Beispiel Alkaios.* Munich.

———. 1990. "*Mnemosyne* in the *Symposion*." In *Sympotica: A Symposium on the Symposium*, O. Murray, ed., 230–237. Oxford.

Rouveret, Agnès. 1989*a*. *Histoire et imaginaire de la peinture ancienne (Ve siècle av. J.-C.– Ier siècle ap. J.-C.).* École Française de Rome.

———. 1989*b*. "Les Lieux de la mémoire publique: Quelques remarques sur la fonction des tableaux dans la cité," *Opus: Rivista internazionale per la storia economica e sociale dell'antichità* 8:101–124.

Saïd, Suzanne. 1989–1990. "Iphigenie à Aulis: Une pièce panhellénique?," *Sacris Erudiri: Jaarboek voor Godsdienstwetenschappen* 31:359–378.

Seale, David. 1982. *Vision and Stagecraft in Sophocles.* Chicago.

Séchan, Louis. 1926. *Etudes sur la tragédie grecque dans ses rapports avec la céramique.* Paris.

———. 1931. "Le Sacrifice d'Iphigénie" *REG* 44:392–421.

Simon, Gérard. 1988. *Le Regard, l'être, and l'apparence dans l'Optique de l'Antiquité.* Paris.

Simondon, Michèle. 1982. *L'oubli et la mémoire dans la pensée grecque jusqu'à la fin du Ve siècle avant J.-C.* Paris.

Sörbom, Göran. 1966. *Mimesis and Art.* Bonniers.

Sousa e Silva, Maria de Fatima. 1985–1986. "Elementos visuaïs e pictóricos na tragédia de Eurípides," *Humanitas* 37–38:9–86.

Steiner, Deborah. 1994. *The Tyrant's Writ: Myths and Images of Writing in Ancient Greece.* Princeton.

Stockert, W. 1982. "Zum Schlussteil der Parodos der euripideische *Iphigenie in Aulis* (v. 277 ff.)," *Prometheus* 8:21–30.

———. 1992. *Euripides, Iphigenie in Aulis.* 2 vols. *Wiener Studien* vol. 16/2. Vienna.

Taplin, Oliver. 1977. *The Stagecraft of Aeschylus.* Oxford.

———. 1978. *Greek Tragedy in Action.* Berkeley.

Trendall, A. D., and T. B. L. Webster. 1971. *Illustrations of Greek Drama.* London.

Walker, Charles, trans. 1958. *Iphigenia in Aulis.* Vol. 4 of D. Grene and R. Lattimore, eds., *Complete Greek Tragedies: Euripides.* Chicago.

Walsh, G. 1974. "Iphigenia in Aulis: Third Stasimon," *CP* 69:241–248.

Webster, T. B. L. 1956. *Greek Theater Production.* London.

Winkler, John W. and Zeitlin, Froma I., eds. 1990. *Nothing to Do with Dionysos? Athenian Drama in Its Social Context.* Princeton.

Yates, Frances. 1966. *The Art of Memory.* London.

Zanker, Grahan. 1981. "Enargeia in the Ancient Criticism of Poetry," *RhM* 124:297–301.

———. 1987. *Realism in Alexandrian Poetry: A Literature and Its Audience.* London.

Zeitlin, Froma I. 1980. "The Closet of Masks: Role-Playing and Myth-Making in the *Orestes* of Euripides," *Ramus* 9:62–77.

———. 1981. "Travesties of Gender and Genre in Aristophanes' *Thesmophoriazousae.*" In *Reflections of Women in Antiquity*, H. Foley, ed., 169–218. London.

———. 1985*a*. "The Power of Aphrodite: Eros and the Boundaries of the Self in Euripides' *Hippolytus.*" In *Directions in Euripidean Criticism*, P. Burian, ed. Durham, N.C.

———. 1985*b*. "Playing the Other: Theater, Theatricality, and the Feminine in Greek Drama," *Representations* 11:63–94. (Also published in Winkler and Zeitlin 1990: 63–96.)

———. 1991. "Euripides' *Hekabe* and the Somatics of Dionysiac Drama," *Ramus* 20: 53–94.

———. 1993. "The Artful Eye: Vision, Ecphrasis, and Spectacle in Euripidean Theatre." In *Art and Text*, S. Goldhill and R. Osborne, eds., 138–196, 295–304. Cambridge.

EIGHT

HISTORICIZING TRAGIC AMBIVALENCE

The Vote of Athena

Richard Seaford

Theory and history are often ignorant, and therefore disdainful, of each other. This is certainly so in the study of Greek tragedy. Real progress (rather than the mere application of formulae or the mere accumulation of detail) will depend in part on their becoming friends. This paper will move from one end of the abstract-concrete polarity to the other and may offend (though not deliberately) against the basic beliefs of many of its readers.

"Tragedy," according to Michelle Gellrich (1988:68), "explores the forces that fragment identity and make moral decidability problematic; its orientation toward the social context is interrogative and even adversarial, for it holds us in the grip of conflicts that various mechanisms of the culture aim to neutralize and dissipate." This remark combines some of the themes typical of a widespread, even perhaps the mainstream, current view of Greek tragedy: that it centers around ambiguity; that it is antistructural; that it resists coherence and closure; that it represents insoluble contradictions; that it subverts cultural norms; and that it asks unanswerable questions.

At the center of this conception is the notion of ambivalence, by which I mean the prevalence of duality over unity. Apparent unity—e.g., of a word or of a person—may also appear as duality—e.g., as two meanings or as male and female. Duality prevails in inverse proportion to the relation of effacement or subordination obtaining between the two elements. Ambivalence may be interrogative by posing two alternatives (justice is x or y), and it may subvert structure and cultural norms because structure and cultural norms are based on distinctions (e.g., between male and female). Frequently the duality will also appear as contrariety. A similar phenomenon (not strictly ambivalence, but sometimes included in "ambiguity") is the prevalence of multiplicity (rather than mere duality) over unity.

"Tragic ambiguity," according to Vernant and Vidal-Naquet (1988:18–19), "is to be found deep within the very language of tragedy, in what has by now for a long time been known as the 'ambiguous discourse' of Ajax, in words that are themselves subject to several interpretations in the interplay explored by the poets between the heroes and the chorus, the actors and the spectators, the gods and the human beings. There is ambiguity between the human way of proceeding in the drama and the plan decided by the gods, between what the tragic characters say and what the spectators understand; ambiguity too within the heroes themselves—for example in the character of Eteocles, between the values of the *polis* and those of the *oikos*." Here tragic ambiguity is envisaged as operating at several interconnected levels, and at some of them it seems to mean little more than "contradiction" (barely qualifying as "ambivalence" as I have defined it). One could, on this basis, go on adding to the list almost indefinitely—notably with the observation that tragic logic, unlike Platonic logic, "is the logic of the orators and sophists that, during the actual years when tragedy was flourishing, still reserved a place for ambiguity since, in the questions it examined, it did not seek to demonstrate the absolute validity of a single thesis but rather to construct *dissoi logoi*, double arguments that, in their opposition, countered but did not destroy each other. Since, at the will of the sophist and through the power of his words, each of the two conflicting arguments could in turn be made to dominate the other."[1]

It is hard to disagree with the views so far described. But they are in danger of becoming a disabling cliché, in which irreducible ambivalence (of various kinds) becomes the final destination of analysis. The discussion needs to move on toward a greater complexity, not only through greater differentiation of types of ambivalence and ambiguity, but above all through a historically informed understanding of the functioning of ambivalence. Such a historical approach will tend to call into question the privileging (not to say fetishization) of irreducible ambivalence, at the impenetrable heart of tragedy, as the object of a unitary, sui generis "tragic consciousness."[2] Such demystification might proceed by pointing for instance to the very different treatment of certain kinds of ambivalence in Aeschylus and late Euripides, a difference determined at least in part by the historical development of the Athenian law courts and of the concomitant awareness of the dangerous power of rhetoric to make both sides of an argument seem equally powerful.

Of course I cannot here carry out in full the project described in the last paragraph. To dislodge antistructure from the throne it occupies in the Western academy so as to reveal its functioning in the social process would constitute the (badly needed) shift of a paradigm held in place by a number of societal and institutional pressures, which include the division of intellectual labor both generally and within the study of antiquity. I want rather to make a tiny contribution to this shift by examining a specific instance of ambivalence cited by Vernant as supporting his influential statement of the view whose limitations I want to expose. This instance is the ambivalence said to prevail at the end of the *Oresteia*. For this purpose some preliminary generalizations of an abstract kind are needed.

To say that at the end of a drama the ambivalences (or contradictions) are resolved is to say that, in the terms of the definition in my second paragraph, the prevalence of duality (or contrariety) over unity is replaced, in the course of the drama, by the prevalence of unity over duality (or contrariety), i.e., by means of the creation of a relation of effacement or subordination between the two elements. This replacement may have the effect of answering the questions posed by the ambivalence (justice is x rather than y) and restoring the cultural norms (e.g., the male-female distinction) and the structure (e.g., male dominates female) subverted by the ambivalence. But how are we to decide whether this shift in prevalence from duality to unity has occurred? The issue of whether resolution or closure has occurred is one on which literary critics are frequently divided. Unfortunately, the critics who make ambivalence a central concern of Greek tragedy are among those who omit to say where they locate the ambivalence. (In the mind of the author? In the text itself? In the mind of the ancient audience? In the mind of the modern reader?) This is a problem in the identification of ambivalence in general, but is particularly acute in the case of unity supposedly constituted by transition from ambivalence (or contrariety) to resolution, inasmuch as the proponent of such unity has to maintain not only that the shift in prevalence occurs but also that the result of the shift prevails over what precedes it. That is to say, even those who allow the prevalence of unity in the ending of a text may nevertheless choose to deny the ending the privileged position of being able to efface or subordinate the earlier ambivalence(s). This path of subjectivity quickly becomes the uninteresting cul-de-sac of undecidability. My own position is, very briefly, that ambivalence (or its opposite) inheres not in the text (or performance) but in the reception of it (although of course the text may be shaped by ambivalence in the mind of the author), and that whereas we cannot entirely escape from our own preconceptions in this (or any other) matter, we should and can make some attempt at understanding what tragic ambivalence might mean in fifth-century Athens, but only by the dual strategy of pondering the formation of our own preconceptions while also discovering what we can about the functioning of ambivalence in Greek culture as a whole. (Much literary criticism of ancient literature is innocent of both these kinds of investigation.)

In the formation of our preconceptions in this matter a key figure is Nietzsche. In the *Birth of Tragedy*, contradiction, Widerspruch, is "the father of things," is at the heart of nature, belongs to the original unity (Ur-Eine).³ Dionysiac cult that gives men access to this Ur-Eine (§4), and Dionysiac tragedy creates a feeling of unity leading back to the very heart of nature (§7). It is in Dionysiac deindividuation that "the contradiction, the joy born of pain declared itself from the heart of nature."⁴ The Dionysiac artist becomes one with the "Ur-Eine, its pain and contradiction," and produces the image of the Ur-Eine as music (§5). Dionysus himself has a "double nature," as a cruel, brutalized demon and as a mild and gentle ruler (§10). It is Dionysiac enchantment that makes the tragic spectator feel contradictory emotions at the suffering of the hero.⁵ One of these contradictions is that "he comprehends deeply the action on stage and gladly escapes into the incomprehensible" (§22). Antithetical to, and destructive of, Dionysiac tragedy is the cheerfulness of the theoretical man, which believes it "is really able to confine the individual man within a very narrow circle of soluble problems" (§17).

This Dionysiac unites men with each other, with nature, with the Ur-Eine—a state of unity in which basic divisions are confused: the animals speak, a man feels himself as a god (§1, §7). Dionysiac tragedy makes the "gulfs between individuals yield to an overwhelming feeling of unity leading back to the very heart of nature" (§7). The point I wish to make about Nietzsche, apart from assembling these early statements of tragic ambivalence and tragic insolubility, is that his "gulfs" between individuals are closely associated, almost identified, with "the state and society."⁶ In general Nietzsche's hostility to the state and society of his own day makes him, given the relationship between Greek tragedy and the *polis,* ill-equipped to understand Greek tragedy. For Nietzsche Dionysiac tragedy and the political-social exclude each other: (§7) "from those purely religious origins [of tragedy] the entire contradiction of people and prince, in general the whole political-social sphere is excluded."⁷

The absurdity of this position comes not only from Nietzsche's own distaste for the "political-social sphere" but also from its directedness—against the Hegelian concept of tragedy.⁸ Now it is no accident that Nietzsche rejects not only Hegel's conception of tragedy as embodying sociopolitical contradiction, but also his conception of the tragic movement from contradiction to reconciliation.⁹ In abstracting tragic contradiction from history and making it a purely metaphysical principle Nietzsche also detaches it from resolution. This metaphysical principle, of eternal unity that is also eternal contradiction, is "the Dionysiac."

The influence of this seductive Nietzschean invention continues to hinder a historical understanding of tragedy and of Dionysus.¹⁰ For it is partly under this influence that the Dionysiac is still often treated as something like a metaphysical principle, even if it is not explicitly called metaphysical. Nietzsche's conception of tragedy as Dionysiac (in itself a fruitful idea) has been welcomed, and (perhaps inevitably) criticized as too compromised by unity or order. Gellrich (1988:266), for example, insisting on the centrifugality of tragedy, complains that "while exploring under the rubric of the 'Dionysiac' various turbulent, agonistic, and unsystematic aspects of experience in Greek tragic plays, Nietzsche nevertheless ultimately submits them to the mediating framework of 'Apollonian' form," and so is in this respect not much better than Hegel. This criticism may in fact miss the mark, because Nietzsche does say that although in tragedy the Dionysiac uses the Apolline as a means of expression, "in the total effect of tragedy the Dionysiac regains the preponderance" (§21), and that Dionysiac enchantment "is able to force the superabundance of Apolline power into its service" (§22).

An interesting adaptation of Nietzsche's Dionysiac, which is again critical of its compromise with unity, is by Oudemans and Lardinois. They cite with justified approval Henrichs' observation that "Nietzsche . . . was far too preoccupied with the larger antithesis between Apollo and Dionysus to pay much attention to differentiation within Dionysus" (at least in *The Birth of Tragedy*), but accommodate this criticism to the Nietzschean notion of the Dionysiac as "self-contradictory force" by taking the coexistence of order and disorder in the Dionysiac as yet another manifestation of the quasimetaphysical principle of Dionysiac contradiction: "Dionysus is a self-contradictory unity of order and disorder." Also, "for Dionysiac logic there is no harmony and no solving of contradictions in any phase of development. It reveals the co-existence of order and disorder."[11] The Nietzschean Dionysiac is both self-contradiction and unity, the latter consisting in "joyful forbearance of ambiguity, in all its negativity and conflictingness. Through all his oppositions and his dreadful aspects Dionysus is embraced and venerated as the eternal affirmation of all things" (1987:226). But Oudemans and Lardinois' extension of the scope of contradiction (so as to cover its own relation to order) eliminates from the Dionysiac even this (somewhat vague) element of unity. And so in maintaining Nietzsche's idea that tragedy is Dionysiac—"tragedy concerns cosmological ambiguity (in its Greek version embodied as the god Dionysus)" (1987:59)—they must nevertheless reject his view that it expressed the joyful forbearance of ambiguity or celebrated the affirmation of unbounded life in the destruction of its heroes, claiming instead that the tragic duality of Dionysus between order and disorder is irreducible, that he cannot be welcomed in his totality.

This irresolvable duality produces "tragic ambiguity," which is to be distinguished from the "controlled ambiguity" characteristic of ritual. In "controlled ambiguity" contact is made with undifferentiated (and so ambiguous) power, for example with the ambiguous power (to pollute or heal) of the scapegoat, but the power is canalized, the negative element separated from the positive. "Tragic ambiguity," on the other hand, occurs when "it is realized that all differentiation, even that of controlled ambiguity, is fed, but also destroyed, by indiscriminate power"; when "it is realised that order resting on differentiation is not self-sustaining." With tragic ambiguity "the relation between power and cosmology [i.e., human ordering] is one of insoluble conflict."

I present this view as the most sophisticated development so far of Nietzsche's conception of the tragic as insoluble ambivalence. This view is valuable in its implication that tragedy subverts the controlled ambiguity of ritual. It deserves a more detailed critique than I can give it here. An obvious objection is that the abstract "realization" by which "tragic ambiguity" is defined (the realization that all differentiation is both fed and destroyed by indiscriminate power) is alien to the Greek mind. Where exactly do Oudemans and Lardinois find "tragic ambiguity"? At the end of *Antigone,* we are told, "tragic ambiguity . . . continues to reign" (1987:159). The civic, purifying Dionysus of the fifth *stasimon* does in a sense, they observe, save the *polis,* but he only does so with the destruction of Antigone and Creon. The tragic ambiguity is that "the city can only continue its existence by sacrificing those who are its most respected representatives, and there is no end to this persistent self-sacrifice" (159). Note here the identification of sacrifice with self-sacrifice, the tacit assumption that the introverted, cursed House of Laius (most respected?) constitutes the city. And in what sense does the self-sacrifice have no end? To be sure, the *polis* persistently enacts, in the tragic theater, the self-destruction of the ruling family (especially the Theban one). But what is enacted is precisely an end, from which the democratic *polis* may persistently benefit, because it is both a paradigm of the political undesirability of the introverted autonomy of the powerful family and a stimulus (nevertheless) to the emotional cohesion of collective pity for those destroyed. In short, Oudemans and Lardinois' notion of tragic ambiguity both overestimates the Greeks' power of anthropological abstraction and takes no account of the historical contradiction between household and *polis.* It is, in anthropological terms, purely intellectualist, to the exclusion of history and of function. "Tragic ambiguity," in my view, turns out to be controlled ambiguity in a special form that arises from the specific needs of the democratic *polis.* The civic Dionysus of the *Antigone*'s fifth *stasimon* was for the Greeks not an embodiment of the irresolvable contradiction between order and disorder, but the god whose (politically vital) rituals performed by the *polis,* at the dramatic festival itself and elsewhere, contrasted with the perversion of ritual by the ruling family in the tragedy. In general the ambivalence of Dionysus between order and disorder is not the manifestation of a quasimetaphysical principle, but inherent in the imperative to perform his collective cult, a special case of the ambivalence of Greek deity in general. If dishonored or ignored, Dionysus will inflict the savagery of his myths. I will return to this point in my conclusion. For we must now finally turn to my specific case of ambivalence, from the *Oresteia.*

In tragedy, according to Vernant, "the world of the city is called into question and its fundamental values are challenged in the ensuing debate. When exalting the civic ideal and affirming its victory over all forces from the past, even Aeschylus, the most optimistic of the tragic writers, seems not to be making a positive declaration with tranquil conviction but rather to be expressing a hope, making an appeal that remains full of anxiety even amid the joy of the final apotheosis. The questions are posed but the tragic consciousness can find no fully satisfactory answers to them and so they remain open."[12] Here again is our mainstream view. In a long endnote Vernant attempts to ground it (pp. 418–420). At the end of the *Oresteia* "conflict persists, in the background, between contrary forces. To this extent the tragic ambiguity is not removed; ambivalence remains." He gives two cases of this persistent ambivalence. One is his view that a majority of the human voters votes against Orestes, with only Athena's vote producing a tie (and thereby acquittal). The other is the emphasis laid on the honors to be accorded to the Furies and on the need to retain terror (τὸ δεινὸν) in the city.

In the same spirit, Simon Goldhill writes that "tragedy's challenge is precisely to the sense of the secure and controlled expression of the order of things that for so many critics in their different ways has constituted the end of the *Oresteia.* The problem of δίκη in this trilogy and its critical reading is not solved but endlessly restated."[13] Important for Goldhill is the figure of the virgin warrior Athena, whose decisive vote for Orestes is based on her lack of a mother, her approval of the male, her strong adherence to her father. As a female who acts like a male, and in her use of persuasive rhetoric, Athena resembles Clytemnestra, with the result that "the final reconciliation of divine and human forces in the city is achieved by a figure who transgresses the boundaries of definition and the definition of boundaries that make up the social order which the reconciliation is intended to achieve. . . . The final reconciled triumph of civic language develops also a powerful sense of its transgressions."[14] Another respect in which the apparent resolution of the conflicts may seem to our sensibility to undermine itself is the sheer arbitrariness of the basis of Athena's decision.

To all this it might be objected that the questions are indeed answered and the conflicts resolved. Orestes is undoubtedly acquitted (752), and with this acquittal are established the law court, patriliny, the cult of the Furies, and the triumphantly celebrated peace and prosperity of Athens. For the postmodern academy, apt to privilege instability, such a simple analysis seems absurdly at odds with the text's manifest complexity and ambiguity, which seem to ensure that the relationship between the elements of disorder (transgression, subversion, questioning, contradiction) and the elements of order (structure, harmony, resolution) is such that the former are (overall, or in the end) not effaced or subordinated by the latter, whether in the mind of the author, in the text itself, or in the ancient or modern reception of the text. How are we to decide whether this is so? In a sense it is already decided for us: we now find it difficult to imagine the textual effacement or control of disorder. The only way of perceiving the sense in which the *Oresteia* might after all subordinate disorder to order is by an effort of historical understanding, of which I will now give an example.

I begin with a critique of the detail with which Vernant supports his generalization. At the end of the *Oresteia*, he writes, "ambivalence remains. Remember, for instance, that a majority of human judges pronounced a vote against Orestes, for it was only Athena's vote that made the two sides equal." Others believe that Athena's vote did not produce the tie but broke it. How does Vernant support his choice of interpretation? He continues: "Cf. line 735 and the scholium on line 746." But the scholium on line 746 is irrelevant. Perhaps he means the scholium on line 743, which states that the Areopagus had thirty-one members. If so, then perhaps he cites it as evidence that the Areopagus had an odd number of members, and so that Athena's vote would produce a tie. But there can hardly be as many as thirty-one jurors voting on stage, and in fact the scholiast derives the number 31 from the Roman period, when the membership was fixed at this level.[15] In Aeschylus' time the Areopagus was composed of all living former archons, and so the number of jurors would vary between odd and even. As for line 735, this is Athena announcing, just after the jurors have voted, that "I will add this voting-counter (ψῆφος) for Orestes." On this Vernant maintains merely that the ψῆφος is indeed a voting-counter (rather than a symbolic vote, presumably), and cites Orestes' words, "Oh Pallas, who has just saved my house" (ὦ Παλλάς, ὦ σώσασα τοὺς ἐμοὺς δόμους, 754), adding "in the same sense, cf. Euripides, *Iphigenia in Tauris* 1469."

Vernant's argument consists then in maintaining that Athena saves Orestes by her vote, which is embodied in an actual voting-counter. But this, as we shall see, does not mean that her vote produces (rather than breaks) the tie. Vernant also cites Euripides *Iphigenia among the Taurians* 1469, where Athena refers to herself as having saved Orestes in the Areopagus by "adjudicating equal votes" (ψήφους ἴσας κρίνασα) and goes on to say that henceforth it will be the custom for equal votes to mean acquittal. Vernant is right to imply that Euripides is here influenced by Aeschylus. But alas the passage tells strongly against his own view of the vote of Athena, because the "equal votes" here cannot include Athena's. That is clear both from the phrase ψήφους ἴσας κρίνασα[16] and from her etiology of the Athenian practice (referred to also in later authors) [17] of taking equal votes (ἰσήρεις . . . ψήφους) to mean acquittal—these "equal votes" did not include Athena's vote (for if they did, it would mean that a human one-vote majority for condemnation would regularly mean acquittal!). This is made even more certain by the occurrence of the same etiology in Euripides' *Electra* without any mention of Athena—it is said merely that as a result of the equal votes acquitting Orestes the practice of equal votes producing acquittal will be established (1265–1269).

So the only point of substance in Vernant's case counts against it. And we may add that Athena is not, after all, one of the jurors. Her position in the court is, it is implied, (if anything) president, for she hears the preliminaries, brings the case to trial, and presides over the debate. [18] In Athenian homicide cases the president was the *basileus archon*, who it seems was (like the archons in other kinds of cases) not also a member of the jury. [19] Athena votes not as a juror but as a deity and was no doubt imagined to ground with her vote the practice of acquittal on equal votes (cf. n. 14), as in Euripides. However, three substantial points have been made in favor of the view that Athena's vote produces a tie, and these I must eliminate before going on to give my own account of the scene.

(1) It seems that the voting of the jurors is accompanied by ten couplets, spoken alternately by Apollo and the chorus, followed by a triplet spoken by the chorus, and then by Athena's statement that she will vote for Orestes (711–743). It has seemed to some that this suggests an odd number of jurors (eleven), with the final juror voting in the first two lines of the triplet, and Athena coming forward in the third line of the triplet. But it is no less likely that the ten couplets accompany voting by (ten) jurors, with the final triplet making a transition to the speech of Athena (and perhaps accompanying her movement to the urns). [20]

(2) In two passages of Lucian the vote of Athena is invoked to produce a tie (*Pisc.* 21, *Harm.* 3). However, unlike the other tradition, there is no early evidence for this one. Moreover, we can explain its invention, either in another version of the myth, in which the jury was the twelve Olympian gods (and so Athena's vote would have produced a tie), [21] or in an era in which the problem of a tied vote was precluded by having a fixed (odd) number of jurors (in the Roman period, we noted, the Areopagus had thirty-one), so that the vote of Athena would make sense only as producing a tie.

(3) The order of events is as follows. The jurors vote. Athena says (probably as she holds her voting counter) that she will vote for Orestes. The votes are counted. And Athena announces that Orestes is acquitted because the votes are equal (ἴσον ἀρίθμα). According to Gagarin, [22] cited with approval by Sommerstein, there is in this announcement "not the slightest suggestion . . . that Athena's vote is not included in this ἴσον ἀρίθμα," and her statement of Ores-

tes' acquittal first and the equality of votes second (752–753) rules out the possibility that she added her counter just after announcing the equality of the voting. But these points have no weight, once it is realized that the audience is already familiar[23] with the mechanism of the "vote of Athena," instituted in this the very first homicide trial, to resolve the problem of a tied vote. In this respect, as in various (though not of course all) others, the trial scene prefigures, and provides mythological grounding for, court procedure. Compare for instance Athena prescribing that the prosecutor should speak first (583–584).[24] Given this familiarity, it does not have to be said by Athena (any more than it does in Euripides) that her vote is not included in the "equal number." Indeed, she does not (having made the position clear before the count) even have to place her counter in one of the two piles. And if she did not do so (or if she did it after 753), it would be clearly seen by the audience that her vote was not included in the "equal number." It is desirable that the abstract practice of acquittal on equal votes should be both concretely grounded (in Athena's vote) and yet prefigured in the respect that the vote is (as in an actual trial) merely imagined as added to the votes for acquittal. And so Athena's early declaration (before the count) of her voting intention did not confuse the Athenian audience as it has some modern scholars. Further, there are good reasons why this declaration should occur before the count. In such contexts rules are more acceptable to the defeated party if laid down before the result is known. The bad news for the Furies is spread over two stages rather than concentrated in a single declaration. This conciliatory function of Athena's early announcement would hardly work if Athena was declaring that she will (in effect) vote twice, first to turn a defeat for Orestes into a tie, and then to turn the tie into a victory for Orestes, with her crucial second vote expressed (apparently as an afterthought) in a single line ("Orestes wins even if he is judged with equal votes," νικᾷ δ' Ὀρέστης, κἂν ἰσόψηφος κριθῇ, 741). But in fact of course this line, as the scholiast realised,[25] makes explicit the consequence of what precedes (735–740).[26] Accordingly, the wrath of the Furies when it comes is not directed against Athena, as it surely would have been had she reversed a majority decision of the jurors.[27]

That the defeated party accepts the verdict is crucial, obviously, both to the resolution of the specific conflict and to the judicial process as a whole, both in the *Eumenides* and in the life of the *polis*. To conciliate the Furies Athena tells them that they have not been conquered, because the votes were equal (οὐ γὰρ νενίκησθ', ἀλλ' ἰσόψηφος δίκη ἐξῆλθε, 795–796). As Thomson notes, "if the votes have only been made equal by the addition of her own, she is adding insult to injury." In response, Sommerstein observes that her argument is disingenuous, for at 741 she says precisely the opposite, namely that Orestes wins (νικᾷ) even if the votes are equal (ἰσόψηφος). Quite so—reconciliation requires a victory that is not a victory, which in turn requires an equal vote. Vernant's preconceived privileging of ambivalence causes him to adopt the view (without feeling the need to consider the arguments) that the majority of human voters vote against Orestes, which, were it so, would indeed constitute an irresolvable contradiction with his acquittal. And so Vernant translates ἰσόψηφος (795) as "un arrêt indécis." But ἰσόψηφος does not mean indecisive. It means equal votes, which in this case are, as Athena has explained, decisive. So far from perpetuating contradiction, the equal votes serve to resolve it, in a highly dramatic way.

None of this is meant to deny the importance of ambivalence in tragedy. My concern is rather to remove ambivalence from its position at the heart of tragedy, where it generally has the appearance of irresolvability, so as to locate it (at least in this case) as a functioning element of the cultural configuration to which tragedy belongs.

The *Oresteia* dramatizes an etiological myth. It concludes in the establishment of the Areopagus court, of the principle of patriliny, and of the cult of the Furies.[28] In this the *Oresteia* is typical of extant tragedy, most of which dramatizes etiological myth, especially of cult.[29] Charles Segal maintains that "tragedy transforms the structures of myth and ritual from an affirmation of order to a questioning of order," and so is able to speak of the "uniqueness of tragic form."[30] But in fact the questioning of order inheres in myth, especially etiological myth.

Here are some examples. We are told that at the altar of Artemis Orthia in Sparta boys were flagellated, sometimes to the point of death.[31] The etiological myth of this ritual says that the four districts of Sparta once quarreled while sacrificing together to Artemis. Many were killed at the altar, and plague killed the rest. Consequently an oracle required that the altar be bloodied with human blood. And so human sacrifice was practiced, until Lycurgus substituted the flagellation of boys, which filled the altar with blood (Paus. 13.6.9–10).

This myth contains several features found generally in etiological myth. Inasmuch as sacrifice by a community expresses and confirms its cohesion, violent conflict at the altar is not only disorder but also a striking transgression, a reversal of the norm.[32] The transgression often causes communal disease,[33] which is cured by the establishment of the ritual. And human sacrifice is a confusion of human with animal. Among the functions of etiological myth are not only to ensure performance of the (socially vital) cult by describing the consequences of its omission, but also to emphasize and clarify, by means of an imagined reversal or confusion, the distinctions necessary to normal practice.[34]

Another example is provided by the eleventh ode of Bacchylides, which tells the etiological myth of the cult of Artemis at Lousoi in Arcadia. The Proitids are driven from their home in a frenzy to roam on the mountainside, like untamed beasts, until they are cured by sacrifice to Artemis, and the sanctuary and cult are founded. The narrative seems to contain various prefigurements of the cult.[35] Here the reversal consists of the escape of females from male control into the wild and of the confusion of human and animal. Apollodorus (*Bibl.* 2.2.2) refers to the Proitids as roaming "with all *disorder*" (μετ᾽ ἀκοσμίας ἁπάσης), and in Hesiod (fr. 133) they suffer a physical disease.

Moving on to Attica, we find transgression and disease in the myth of the founding of the cult of Artemis at Brauron,[36] and in the stories about the arrival in Attica of Dionysus. The cult of Dionysus Melanaigis was founded to cure the frenzy (and probably the roaming in the wild)[37] of the daughters of Eleuther. And when the Athenians failed to honor the newly arrived Dionysus Eleuthereus (the god of tragedy), they were smitten with a disease of the genitals, which was cured by the institution of phallic processions in the god's honor.[38] We have more detail where the myths survive in poetic versions—Bacchylides on the Proitids, for example, or the myth of the foundation of Dionysiac cult in Thebes dramatized in Euripides' *Bacchae,* in which there is a multiple reversal of norms: in what is described as a "disease"[39] the females of Thebes abandon their homes for the wild, where they act like males (as hunters, or as warriors who actually defeat a band of Theban males), the male (Pentheus) dresses as a female, there is much confusion of human and animal, a mother kills her son, and so on.

In a tradition preserved by Diogenes Laertius (1.110) various altars in the Attic demes commemorate the sacrifice by which Epimenides put an end to a communal disease. According to some writers, he adds, the disease was caused by the Cylonian pollution. We read in Plutarch (*Sol.* 12) how this pollution, and the fears and strange apparitions that accompanied it, was caused by civil conflict and cured by Epimenides with purifications and founding of cults. Here the etiological disorder (including disease) is caused not by dishonor done to deity but by reciprocal violence in the *polis.* The etiological transition from disorder to cult has been historicized. Plutarch's narrative also contains a role for judicial action as a way of resolving the conflict. The Cylonian pollution is caused specifically by the murder of men who were persuaded to leave sanctuary to stand trial. But the judicial principle does make some progress: with his entreaties and arguments Solon persuades the murderers to submit to trial, and to abide by the decision of the jurors chosen from the best men (12.2), which results in their banishment. The insertion by the Athenian *polis* of its judicial process into the ancient pattern of etiological myth is to be found also in the myth of Erigone, the daughter of Orestes' victim Aegisthus. She prosecutes Orestes, hangs herself after his acquittal, and becomes a spirit seeking revenge on the Athenians, who then on instructions from an oracle found a cult for her:[40] as in the *Oresteia,* resentment of the judicial decision causes a crisis, which is resolved by the foundation of cult, this time the Dionysiac cult of the Aiora.

The *Oresteia*, like Plutarch's narrative of the Cylonian events, exemplifies the historicization of etiological myth. I cannot here go into the similarities between them, which include a similar role for the Furies *(Semnai)*.[41] In etiological myth the deity is generally dishonored, and so causes disease to land and community, which is ended by the foundation of cult. So too in the *Oresteia* the dishonor felt by the Furies, who consequently threaten the land and community with disease,[42] is denied by Athena (824, 884), who founds their cult. But the Furies, as agents of reciprocal violence,[43] are exceptional deities. The havoc (described in medical terms)[44] they wreak on the House of Atreus does not need to be motivated by dishonor and cannot be resolved merely by founding a cult. Rather, their sphere of operation is limited by founding the law court, and it is out of this etiology that there arises the dishonor (in myth generally unmotivated) canceled by the founding of cult. The elements of etiological myth are in their historicization reconfigured.

In etiological myth it is not only disease that is ended by the foundation of cult but also, we saw, transgression, and the confusion of normally distinct categories,[45] as for example in the confusion of gender roles in the *Bacchae*. The belligerent autonomy of maenads makes it appropriate that Clytemnestra's champions the Furies are called "maenads" in the *Eumenides* (500). Maenads are not the only women who perpetrate such transgression and gender confusion in etiological myth. One thinks for example of the women who, in an etiological myth of cult,[46] kill their husbands and for a time rule Lemnos, a crime compared in the *Choephori* (631–634) to the behavior of Clytemnestra. The etiological themes of gender confusion and of disease may be associated with each other, as when in the *Bacchae* maenadism is called a "disease" or when the Proitids are "cured" of their Dionysiac frenzy,[47] or when in the *Choephori* the death of Orestes is said to have destroyed the hope of "curing the bacchic revel in the house" perpetrated by Clytemnestra—i.e., her domination of the house after killing her husband.[48]

The resolution of gender confusion at the end of the *Oresteia* is typical of etiological myth. But the etiological crisis of the *Oresteia* does not, we noted, arise from the usual cause, the dishonoring of deity. It is rather a social crisis.[49] The *polis* adapts etiological myth to reflect on its own contradictions and to ground its own creation. The contradiction and confusion of genders belong to the reciprocal violence. Accordingly, the resolution is only in part the traditional one of founding cult. The normal (patrilineal) differentiation of genders is established by the decision, after discussion, of the law court. And judicial deliberation is, though it may be reinforced by divine sanctions, a human (political) activity. On the other hand the traditional form of etiological myth is apparent, not only in that the foundation and decision of the law court is accompanied by the foundation of the Furies cult, but also in that the crucial decision(s) are in fact taken by deity. Just as in the normal etiological myth it is deity who (generally by means of an oracle) prescribes the cult, so in the *Oresteia* it is Athena who founds the court and its procedures, bids the jurors to respect for all time the ordinance of the oaths (483–484), delivers the casting vote, and offers the Furies cult. As for the establishment of patriliny, the balance of human votes not only helps (as we have seen) to reconcile the Furies, but also allows the issue to hang on the decision of deity. The intrahuman ambivalence activates another ambivalence, a shared responsibility between human and divine, that has already been expressed in Athena's statement of her motives for founding the Areopagus: "The matter is too great, if any mortal thinks to judge it. Nor indeed is it right for me to give a decision in the case of sharp-angered murder" (470–473). A human majority (as imagined by Vernant) would not have required a divine vote, and the reversal of a human majority by a divine vote (also imagined by Vernant) would destroy both the intrahuman and the human-divine balance.

Just as the intrahuman ambivalence permits a human-divine ambivalence, so the latter in its turn permits an ambivalence between male and female. The reason Athena gives for voting for Orestes is: "There is no mother who gave me birth, and I praise the male in all things (except that I do not marry) with all my heart, and am strongly of my father. So I will not give greater weight to the death of a woman who has killed her husband, guardian of the house." However inappropriate we may find this argument, we should not infer that Aeschylus is undermining the case for acquittal. The motherlessness of Athena has already been cited by Apollo as evidence for his view that the father is parent of the child (658–666). But perhaps the myth, in the mouth of Athena, was more powerful than any physiological speculation. Myths about deity are not irrelevant to human contradictions, but may rather be shaped precisely to resolve them.[50] The myth adduced by Athena here would be for the male audience no less decisive than the one she mentions in her first words in the play: the leaders of the Achaeans have given to her in perpetuity, she says, the land around the river Skamander, to be a gift for the offspring of Theseus (398–402). Herodotus (5.94) tells us that the Athenians used the Trojan legend in their conflict with the Mytileneans over this territory.

It is also important to the persuasiveness of Athena's argument that she is not only the guardian of the Athenian *polis* but, as a virgin warrior, as close to being male as a female can be, "like a bold man (ἀνήρ) in military command" (296). In this aggressive maleness (N.B. 296), this confusion or ambivalence of gender, she resembles not only Clytemnestra, as others have observed (n. 14), but also the Furies. And like the Furies, she is a virgin—a similarity hinted at in their first address to her as "daughter of Zeus" (Διὸς κόρη, 415), for they are themselves κόραι (68) and "daughters of Night" (κόραι . . . Νυκτὸς, 791, 821). Important to the acceptance of the verdict by the defeated party is the absence of one-sidedness not only in the human vote but also in the gender of the figure whose vote decides the issue. Just as Vernant maintains that the resolution of the *Oresteia* is undermined by the ambivalence of voting, so Goldhill implies, we saw, that it is qualified by the gender ambivalence of Athena. But we should say rather that gender ambivalence in the *Oresteia* is present both as an element in the etiological crisis (Clytemnestra, the Furies) and as a means of its resolution (Athena).[51] Indeed all three closely interrelated ambivalences—between the human jurors, between human and divine, and between male and female—are important both to the acquittal and to its acceptance by the Furies, i.e., to the resolution of the etiological crisis.

According to another Athenian etiological myth of patriliny, preserved by Varro (from Aug. *De civ. D.* 18.9), when the Athenians voted on which deity to name their city after, the women voted for Athena and the men for Poseidon, with the result that Athena won by one vote. Poseidon then angrily devastated the land and was appeased by the institution of patriliny and by the removal of political rights from women, whom Athena, it is noted, failed to help. Here, as in Aeschylus, we have the sequence: (1) female power (Clytemnestra, the Furies, the women of Attica); (2) a very close vote producing divine anger that has to be appeased; and (3) a settlement in which the female principal, abandoned by Athena, loses power, suffers the institution of patriliny, and yet has gained something (the cult of the Furies, the name of Athens). To find this same sequence of balances producing patriliny in two otherwise very different narratives confirms our view of its etiological significance.

Of the two cases given by Vernant of the persistence of ambivalence at the end of the *Oresteia*, we have so far examined only one, the vote of Athena. The other was the emphasis on the honors to be given to the Furies and on the need to retain terror (τὸ δεινὸν) in the city. Suffice it to say that here too the ambivalence, between the final benevolence of the Furies and their continuing power to create havoc, is characteristic of etiological myth, which, in addition to its other functions, indicates what happens when you do not perform the cult. To provide itself with the emotional cohesion needed for survival a *polis* must perform collective cult, a necessity expressed in the deity's beneficence if venerated and maleficence if ignored. This is especially true of the Furies, because they are the agents of reciprocal violence, and so will if ignored tear apart the *polis*. Conversely, they will if honored bring to the *polis* the concord that they eventually pray for, as a "cure," in the *Eumenides* (976–987). The final ambivalence noted by Vernant is therefore profoundly practical. We must accordingly resist his confusion of the final anxiety with a sui generis, ahistorical "tragic consciousness" unable to answer the questions posed, which therefore "remain open." There is no doubt that at the end of the *Eumenides* the questions are answered, however much we may dislike the answers, the way they are arrived at, or the idea of questions being answered. But answered questions are quite consistent with the persistence of the salutary anxiety inherent in etiological myth.

Finally, we are now in a position to return to Dionysus, so as to explain his ambivalences, not as the manifestation of a quasimetaphysical principle, but as the ambivalences of etiological myth. In etiological myth (and even sometimes, although always in a limited way, in its ritual) basic differentiations are affirmed and clarified by their temporary confusion or inversion, and the mythical catastrophe (the cruel deity) ensures the continued performance of the cult (the gentle deity). Dionysus, like the Furies, is of special importance to the cohesion of the democratic *polis*. Much of his activity can be comprehended as enforcing this cohesion: his coming as an (impartial) outsider, his rejection by the royal family, his extraction of the royal females from their homes to perform collective cult, his imposition of frenzied self-destruction on the royal family, his demand for cult "from everybody," "mixed up together," his foundation of *polis* cult.[52] And this is also one of the characteristics that qualifies him to preside over the democratic genre of tragedy.[53]

NOTES

1. Vernant in Vernant and Vidal-Naquet 1988: 417–418.

2. For this "tragic consciousness" see esp. the influential essay of Vernant entitled "Tensions and Ambiguities in Greek Tragedy," reprinted in Vernant and Vidal-Naquet 1988: 29–48. Paradoxically, Vernant's basically ahistorical conception of "tragic consciousness" is his development of Gernet's historical account of tragedy as embodying the contradiction between heroic myth and the legalism of the *polis*.

3. ". . . des ewigen Widerspruchs, des Vaters der Dinge . . . ," "dem Ur-Einem, seinem Schmerz und Widerspruchs," and the passage quoted in the next note.

4. ". . . der Widerspruch, die aus Schmerz geborene Wonne sprach von sich aus dem Herzen der Natur heraus."

5. Note the passage in §24 from "die qualvollste Gegensätze der Motive" to "an diesem allen eine höhere Lust perzipiert wird?" and in §22 from "Er schaut die verklärte Welt der Bühne und verneint sie doch" to "aus dem *dionysischen* Zauber," (especially the sentence "Er schaudert vor den Leiden, die den helden treffen werden, und ahnt doch bei ihnen eine höhere, viel übermächtigere Lust").

6. "Und dies ist die nächste Wirkung der dionysischen Tragödie, dass der Staat and die Gesellschaft, überhaupt die Klüfte zwischen Mensch und Mensch einem übermachtigen Einheitsgefühle weichen, welches an der Herz der Natur zurückführt."

7. It is ironic, given Nietzsche's attitude to Christianity, that, as Barbara von Reibnitz (1992: 188) points out, this absolute division has its "argumentativischen Ort" in

the Christian-theological definition of religion as the realm of the "entirely Other" separate from culture, society, and politics, a separation for which there is no evidence in antiquity.

8. Silk and Stern (1981:68 and 395) refer in this connection to Hegel's *Ästhetik*, ed. F. Bassenge (Berlin, 1955), 1083–1084.

9. For this movement see the collection of passages in Paolucci 1962:71: "The true course of dramatic development consists in the annulment of *contradictions* viewed as such, in the reconciliation of the forces of human action, which alternately strive to negate each other in their conflict"; 73: "The higher conception of reconciliation in tragedy is . . . related to the resolution of specific ethical and substantive facts from their contradiction into their true harmony." See also 51–52, 74, 324–326.

10. And for its significant influence also on twentieth-century philosophy see Habermas 1987:91–106, 131–136.

11. Oudemans and Lardinois 1987:216, 227; Henrichs 1984:220. Similarly, writing on the City Dionysia, Simon Goldhill (1987:76) claims that "it is the *interplay between norm and transgression* enacted in the tragic festival that makes it a Dionysiac occasion."

12. In Vernant and Vidal-Naquet 1988:33.

13. Goldhill 1986:56.

14. Goldhill 1986:31, following Winnington-Ingram 1983:125–131.

15. Busolt 1926:936.

16. Her claim is to have saved Orestes, and so if she had voted to produce a tie, she would have said so. Gagarin (1975:125) calls the passage "ambiguous," but the only ambiguity is in his translation "deciding equal votes." In fact κρίνασα unambiguously means *adjudicate*. Eur. *IT* 965–966 says that Pallas counted equal votes.

17. Aristid. 2.24 explicitly connects the practice to Athena at Orestes' trial of adding her vote to a tied human vote. See also Julian *Or.* 3.114d, and further passages cited by Thomson (1966) on *Eum.* 734–743. For secular explanations of the practice see Arist. *Pr.* 13, 29. See also Antiphon *De Caede Herodes* 51. Sommerstein's case for Athena's vote producing a tie suffers from ignoring this issue (and the Euripides passages) entirely.

18. This was pointed out long ago by K. O. Müller (1835:176–179).

19. Macdowell (1963:37–38) convincingly refutes the suggestion that he voted.

20. I do not know why Sommerstein finds this "bizarre." Athena is not just another juror (nor, if she moves to the urns, would she do so from the same location as the jurors).

21. Hester 1981:268.

22. Gagarin 1975:123. He tries to dismiss the evidence of Euripides on this point by saying that "Euripides was fond of linking mythical events to historical practices." But where another source happens to survive (e.g., Paus. 2.32.1–4; cf. Eur. *Hipp.* 1423–1430), we can see that (as one might expect) Euripides did not invent the link. And indeed here we have the extra evidence of Aristides et al.: see n. 17 above.

23. This familiarity cannot be proved, but is very likely: Eur. *IT* 1469–1472 surely refers to a traditional practice.

24. See also Thomson 1966:I.54 and II on lines 397, 429, 485–486, 579–580, 588–593, 609, 674–675.

25. Ad 735: ἐγὼ προσθήσω τὴν ἐσχάτην ψῆφον, ᾗ, ὅταν ἴσαι γένωνται, νικᾷ ὁ

κατηγορούμενος (ἢ ὅτι ἂν M; ἢ ὅταν Hermann); ad 741: κἂν ἴσαι δὲ γένωνται αἱ ψῆφοι, ὁ κατηγορούμενος νικᾷ.

26. West (1990:288) would make the consequence of explicitly universal application by reading ὁ φεύγων in 741 (with Ὀρέστης as an intrusive gloss). He also reads ἰσόψηφον (neut. acc. adverbial), but this does not affect my argument.

27. Hester 1981:270–271. Sommerstein objects that "if Athena is one of the jury, why should Orestes or the Erinyes draw distinctions between her and her human colleagues?" But the distinction is already there, at many levels. Unlike the human jurors Athena is a deity, presides over the court, makes the rules, and declares and explains her voting intention.

28. One might add a permanent Argive debt of friendship to Athens (762–774), the procedures of the court, et cetera.

29. Seaford 1994:7§f.

30. Segal 1986:59, 75.

31. Pl. *Leg.* 633b; Xen. *Resp. Lac.* 2.9; Cic. *Tusc.* 2.34; Nik. Dam. 90 (*FGH* 103); Plut. *Mor.* 239d; etc. (sources and discussion in Brelich 1969:133–136).

32. In another etiology of the same ritual this is expressed in a different way: before the battle of Plataea, Pausanias, while sacrificing (and so without weapons), beats off with sacrificial rods and whips a Lydian attack (Plut. *Aristides* 17).

33. By the word "disease" I may include (like the Greeks with λοιμός) also crop failure and the failure of humans and animals to reproduce.

34. We may add, although this does not affect the argument of this paper, that the etiological myth may also comment on the ritual by containing the extreme actualization of what in the ritual is necessarily limited to the symbolic level: e.g., at Sparta the idea of the flagellation of the boys as a kind of death is represented in the myth as actual human sacrifice. This does not mean that the boys never actually died, although the reports of this may be influenced by the idea that the flagellation was a kind of death (cf. Brelich 1969:136). So too this ritual (unusually) itself contained an expression of disorder, in the requirement that the boys steal from the altar.

35. Seaford 1988:121.

36. Sources in Brelich 1969:248–249.

37. With the phrase ἐξέμηνεν αὐτάς in Suidas, s.v. Μέλαν, cf. Eur. *Bacc.* 36 (. . . ἐξέμηνα δωμάτων).

38. Schol. Ar. *Ach.* 243. Note also the etiology of the Aiora ritual at the Athenian Anthesteria: Icarius, given the vine by Dionysus, makes his neighbors drunk, with the result that they, thinking the wine to be poison, killed Icarius. His daughter Erigone consequently hanged herself, and this caused an epidemic of self-hanging among Attic maidens that was ended by the foundation of the Aiora.

39. ὃς ἐσφέρει νόσον/καινὴν γυναιξὶ (353–354). I suggest we read κοινήν, to give the meaning "epidemic" (cf. Theophr. *Phys.* 12. 168; Eur. *Hipp.* 730–731; etc.). For the same corruption see A. fr. 389, Bond on Eur. *HF* 831.

40. *Etymologicum Magnum* 42.4, s.v. Ἀιώρα . . . ἀπολυθέντα δὲ, ἀναρτήσασαν ἑαυτήν, προστρόπαιον τοῖς Ἀθηναίοις γενέσθαι. κατὰ χρησμὸν δὲ ἐπ᾽ αὐτῇ συντελεῖσθαι τὴν ἑορτήν. Cf. *Marmor. Parium.* 25; Apollod. *Epit.* 6.25. In another (Dionysiac) version the Erigone whose self-hanging causes a crisis is the daughter of Icarius (see n. 38 above).

41. Seaford 1994:ch. 3.

42. Note esp. 780–787, 792, 810–815.

43. That is why at Argos they appear to be on both sides: e.g., *Cho.* 283, 402–404, 577, 692, 1054.

44. *Cho.* 471–475, 539, etc. In an unpublished paper A. Callinicos shows that "tragedy was the first genre to use disease metaphor extensively" (in sharp contrast to Homer), including the idea of the diseased *polis*.

45. The disorder may though be enacted in the ritual itself (see e.g., n. 34 above), albeit in a circumscribed way.

46. Burkert 1970.

47. Apollod. *Bibl.* 2.2.2. At Hes. fr. 133 they have a physical disease.

48. Aesch. *Cho.* 698–699 (ἐν δόμοισι . . . ἰατρὸς ἔλπις); cf. Aesch. *Ag.* 1235 (''Αιδου μαινάδ') and Seaford 1989.

49. It might indeed be argued (see esp. Girard 1977) that it was precisely the social crisis of reciprocal violence that gave rise to the etiological myths of disease ended by cult. If so, then the *Oresteia*, in making the crisis one of reciprocal violence (albeit impelled by the Furies and described in terms of disease), exposes the reality underlying such etiological myths.

50. E.g., why do men sacrificing give only a poor portion to the gods? Because of Prometheus' trick, says Hesiod's *Theogony* (556–557).

51. From an etiological perspective the same point can be made about the "persuasive rhetoric" that, Goldhill notes, is common to Clytemnestra and Athena: an element of the reversal of order becomes, when employed by the *polis* deity, a means of creating order.

52. Seaford 1994:chs. 7 and 8.

53. My thanks go to André Lardinois, Alan Sommerstein, and John Wilkins for their comments on an earlier draft of this paper.

REFERENCES

Brelich, Angelo. 1969. *Paides e Parthenoi*. Rome.

Burkert, Walter. 1970. "Jason, Hypsipyle, and New Fire at Lemnos," *CQ* 20:1–16.

Busolt, Georg. 1926. *Griechische Staatskunde*, vol. 2. 3d ed. Munich.

Gagarin, Michael. 1975. "The Vote of Athena," *AJP* 96:121–127.

Gellrich, Michelle. 1988. *Tragedy and Theory: The Problem of Conflict since Aristotle*. Princeton.

Girard, René. 1977. *Violence and the Sacred*. Baltimore and London. (Translation of *La violence et le sacré*, Paris 1972.)

Goldhill, Simon. 1986. *Reading Greek Tragedy*. Cambridge.

Goldhill, Simon. 1987. "The Great Dionysia and Civic ideology," *JHS* 107:58–76.

Habermas, Jürgen. 1987. *The Philosophical Discourse of Modernity*. Cambridge.

Henrichs, Albert. 1984. "Loss of Self, Suffering, Violence: The Modern View of Dionysus from Nietzsche to Girard," *HSCP* 88:205–241.

Hester, D. A. 1981. "The Casting Vote," *AJP* 102:265–274.

Macdowell, Douglas M. 1963. *Athenian Homicide Law in the Age of the Orators.* Manchester.

Müller, Karl O. 1935. *The Eumenides of Aeschylus.* Cambridge.

Oudemans, T. C. Wouter, and Lardinois, André P. M. H. 1987. *Tragic Ambiguity.* Leiden.

Paolucci, A. and H. 1962. *Hegel on Tragedy.* New York.

Seaford, Richard. 1988. "The Eleventh Ode of Bacchylides," *JHS* 108:118–136.

————. 1989. "The Attribution of Aeschylus, *Choephoroi* 691–9," *CQ* 39:302–306.

————. 1994. *Reciprocity and Ritual: Homer and Tragedy in the Developing City-State.* Oxford.

Segal, Charles. 1986. "Greek Tragedy and Society." pp. 43–75 in *Greek Tragedy and Political Theory.* Edited by J. P. Euben. Berkeley and Los Angeles.

Silk, Michael S., and Joseph P. Stern. 1981. *Nietzsche on Tragedy.* Cambridge.

Sommerstein, Alan. 1989. *Aeschylus Eumenides.* Cambridge.

Thomson, George. 1966. *The Oresteia of Aeschylus.* 2 vols. Amsterdam and Prague.

Vernant, Jean-Pierre, and Pierre Vidal-Naquet. 1988. *Myth and Tragedy in Ancient Greece.* New York. (Combined translation of *Mythe et tragédie en Grèce ancienne* [Paris 1972] and *Mythe et tragédie en Grèce ancienne* II [Paris 1986].)

von Reibnitz, Barbara. 1992. *Ein Kommentar zu Friedrich Nietzsche 'Die Geburt der Tragödie aus dem Geiste der Musik' (Kapitel 1–12).* Stuttgart and Weimar.

West, M. L. 1990. *Studies in Aeschylus.* Stuttgart.

Winnington-Ingram, R. P. 1983. *Studies in Aeschylus.* Cambridge.

NOTES ON CONTRIBUTORS

HELENE FOLEY is Olin Professor of Classics at Barnard College, Columbia University. She is the author of *Ritual Irony: Poetry and Sacrifice in Euripides* (Cornell, 1985) and editor of *Reflections of Women in Antiquity* (Gordon and Breach, 1981). She has published numerous articles and reviews on Greek tragedy and on women in antiquity. Her most recent books are *The Homeric "Hymn to Demeter": Translation, Commentary, and Interpretive Essays* (Princeton, 1994) and, as coauthor, *Women in the Classical World: Image and Text* (Oxford, 1994).

MICHELLE GELLRICH teaches in the Departments of English and Classics at Louisiana State University. She is the author of *Tragedy and Theory: The Problem of Conflict since Aristotle* (Princeton, 1988) and has published articles on Aristotle, Plato, and Greek drama. Her present project is entitled *The Spell of Persuasion: Magic and Rhetoric in Antiquity and the Renaissance.*

BARBARA GOFF, the editor of this volume, teaches classics at the University of Texas at Austin. She is the author of *The Noose of Words: Readings of Desire, Violence, and Language in Euripides' Hippolytos* (Cambridge, Eng., 1990) and of several articles on tragedy.

PETER W. ROSE is Professor of Classics at Miami University of Ohio. He has published on Homer, Pindar, and tragedy, and is the author of *Sons of the Gods, Children of Earth: Ideology and Literary Form in Ancient Greece* (Cornell, 1992).

DAVID ROSENBLOOM teaches classics at the Victoria University of Wellington, New Zealand. He is completing a book on Greek drama and the origins of Athenian imperialism.

RICHARD SEAFORD is Reader in Greek Literature at the University of Exeter. He is the author of an edition with commentary on Euripides' *Cyclops*

(Oxford, 1984) and of numerous articles and reviews on Greek literature and culture. His most recent book is *Reciprocity and Ritual: Homer and Tragedy in the Developing City-State* (Oxford, 1994).

BERND SEIDENSTICKER is Chair of Greek at the Freie Universität, Berlin. He is the author of *Die Gesprächsverdichtung in den Tragödien Senecas* (Heidelberg, 1969) and *Palintonos Harmonia: Studien zu komischen Elementen in der griechischen Tragödie* (Göttingen, 1982), as well as of numerous articles and reviews on Greek and Roman drama.

FROMA I. ZEITLIN is Charles Ewing Professor of Greek Language and Literature at Princeton University. She is the author of *Under the Sign of the Shield: Semiotics and Aeschylus' Seven against Thebes* (Rome, 1982) and of numerous articles and reviews on Greek and Roman literature. She is coeditor of *Before Sexuality: The Construction of Erotic Experience in the Ancient Greek World* (Princeton, 1989) and of *Nothing to Do with Dionysos? Athenian Drama in Its Social Context* (Princeton, 1990), and editor of *Mortals and Immortals* (Princeton, 1991), a collection of essays by J.-P. Vernant. Her own collection, *Playing the Other: Gender in Greek Literature and Society,* is forthcoming from the University of Chicago Press (1995).

INDEX

Aelian, 191
Aeschines, 139
Aeschylean drama, 22, 27, 66, 67, 91, 92–
  95, 98, 105–106; *Agamemnon*, 71, 106–
  110, 112, 113, 114, 158–159, 160–161;
  Choephori, 91–92; *Eumenides*, 31,
  35 n.36, 94, 97, 110–111, 113, 114–116,
  174–175, 208–212, 214, 215, 216–217;
  Oresteia, 27, 32–33, 45, 94, 105, 115,
  208–209, 212, 214, 215, 216; *Persians*,
  93–94, 158; *Prometheus Bound*, 73, 92,
  192–193; *Septem*, 112, 113, 140
Agatharchos, 174
Althusser, Louis, 11–12, 62, 70, 77
ambiguity and ambivalence, as critical
  principles, 26, 30–31, 52, 53, 60, 81 n.14,
  131, 143–144, 166, 202–221
anthropological theory, 19, 23, 24, 25, 131
Areopagus, 115–116, 209, 210, 212, 215
Aristophanic drama, 100
Aristotle, 52, 53, 55, 133, 138, 141, 152, 188
Artemis Orthia, 212
Athena, vote of, in *Eumenides*, 209–212
Athens: burial practices, 133, 134, 136, 139,
  142, 146 n.11; democracy, 24, 70–71, 73,
  95, 105–106, 116, 217; empire, 22, 26, 27,
  67, 71, 72, 78–79, 85 n.43, 92, 93–94,
  96–97, 99, 102, 105; etiological myth,
  216; funeral oration at, 78, 100, 138,
  140–141, 142; identity, 98–99, 105; naval hegemony, 27, 94–98, 104–106, 112,

115; politics, 26, 69–71; *strategoi*, 69–71,
  117, 134. *See also* ideology; tragedy
audience, 8, 11, 19, 23, 28, 132, 135, 143. *See
  also* spectator
Austin, J. L., 4
authorial intention, 2, 3, 4, 11, 14, 21, 23,
  24, 25, 26, 39, 49, 132, 165

Bacchylides, 212–213
Baker, Houston, 9
Bakhtin, M. M., 46
Balzac, Honoré de, 74
Benjamin, Walter, 79
Bennett, Larry, 28, 132–133, 140–142, 143
binary polarity, 2, 3, 14, 25, 40, 43, 44, 45,
  51–54, 76. *See also* structuralism
Boeckh, August, 38, 46; and Romantic
  hermeneutics, 41

Calder, William, 132
City Dionysia, 22, 42, 95, 104–105
classics: and deconstruction, 4, 25, 39;
  and new historicism, 17, 31–32, 38, 59;
  and structuralism, 25; and theory, 1,
  15–17, 38
Cold War, end of, 5
comedy, Athenian, 137
Connor, W. R., 95
context: definition of, 40; role of, 1, 25, 41,
  45, 47, 50
Culham, Phyllis, 60